Carmarthenshire air crashes

Steven H. Jones

BRYNGOLD BOOKS

Published in Great Britain in 2015 by Bryngold Books Ltd.,
100 Brynau Wood, Cimla, Neath, South Wales SA11 3YQ.

Typesetting, layout, editing and design
by Bryngold Books.

ISBN 978-1-905900- 37-4

Printed and bound in Wales

www.bryngoldbooks.com

Appreciation

There is no doubt that this book wouldn't have been possible without a great deal of help and assistance from many people for which I will always be grateful.

Among them are: Alun 'Airfix' Evans, Dewi & Mair Evans, Dorothy Jones, Mair Thomas, Howell Rees, Roy & Nerys Edwards, Emyr Edwards, Pat Rowlands, Dennis Rogers, Bill Wainwright, Dan Gravell, Verdun Williams, Vincent Davies, Myra Jones, Ken Phillips, Paul Liiv, Percy Jones, Hugh Bonnell, Wyn Evans, Owen Griffiths, Glyn & Irfon Davies, Ita & Millia Mosses, Lilian Mosses, John Thomas, Donald Evans, John Davies, Evan Thomas, Elgan Jones, Melfydd Jones, Peter Foot, Meirion & Anna Thomas, Islwyn Jones, Emrys George, Donald Jones, Tom Gallagher, Gethyn Thomas, Ernie & Mary Randall, Emily Conary, Lloyd Davies, Tony & Mair Lockley, Myrddin Jones, Ralph Carpenter, Wojtek Matusiak, Gayle Marsh, Elizabeth Gabszewicz, Dave Quigley, Terry Williams, Violet Stanyer, Frank Cave, Ryan Rowlands, Patrick Nelson-Edwards, Rolf & Kirsten Riise, Ralph Shoop, Patrick & John Reiss, Gwen Scoggins, Shirley Wetzel, James Wilkinson, Sean Brady, Barbara McAllen, John, Judy & Peter Crozier, Bruce Thomson, Ron Dear, Frank Ford, Alexander Hay, Stan Kreciala, Claude Fryer, Jeffrey Crocker, David Wakeford, John York, Mike Allaby, Johnnie Robertshaw, Ivor & Edna Jones, Eddie Doylerush, Cecil Jones, Islwyn Thomas, George Walsh, Stephen Knapp, Johnnie Walker, Jane Wallance, Fred Williemsen, Mike Freer, Shaun Connor, Howard Muncy, Neil Stevens, The Imperial War Museum, National Archives and also the helpful staff at Carmarthen and Llanelli libraries and Carmarthenshire Archives.

Steven H. Jones

Dedication

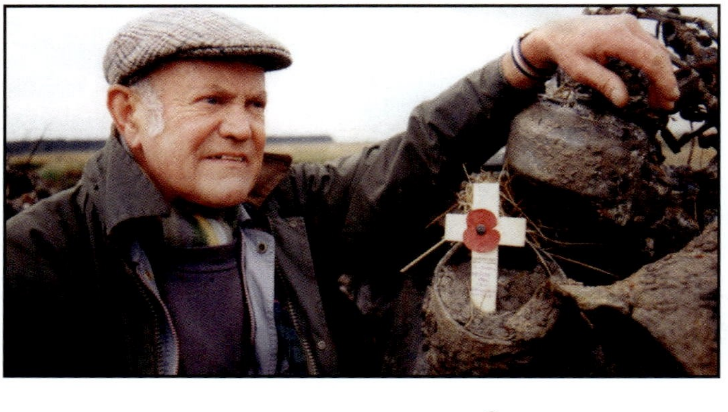

For Fred Lyne. Treasured memories of a good friend.

Introduction

On a clear day, flying my paraglider just a few hundred feet above the Graig Fawr ridge near the west Wales town of Ammanford affords the most glorious view across almost the entire length of the county of Carmarthenshire.

With the exception of the high ground to the east, around Brynamman, known as the Carmarthen Fans, the county mainly consists of low hills and gently undulating farmland – not the terrain you would usually associate with aircraft losses. Despite this however, more than 60 aircraft accidents have occurred, resulting in the loss of 78 airmen within the county's boundary. The highest concentration of these was on the periphery of its only designated airfield at Pembrey.

Opened as a Royal Air Force Fighter Command sector station at the beginning of Second World War, Pembrey airfield's association with the RAF can be divided into three distinct periods each of which can be linked to the different aircraft types which operated from there.

During the summer of 1940 Spitfires of 92 Squadron flew briefly from the airfield's grass strip, before being replaced in September by the Hurricanes of 79 Squadron. In February 1941 a new unit – 316 (Polish) Squadron – made up of personnel of the 1st Warsaw Air Regiment who had fled the German invasion of their country, was formed at the base. The main role of both Hurricane squadrons was that of convoy escort, a task that required pairs of aircraft to provide air cover for shipping convoys in the Bristol Channel. During the Spring of 1941 Lysander aircraft of a new Fighter Command initiative, the Air-Sea Rescue Service, were also to be seen at Pembrey.

The second phase began on June 15, 1941, when the airfield became non-operational and passed from RAF Fighter Command to Training Command. At that point 79 Squadron made the short hop across the Loughor Estuary to the recently-opened RAF Fairwood Common, near Swansea, and 316 Squadron left for RAF Colerne, near Bath. At the same time the war weary Blenheim aircraft of 1 Air Gunners' School arrived.

Initially the Blenheims were among aircraft utilised as both target drogue-towing aircraft and as gun-firing platforms for trainee air gunners. In March 1943 the situation changed when Martinets – purpose-built drogue towing aircraft – made their debut at the base. Towards the end of the war Ansons and Wellingtons replaced the gunnery school's ageing Blenheim fleet while Spitfires, used in fighter affiliation exercises for the trainee air gunners, also made a return to Pembrey. With the ending of hostilities in Europe in May 1945 the demand for air gunners in the RAF declined and on June 14, 1945, exactly four years after it's inception, 1 Air Gunners' School was disbanded.

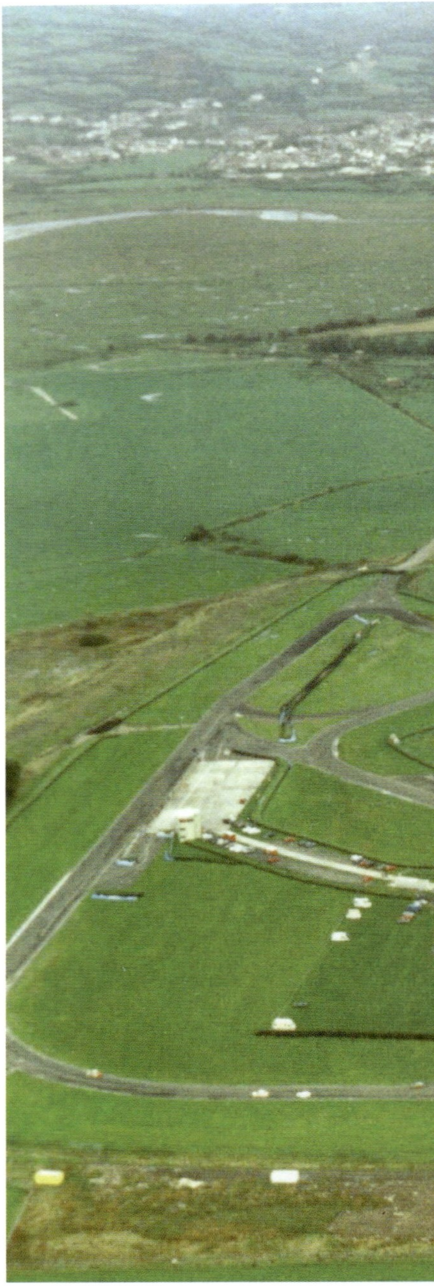

The next visitors to Pembrey were the Spitfires, Vampires and Martinets of 595 Squadron, an Army Co-operation Unit previously based at Fairwood Common. Because of the deteriorating conditions of the facilities at Fairwood, the longer runways available at Pembrey, needed for the squadron's newly acquired Vampire jets, and the closer proximity of the airfield to the Army's artillery range at Manorbier near Tenby, the move was perhaps inevitable. For three years, from October 1946 until October 1949, the squadron flew target duties for the Manorbier range. The artillery range is still active today, though radiocontrolled model aircraft now seem a more economical, and much safer, method of providing targets for the Army.

The final phase of the airfield's association with the RAF began in the autumn of 1952. As a direct result of the Korean War, the Ministry of Defence became aware of a shortfall in the number of its fighter-bomber aircraft and the pilots required to fly them. To this end 233 Operational Conversion Unit was formed at Pembrey in October 1952. The unit's motto was Ymlaen – the Welsh word for forward – which it tried to instil into its student pilots. Vampires and Meteors for student pilots could be seen at the airfield, augmented by Tempests for use as target tugs by the staff pilots. By 1956 Hunter jets were replacing the Vampires for students, while Mosquitos had already replaced the Tempests and were about to be replaced themselves by Meteors and Balliols.

The year 1957 was a crucial one for the RAF, for the then government minister for defence, Duncan Sandys, produced a White Paper which recommended a dramatic reduction in the strength of Fighter Command.

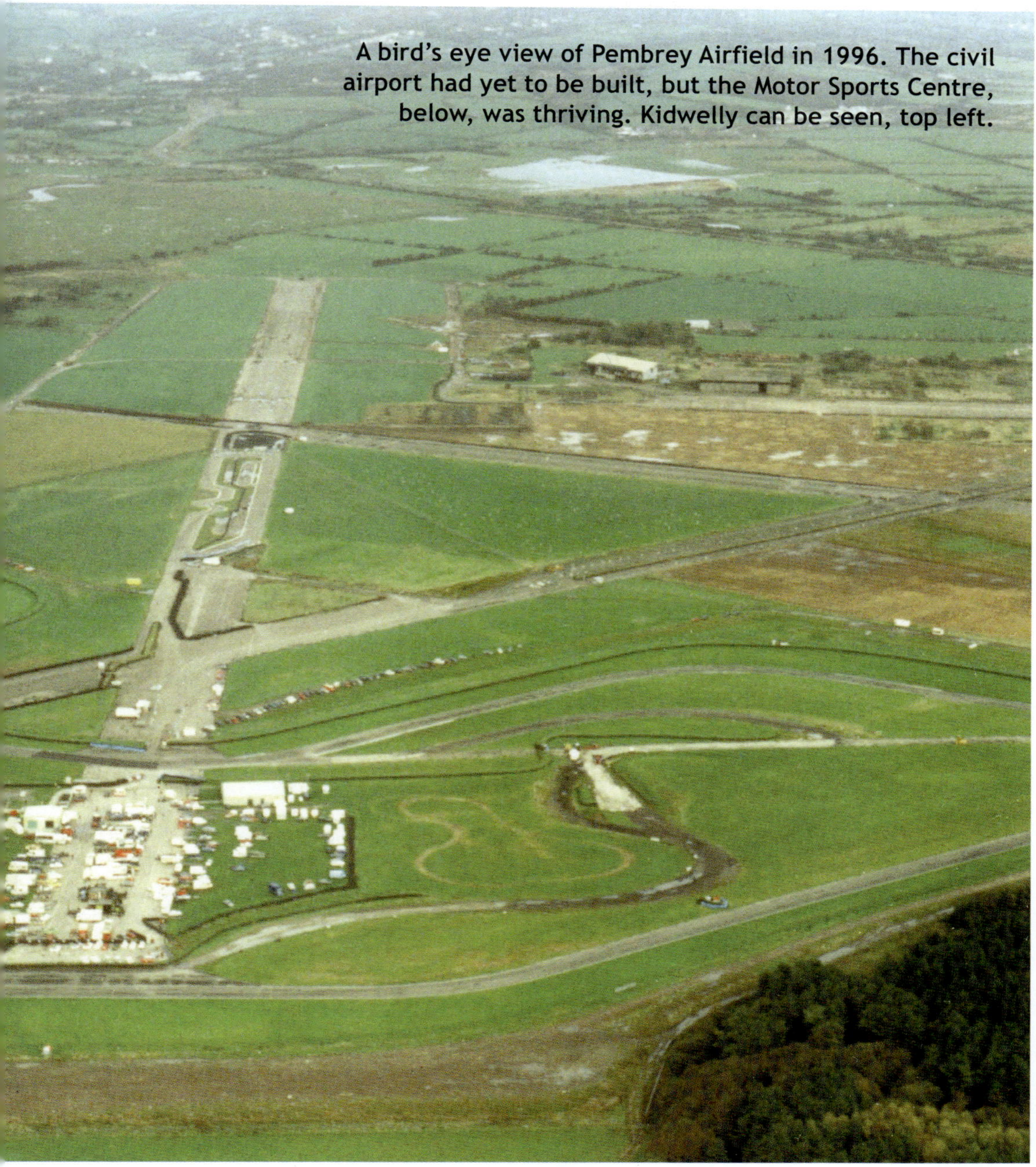

A bird's eye view of Pembrey Airfield in 1996. The civil airport had yet to be built, but the Motor Sports Centre, below, was thriving. Kidwelly can be seen, top left.

This suggested that ground-based missiles were a more effective way of achieving aerial supremacy in any future conflict. As a result, and to the consternation of many fighter pilots in the RAF who had to transfer to other Commands, 233 OCU was disbanded at Pembrey on July 13 that year.

The disbanding of this unit also marked the end of the RAF's presence at the airfield, though the air-to-ground firing range on marshland at the northern edge of Cefn Sidan beach, is still maintained by the RAF.

Guide to abbreviation

The following abbreviations are used within the pages of this book:

C.O.	Commanding Officer
W. Cmdr.	Wing Commander
Sqn. Ldr.	Squadron Leader
Flt. Lt.	Flight Lieutenant
F.O.	Flying Officer
P.O.	Pilot Officer
W.O.	Warrant Officer
Flt. Sgt.	Flight Sergeant
S. Sgt.	Staff Sergeant
Sgt.	Sergeant
LAC	Leading Aircraftman
LACW	Leading Aircraftwoman
AC	Aircraftman
AC2	Aircraftman Second Class
AG	Air Gunner
W.Op.	Wireless Operator
WAAF	Womens' Auxillary Air Force
KIA	Killed in action
POW	Prisoner of war

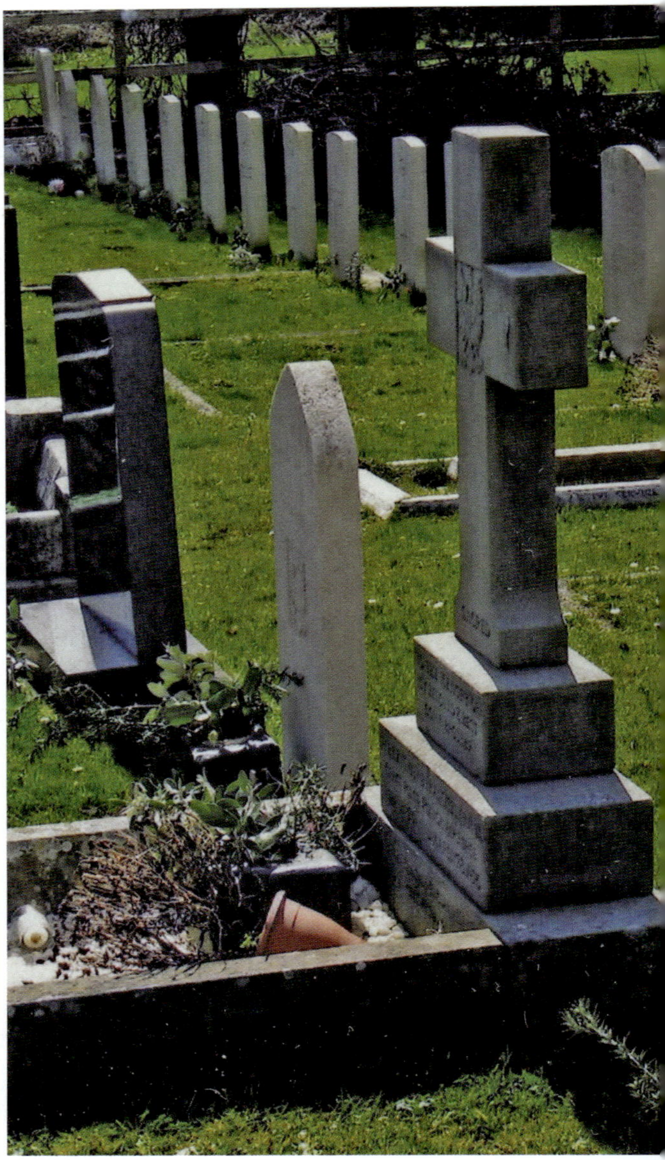

The causes of the accidents which occurred over Carmarthenshire are varied. Engine failures feature prominently throughout the time scale of the book, although unanticipated poor weather affecting aircraft transiting the county along with pilot error, also took their toll. Surprisingly, no losses are directly attributed to combat; even the demise of the Luftwaffe JU88, Werke No. 140715, on August 5, 1942 remains unexplained.

At the Commonwealth War Graves Commission plot in St Illtyd's Churchyard, Pembrey village, there is a more poignant record of the airfield's past. Here lie fallen aviators from all corners of the world whose passion for flying and fate somehow brought them to South Wales. While their comrades made the journey home, they shall stay forever.

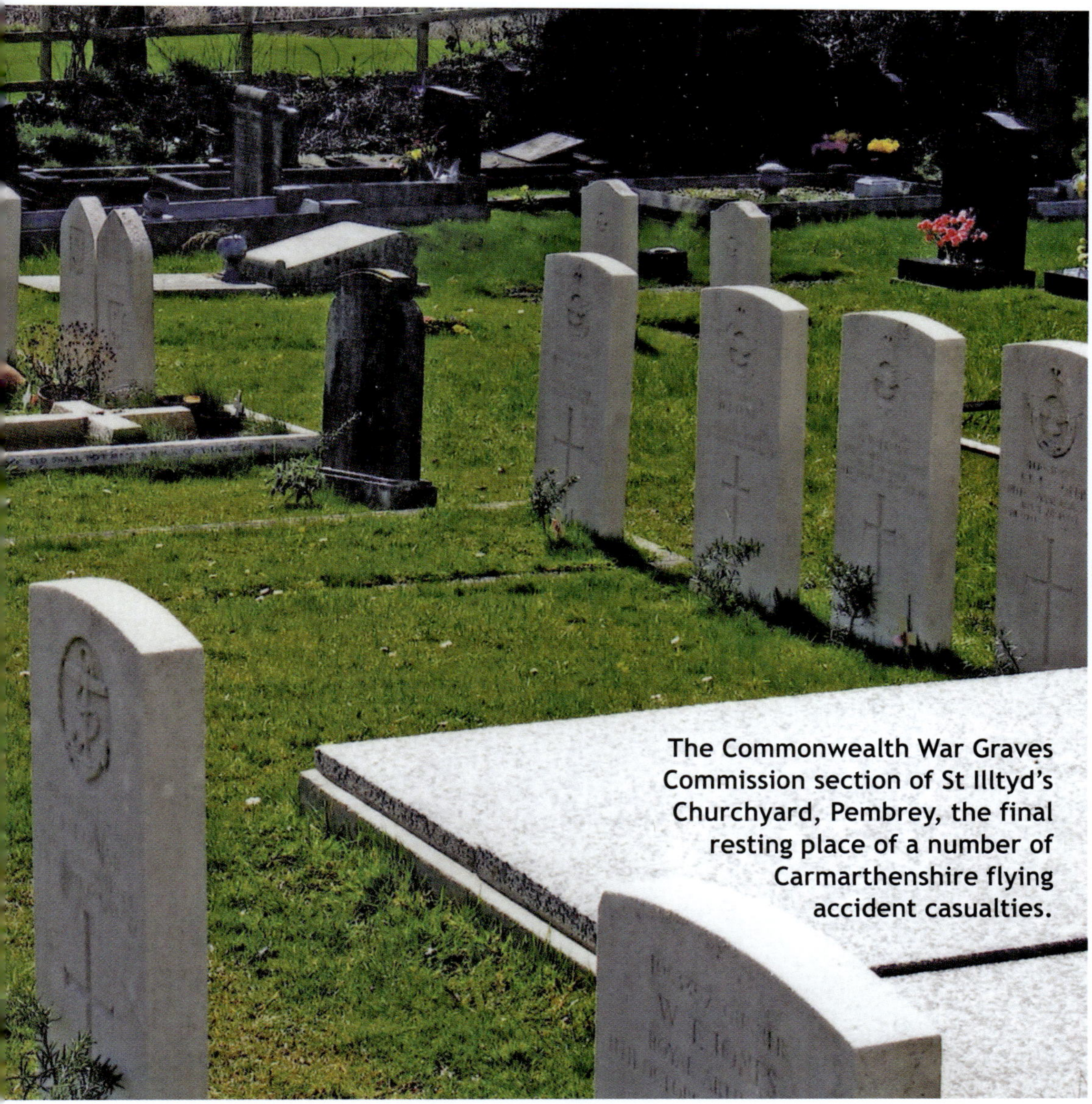

The Commonwealth War Graves Commission section of St Illtyd's Churchyard, Pembrey, the final resting place of a number of Carmarthenshire flying accident casualties.

Early memories of an abandoned airfield

My earliest memories of the former RAF base at Pembrey stretch back to the 1970s, when, as a teenager, I accompanied my father on fishing trips to the vast stretch of Cefn Sidan beach. Access to it by car was by a network of concrete perimeter tracks and runways of the former airfield. Dotted around the base at that time were the giant chicken sheds of the Eastwood poultry farm. Before leaving the airfield and entering the maze of tracks in the forestry plantation, we would pass the derelict control tower. With its rusting and broken window frames it seemed an intimidating building to enter and explore to a youngster such as myself. After all, perhaps it was haunted! I recall while returning from one such fishing trip on a damp and dark evening, our car spluttering to a halt inside a cavernous hanger on the airfield's apron. While my father tinkered under the car's bonnet, my thoughts turned to all the different aircraft types which might also have been repaired and serviced in that very building.

In the years that followed I would again find myself spending time with my father at the airfield. My memories this time are of long, sunny, Sunday afternoons in the summertime, watching my father's home-built, radio controlled model aircraft tearing down the runway and climbing high into the clear blue sky. It was during this time that I first heard mention of Armin Faber's unscheduled arrival at Pembrey in his Focke-Wulf 190. A fascinating story which I would later research in more detail.

The fascinating quest to discover the facts

The research for this book started in much the same way as that for my first book, Fallen Flyers. By visiting St Illtyd's Churchyard in Pembrey I was able to note from the headstone inscriptions of the airmen interred there, names, dates and units. Armed with this information I made many visits to the National Archives at Kew and the RAF Museum in Hendon.

It was here, after consulting unit diaries and accident reports, that a clearer picture of exactly what fate had befallen these airmen unfolded. Local newspapers held at both Llanelli and Carmarthen libraries also provided a wealth of information, especially when it came to post-war incidents and a period when there was no wartime press censorship.

One of the most fascinating and also rewarding aspects of the research came from interviewing local people, many of whom had witnessed the events mentioned in this book.

In a few cases I was also lucky enough to trace aircrew, who gave intriguing accounts of how they survived their near death experiences.

Sadly, as the years progress, these witnesses and survivors dwindle in number and become harder to track down; a good reason for putting pen to paper perhaps.

Finally, the most important group of people associated with my research have been the relatives of the airmen mentioned within the pages of this book. They provided anecdotes and photographs of their lost loved ones, unobtainable in any archive, or reference library.

JULY 7 1917

AIRCRAFT: **BE2 A1278**

Lost hero's aerial arrival had farmworkers gasping

On Saturday July 7, 1917 farm workers in fields around the village of Saron on the outskirts of Ammanford, gazed skywards to see an aircraft heading their way. Many gasped and feared the worst, thinking that the pilot was a German who had somehow become separated from his squadron on the Continent. That wouldn't have been surprising, for by 1917 the First World War threat of aerial bombing over Britain was very much a reality and by strange coincidence on this very day London was raided in broad daylight by a force of 22 Gotha bombers. During the attack 54 people lost their lives and nearly 200 were injured.

At the controls of the aircraft flying over Ammanford however, was Sgt. Charlie Butler, an 18-year-old trainee Royal Flying Corps pilot who had earlier taken off from his base at Yatesbury in Wiltshire and become lost.

On landing in a nearby field Sgt. Butler himself feared that he was about to meet up with the enemy, as the locals seemed to converse in a strange language which was of course Welsh!

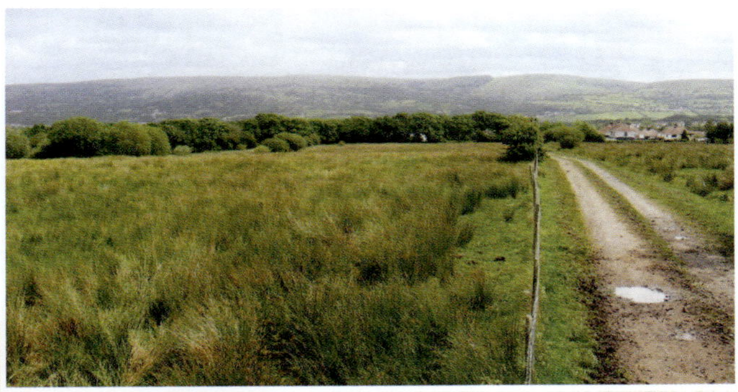

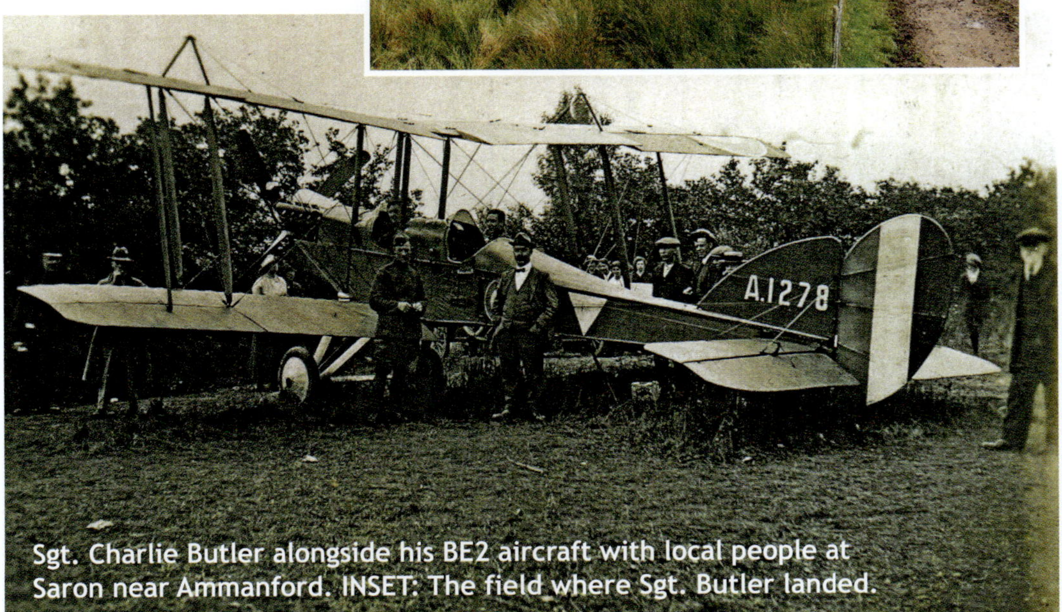

Sgt. Charlie Butler alongside his BE2 aircraft with local people at Saron near Ammanford. INSET: The field where Sgt. Butler landed.

However, he was soon assured that he was still on British soil and in the following few days became something of a local celebrity. Later in the week his aircraft was refuelled and he took off from the field, making his way back to Yatesbury via Bristol to continue his flying training. Prior to training as a pilot Sgt. Butler had distinguished himself flying as an observer over the Western Front for which he was awarded the Croix de Gerre. On October 21, 1917 he failed to return from a sortie somewhere over France. Thankfully, a short time later, news reached his family in Merstham, Surrey that he was a prisoner-of-war. He was repatriated in January 1919.

The long and narrow field where Sgt. Butler force landed in 1917 lies just yards off the main road which today runs through Saron village.

SEPT 12 1919

AIRCRAFT: Avro 504 G-AEDN

Jealousy may have caused county's earliest crash

At the National Archives in London are a group of files under the heading of AVIA 5. These documents were created by the government in the era immediately following the First World War to help prevent the recurrence of aviation accidents. Listed in Section 1 of AVIA 5 is Carmarthenshire's earliest recorded flying accident. Ironically, its sole casualty wasn't even on board an aircraft at the time.

In the late afternoon of Friday, September 12 1919, David Watts, a 71-year-old retired china dealer, from Victoria Road, Llanelli, was out on the sands at Llanelli Beach, touting for business for his penny horse-buggy rides along the beach, near the modern North Dock development.

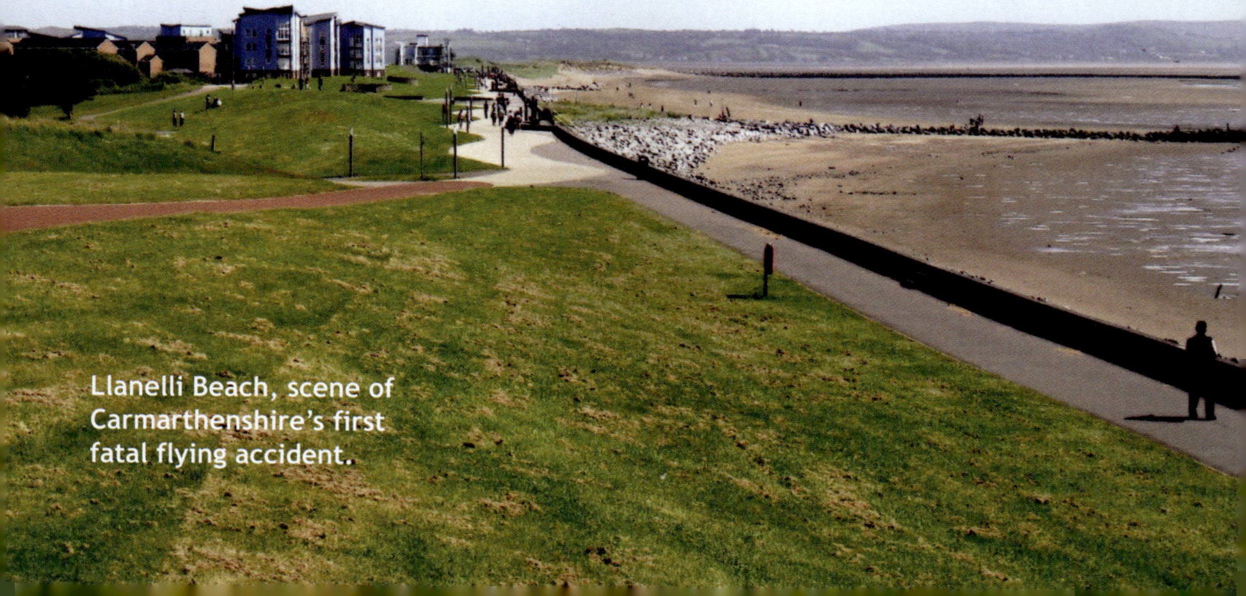

Llanelli Beach, scene of Carmarthenshire's first fatal flying accident.

Also offering pleasure trips from the beach that day was Mr. T.B. Bruce, the pilot of an Avro 504 bi-plane. There was much curiosity about this new attraction and the aircraft drew a crowd of about 150.

Perhaps with a little jealousy, Watts was heard to ridicule his new competitor's 'flying machine' and protested that thrill-wise, his penny rides offered by far the best value for money.

In an attempt to prove this, when the Avro next started its take off run Watts raced alongside it. After initially overtaking the Avro he then steered his buggy, which had three children seated in the back, in front of the aircraft's flight path as if to push it off course.

Unknown to Watts the Avro had just become airborne and at this critical time the pilot's attention had been drawn to some children playing on the beach on the opposite side. Losing sight of the buggy, which was now directly in front of and underneath the Avro, the pilot continued on his take off track. As the aircraft gained speed it flew over the buggy fatally striking Watts on the back of the head.

When the horsedrawn buggy came to rest David Watts was taken, unconscious, to his nearby home in Victoria Road. He never regained consciousness and died as a result of his injuries six days later; reluctantly becoming the first person in Carmarthenshire to lose his life in a flying accident. Today his crumbling headstone stands inconspicuously among hundreds of others at Llanelli's Box cemetery.

OCT 6 1919

AIRCRAFT: **BE2 4577**

Fuel crisis brought the mail back down to earth

Uncannily, on October 6, less than a month after the death of David Watts, another flying accident occurred on the same stretch of coastline. Fortunately this time there were no casualties. The aircraft involved was a BE2 bi-plane, named Sumflia which was owned by the newly formed Royal Air Force.

While on a mail delivery flight from Salisbury to Pembroke Dock the aircraft ran low on fuel. Accordingly, the two crew on board, Lieutenants Lloyd and Thomson, decided to make a precautionary landing in fields to the west of Llanelli Steelworks, near to what is now the Beach Road area of the Millennium Coastal Path. All went well until the BE2 overshot the intended field and hit an earth bank. The two crew emerged unhurt, but the aircraft was severely damaged and had to be taken away by rail.

JUNE 18 1928

AIRCRAFT: **Fokker F.VIIb**

Touchdown marked first non-stop seaplane hop

After the Atlantic ocean had been crossed non-stop by Alcock and Brown in 1919, 'jumping the pond' as it was referred to, soon became one of the quintessential flights to be made by any budding aviation pioneer in the early 20th Century.

On June 17, 1928 Wilmer Stultz and two fellow American aviators took off from Trepassey, Newfoundland in an attempt to set a world record for crossing the Atlantic non-stop in a seaplane.

At 12:40 hrs the following day, June 18, their Fokker tri-motored monoplane, named Friendship, touched down in the waters of the Burry Estuary just off Burry Port to claim the first, non-stop, Transatlantic flight by a seaplane. However, Stultz's achievement was overshadowed by the fact that one of his passengers was a young female aviator, a Miss Amelia Earhart, who had now become the first woman to have flown across the Atlantic.

On completion of their arduous 20 hour and 49 minute flight, Wilmer Stultz, Louis Gordon and Miss Earhart stayed overnight at the Ashburnham Hotel. The following day as they prepared to fly on to Southampton, their intended destination for the record attempt, they were greeted by hundreds of well-wishers who had descended on Burry Port harbour to bid them farewell. Unexpectedly, Sir Arthur Whitten-Brown and his family, at the time resident in Swansea, had turned up in the hope of meeting his fellow Atlantic adventurers, but by the time he made himself known to the authorities, the trio had already set off by boat to board the anchored 'Friendship'. Another boat was summoned, only to reach the vicinity of the aircraft as it took off.

On May 21, 1932, Amelia Earhart claimed another aviation milestone

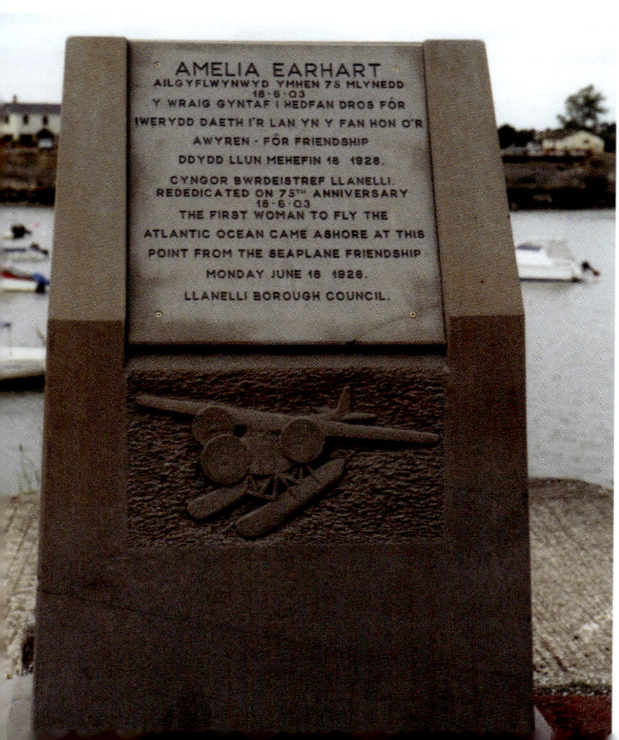

The Amelia Earhart commemorative stone at Burry Port harbour.

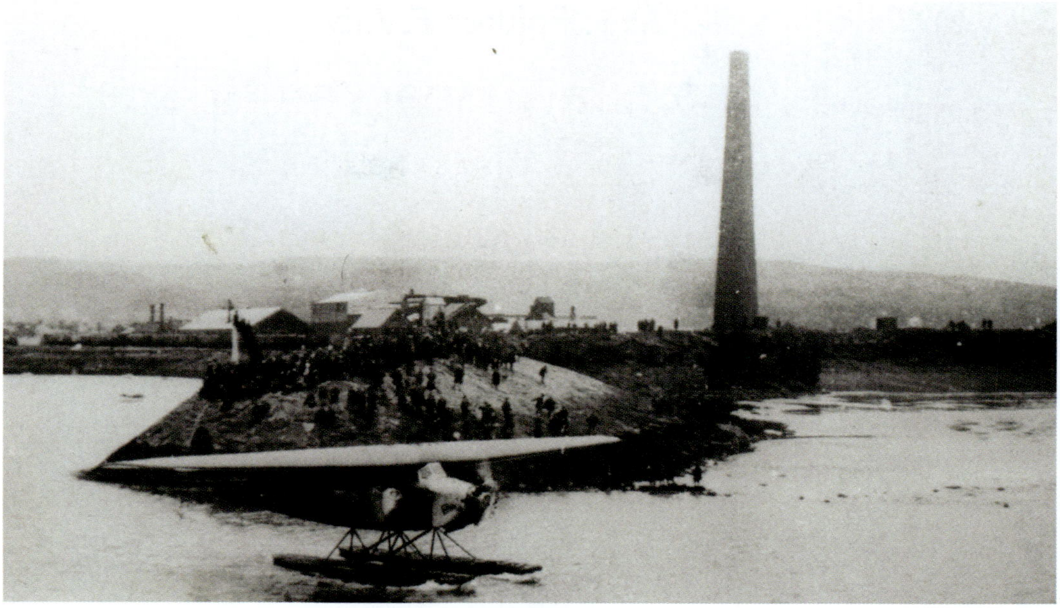

The Fokker tri-motor aircraft 'Friendship' leaving Burry Port harbour, June 1928.

by becoming the first woman to fly solo across the Atlantic. She was dubbed 'Lady Lindy' after the exploits of Charles Lindberg five years earlier. Sadly, in July 1937 she disappeared over the Pacific while attempting to circumnavigate the world around the equator. The cause of her disappearance still remains one of aviation's great mysteries.

SEPT 3 1936

AIRCRAFT: Vultee V1 NC13770

County proved a safe haven for dare devils

In the years that followed Amelia Earhart's unscheduled arrival at Burry Port a number of other Transatlantic aviators inadvertently touched down in Wales. In 1936 it was Carmarthenshire once again that provided a safe haven for two Americans.

At 21:30 hrs on September 2, 1936 a Vultee V1, single-engined, passenger aircraft named Lady Peace took off from Floyd Bennett Airport, New York bound for Croydon, near London. In modern times this journey would be considered routine, but the purpose of the flight in 1936 was to set yet another world record, this time for the first round trip, non-stop crossing of the Atlantic.

On board the fuel-laden Lady Peace were the pilot, Henry 'Dick' Merrill, the instigator of the record attempt, and the aptly named owner of the aircraft, Harry Richman, a successful Broadway entertainer and part-time

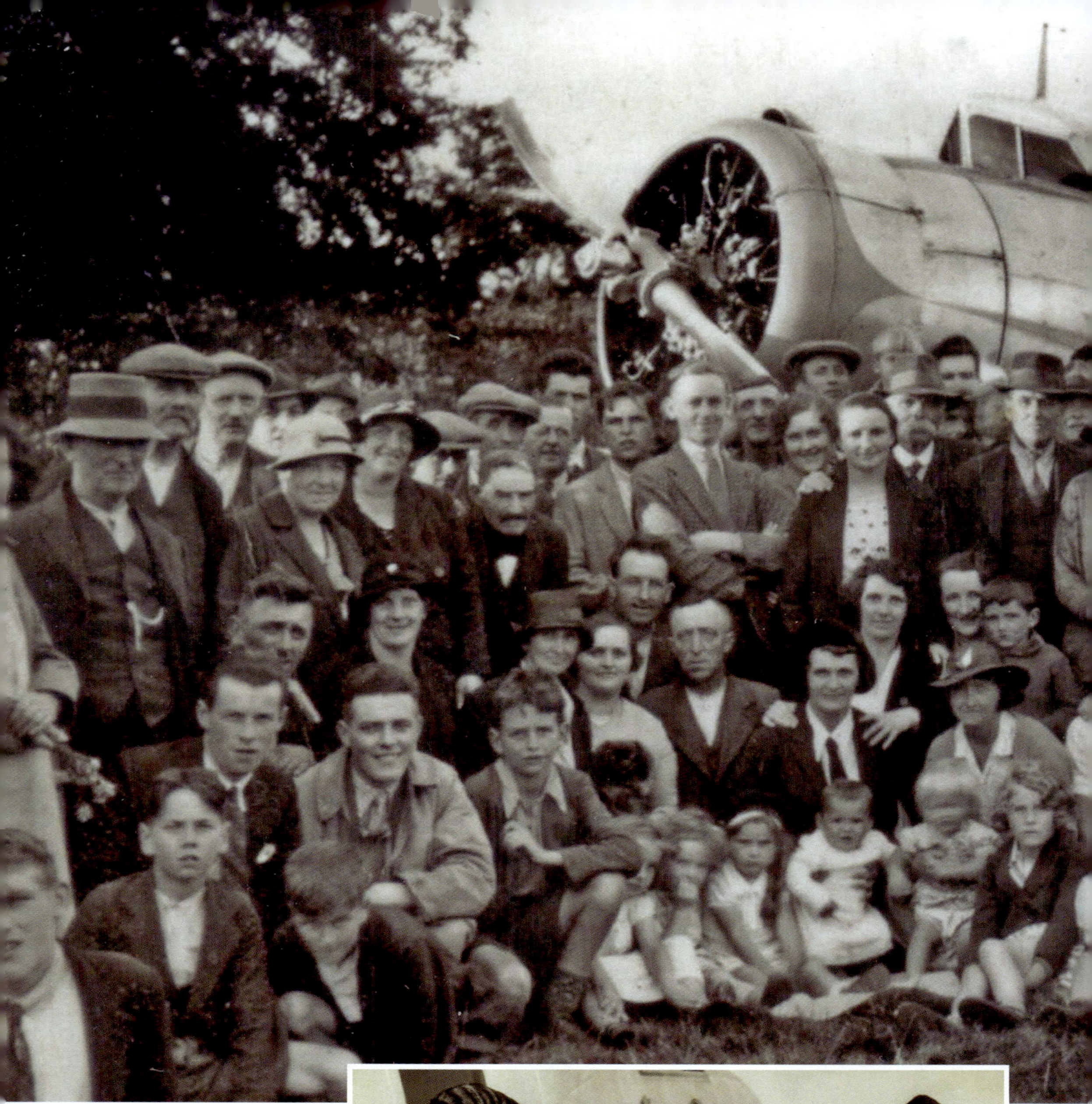

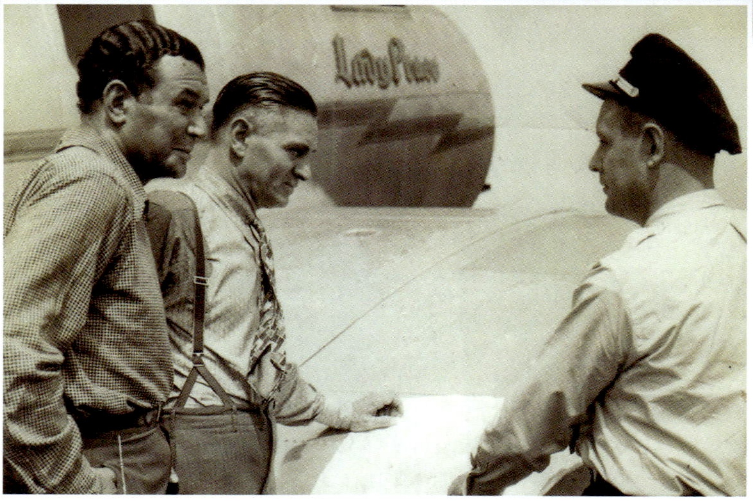

Harry Richman, left, Dick Merrill centre, and John Quigley, an Eastern Airlines pilot and meteorologist, planning the 1936 record attempt on August 20, 1936.

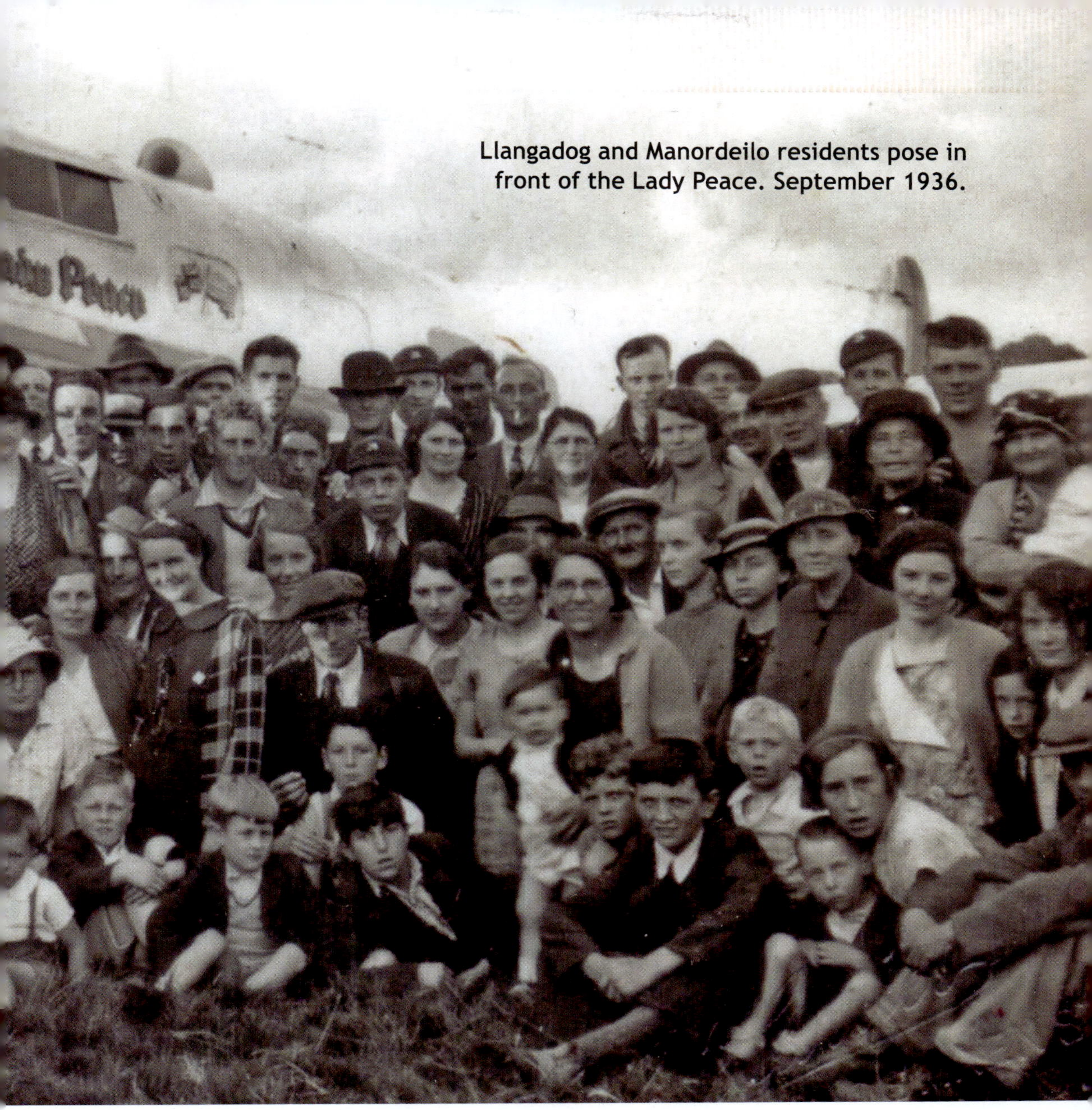

Llangadog and Manordeilo residents pose in front of the Lady Peace. September 1936.

pilot. As well as supplying the aircraft for the record attempt, Harry Richman also provided the financial backing for the venture, estimated to be in the region of $360,000. Besides the replacing of the passenger seating with auxiliary fuel tanks, another unusual feature of the Lady Peace was the 30,000 table-tennis balls crammed into the dead-spaces of her airframe. Richman reasoned that should they be forced-down on to the sea, the balls would provide sufficient buoyancy to keep the aircraft afloat – a phenomenal mathematic equation to work out! He had named the aircraft Lady Peace in deference to the mounting prospect of a global conflict.

The first few hours of the record attempt were uneventful, but when about 600 miles west of Ireland the Lady Peace flew into a thunderstorm and the crew spent some time being buffeted about by the ensuing turbulence. As a consequence the aircraft consumed more of its precious fuel than planned and instead of landing at Croydon to the fanfare of a band and hordes of spectators who were anticipating their arrival, Merrill and Richman were forced to put down in a quiet, grazing meadow on the banks of the River Towy near Manordeilo.

The Lady Peace was first sighted in the Towy valley just before 16:00 hrs on September 3, flying on a south westerly course down the valley from the direction of Llangadog. It was then seen to turn back up river near Llandeilo and attempted to land near Glan Towy Farm. Overshooting the intended field it crossed the river and landed in a triangular shaped field bordering the River Towy near Glanrhyd Saeson Farm.

Though weary from their ordeal both Merrill and Richman wanted to refuel the Lady Peace immediately and head for Croydon before sunset, but the reality of obtaining aviation fuel at short notice in rural Carmarthenshire curtailed their plans. Instead, the pair lodged overnight at the Cawdor Arms in Llandeilo, while the local police stood guard over their aircraft.

By the following morning, September 4, a supply of fuel had been conveyed to the field and the Lady Peace was partially refuelled. News of the arrival of the aircraft had spread like wildfire and a large crowd of inquisitive locals had gathered at Manordeilo to watch the Americans depart. Despite the

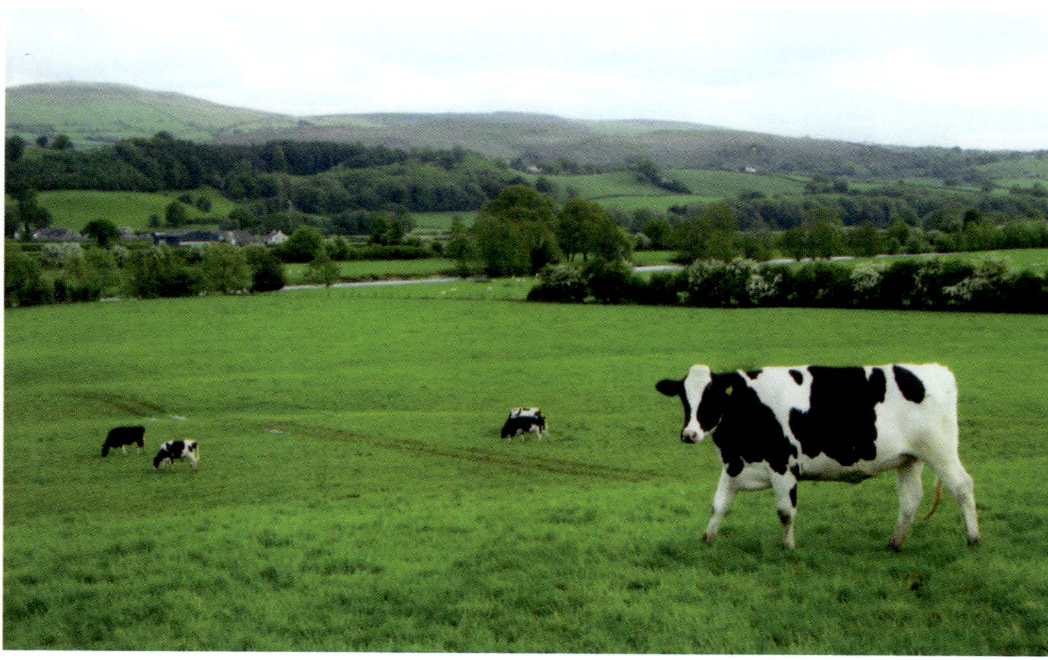

The field where the Lady Peace landed, now part of Bryn Fedwen Farm, Manordeilo. The missing hedgerow, in the centre of the picture running towards the river, was uprooted overnight to give the aircraft a longer take off run.

huge numbers of people present the police appear to have done an excellent job of keeping order. Though now minus her landing lights, removed overnight by stealthy souvenir hunters, and sporting some graffiti on her fuselage in the form of local signatures, the Lady Peace was ready to resume her journey. On arrival at the field Merrill and Richman were greeted to the sound of hymns and the Welsh national anthem being sung by the crowd. Both expressed their gratitude to the local people for coming to their aid, before climbing aboard the aircraft.

To ensure that the Lady Peace took off safely from the Towy valley, the hedgerow to an adjoining field had been uprooted overnight and smoothed over, thus extending its take off run. Just before midday the pair took off from their improvised airstrip and headed for Bristol Airport to fully refuel their aircraft. The take off itself was not without incident. Dick Merrill was later to describe the moment a television camera van hurtled across his flight path as the most heart stopping moment of the entire venture. The aircraft missed the van by a matter of inches. With a second aircraft acting as an escort this time, the Lady Peace flew to Bristol, refuelled and finally landed at Croydon at 15:00 hrs.

Their flight time from New York to Manordeilo was 18 hours and 36 minutes; the fastest crossing of the Atlantic at that time. The 3,500 mile journey had been made at an average speed of 200 miles per hour.

Their return flight to New York was equally eventful. After 10 days of waiting for favourable weather the Lady Peace departed Britain from Southport Sands near Liverpool at 03:30 hrs on Monday, September 14.

Somewhere over the Atlantic Richman accidentally jettisoned a full fuel tank, mistaking it for one that was empty. This once again caused the Lady Peace to force land short of its destination. On this occasion the impromptu landing ground was a swamp near Musgrave Harbour on the Newfoundland coast. So remote was the location that it took a whole week to repair and refuel the aircraft before the Lady Peace finally maked it back to Floyd Bennett Airport on September 21.

The following year Dick Merrill set another Atlantic record, the first commercial round trip, non-stop crossing of the Atlantic. In mid-May 1937, with Jack Lambie as co-pilot, he flew to Britain, collected newsreel footage of the Coronation of King George VI and returned to the United States. For this flight he was awarded the prestigious International Harman Trophy. In his 33-year flying career he amassed more than 36,000 hours of airtime and became chief pilot of America's Eastern Airlines.

Harry Richman continued in show business and whenever anyone was willing to listen he would retell with great enthusiasm the story of his 1936 Atlantic adventure. As a spin-off to the flight he later sold autographed table tennis balls from the Lady Peace, whether he sold all 30,000 is not known. Today these autographed balls sometimes appear for sale on internet auction sites.

Ironically, the Lady Peace, named in an attempt to discourage conflict, herself ended up in a war zone. The aircraft was captured by rebel Nationalist forces in the Spanish Civil War and was renamed Captain Haya after a famous Nationalist pilot. She survived the war only to be scrapped by the Spanish Air force in 1953.

The only remaining example of a Vultee V1, NC16099, is displayed at the Virginia Air Museum in the United States. In honour of Dick Merrill's 1936 flight, known in aviation history as the 'ping pong' flight, this last surviving airframe is named Lady Peace II.

The field near Manordeilo where the original Lady Peace touched down after crossing the Atlantic has changed little in almost eight decades and the hedgerow removed to extend her take off run is still noticeable.

JUNE
18
1940

AIRCRAFT: **Spitfires & Hurricanes**

Opening of Pembrey brings increased aerial activity

After the outbreak of the Second World War in September 1939 aerial activity around Britain increased significantly. The skies above Carmarthenshire were no exception. With the opening of RAF Pembrey on the edge of the Gwendraeth marshes near Kidwelly, aircraft became a common sight for the local population. Along with this increase in aircraft movements came the inevitable accidents.

The first operational flying unit to move into Pembrey was 92 Squadron with its Spitfires. After being in the frontline during the evacuation of Dunkirk, the squadron was posted to Pembrey on 18 June 1940 to recuperate from its losses. During its time at Pembrey it was given the duty of carrying out convoy patrols around the Welsh coast. Luftwaffe bomber units by then based on the Brest Peninsula were within striking distance of the busy industrial ports of South Wales. Most of 92 Squadron's aircraft losses while at Pembrey were attributed to the hazards of flying Spitfires at night, in particular minor landing accidents. Two aircraft were lost as a result of combat with enemy bombers during the month of August, but they occurred outside the county. In each case the pilot was able to force land.

On September 8, at the height of the Battle of Britain, 92 Squadron replaced 79 Squadron at RAF Biggin Hill and the latter, with its Hurricanes, moved into Pembrey.

AUG 9 1940

AIRCRAFT: **Anson K6285**

Solo night flight pilot escaped with a soaking

Just after midnight in the early hours of August 9, 1940 Sgt. J.P. Bielfeldt of 321 Squadron, Royal Netherlands Naval Air Service, based at RAF Carew near Tenby, took off on a solo night flying exercise.

The aim of the flight was to make the pilot more proficient at taking off and landing in the dark. In the total blackout conditions that prevailed in the countryside below him, he soon became disorientated as to his position from the airfield. Recognising the long stretch of beach at Pendine ahead of him, Sgt. Bielfeldt attempted to force land on the foreshore. Ironically, the Anson hit one of the many anti-glider poles placed near the low water mark of the beach to deter enemy glider aircraft from landing there. The aircraft ended up in the shallow water and Sgt. Bielfeldt was able to wade ashore uninjured. Though K6285 was recovered from the beach it never flew again, instead it was used an instructional airframe.

SEPT 17 1940

AIRCRAFT: **Hampden P4311**

Bomber came to grief on Gwendraeth marshes

As well as being a fighter station during the Battle of Britain, Pembrey was also home to a small detachment of Hampden bombers from 14 Operational Training Unit based at RAF Cottesmore near Leicester. These units were formed by the RAF to train newly qualified aircrew in the operational use of specific aircraft, in the case of 14 OTU the aircraft concerned were Hampden and Hereford bombers. From a distance the two aircraft types appeared identical, the only difference being that the Hampden was powered by two Bristol Pegasus radial engines, while the Hereford had Napier Dagger in-line engines. Nicknamed the ‘flying suitcase’ because of its narrow, high ceilinged fuselage, the Hampden alongside the Whitley and the Wellington aircraft formed the backbone of Bomber Command during the early war years.

On the morning of September 17 Hampden P4311 was returning to Pembrey on completion of an air-to-air firing exercise. While approaching to land from the direction of Kidwelly, the starboard engine cut out and a strong, gusting crosswind forced the aircraft off track. Unable to retract the lowered undercarriage due to the hydraulic system being powered by the unserviceable engine, the aircraft lost height and at 10:50 hrs was seen to crash and burst into flames on the edge of the Gwendraeth marshes, about half a mile south of Kidwelly Quay.

Due to the remote location and boggy terrain, it took a while for the emergency services to arrive at the scene, by which time the crew had all perished in the flames. One would-be rescuer, Bill Wainwright, said of the crash:

"On the day in question I was close to the cookhouse when an aircraft was seen approaching the camp in trouble from the direction of Kidwelly. It disappeared from view and immediately a large volume of black smoke was seen rising from the salt marsh. I don't remember any general crash alarm being given. Those of us who had witnessed the aircraft's mishap simply commandeered a truck and drove away from the RAF camp, with others clambering on board as we picked-up speed. We numbered six as we headed in the general direction of Kidwelly.

"Not knowing the area to which we should go, we desperately sought an opening in the hedge which would enable us to drive as close to the scene of the crash as possible. Eventually we found a lane next to a farm at Tycoch near Kidwelly which led, via a bridge over the main railway line, to a marshy area.

"The truck could be driven no further than the bottom of the lane, from there we had to walk over some very wet and boggy ground, taking about 30 minutes before reaching the crashed aircraft. Other services had reached

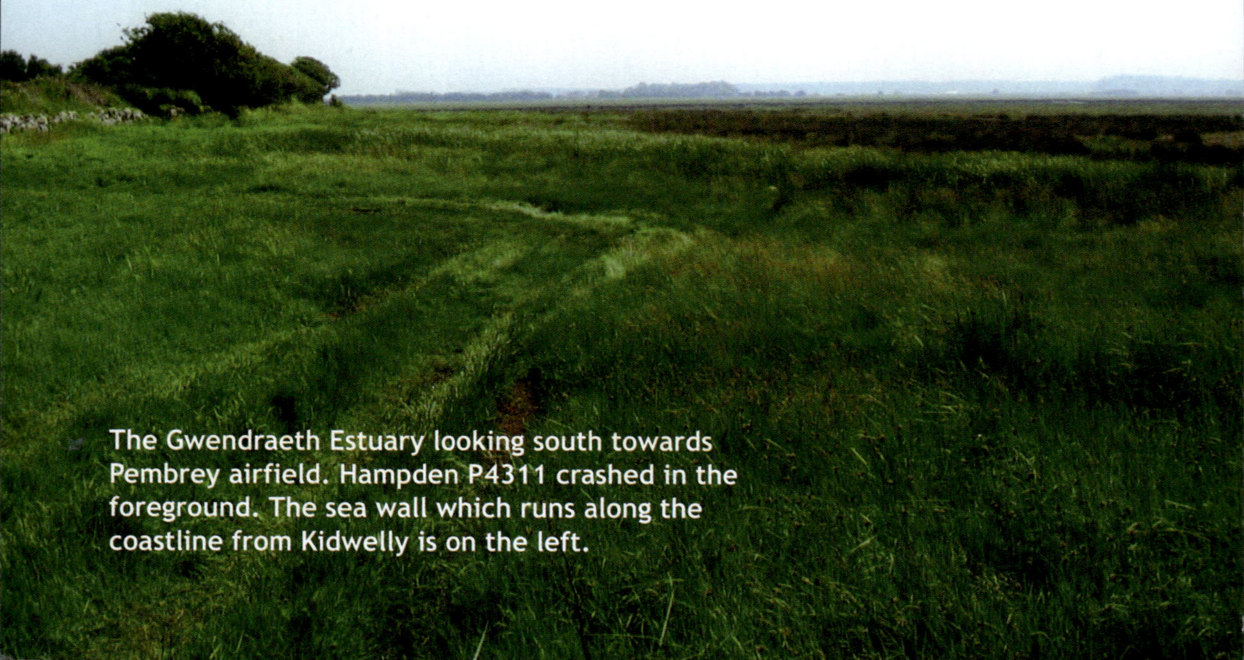

The Gwendraeth Estuary looking south towards Pembrey airfield. Hampden P4311 crashed in the foreground. The sea wall which runs along the coastline from Kidwelly is on the left.

the scene before us and ammunition was still exploding from the heat of the smouldering wreckage."

A subsequent inquiry into the accident came to the conclusion that had the port engine been fitted with a hydraulic pump, then it may have been possible for the pilot to raise the undercarriage, thus allowing the Hampden to pick up speed, gain height and possibly reach the airfield. All four crew are buried alongside each other at St Illtyd's Churchyard, Pembrey. At the location where the aircraft burned out, small pieces of corroded aluminium can still be found in the boggy ground.

CREW LIST: P.O. Sowter BY, Pilot; Sgt. Blair DJ, Co-pilot; Sgt. Brown GW, W.Op/Ag; Sgt. Cooper JDL, W.Op/Ag.

SEPT 30 1940

AIRCRAFT: Hereford L6036

Trainer crashed on its approach to Pembrey

Though never used operationally, the Hereford aircraft was popular with Hampden training units. Just two weeks after the loss of Hampden P4311, Hereford L6036 also crashed while on its approach to Pembrey. On September 30, Flt. Lt. N.W. Timmerman was ferrying the aircraft from RAF Cottesmore. Just after 19:00 hrs, and within sight of Pembrey airfield, the Hereford suffered an engine failure. Flt. Lt. Timmerman, the sole occupant of the aircraft, was able to force land the Hereford onto a coppice of small trees near Caerbigyn Farm on the outskirts of Five Roads. Though the aircraft was a write-off he was able to climb out of the wreckage unhurt. The coppice where the unfortunate Hereford came down has since been cultivated into a grazing field which runs alongside Tir John bungalow.

In October 1940 Pembrey lost three personnel in accidents outside the county. On October 8 the Commanding Officer of the base, Wing Commander Hutchinson, along with a passenger, F.O. Hicks, were en-route to RAF Northolt, on the outskirts of London, in Magister P6347 when it struck a barrage balloon cable in poor weather near Langley, Buckinghamshire. The Magister crashed not far from the main A4 road killing the crew.

The third casualty was P.O. Stanislaw Piatkowski, a Polish pilot on the strength of 79 Squadron. On October 25 while on a routine convoy patrol his Hurricane, N2708, suffered an engine failure off the Pembrokeshire coast. Gliding to shore he found a large field near the village of Milton and attempted a wheels down forced landing. Unknown to him the field had a steep downward incline. As he touched down his Hurricane gained momentum over the ground and struck a hedge at the bottom of the field. It overturned trapping him in his cockpit and burst into flames.

Had the Hurricane been able to glide a little further P.O. Piatkawski would have been able to land safely on the runway at RAF Carew; a few hundred yards from where the aircraft came down.

During December 1940, 78 Maintenance Unit was formed at Bynea near Llanelli. The unit was responsible for the recovery of crashed aircraft in the South Wales area and the salvage of re-usable parts from them. Most of the wartime accidents recorded in this book were attended by the unit.

JAN 12 1941

AIRCRAFT: Hurricane P3871

Flight collision ended in death of a pilot

The first six months of 1941 brought with them a number of Hurricane losses for Pembrey. Not all were 79 Squadron aircraft for in mid-February a new unit, 316 (Polish) Squadron, was formed at the base and from April until June, 32 Squadron was also resident there. The year was only 12 days old when 79 Squadron lost another Hurricane, and sadly its pilot. At 11:35 hrs on January 12 F.O. Alec Chapple was leading a formation of three aircraft on a practice flight at 1,000ft over the airfield. Changing his position in the formation, a new pilot – Sgt. Boucher – in Hurricane P3716, came in a little too fast, overshot, and collided with the leader's wing. Chapple's Hurricane turned over onto its back and crashed on the airfield.

FEB 24 1941

AIRCRAFT: Hurricane P3122

Pilot failed to pull-up from a strafing dive

On February 24 another training accident involving a new pilot occurred on Cefn Sidan beach. At 15:20 hrs Sgt. C.A. Venn was practising air-to-ground strafing techniques when he failed to pull up in time to avoid an obstruction on the beach, probably an anti-invasion pole, and crashed into the sea. The cause of the accident was attributed to him diving too low and firing his guns for too long. Sgt. Venn had gained his 'wings' the previous November and had flown a total of 12 hours on Hurricanes. He is buried at St Illtyd's churchyard.

APRIL 4 1941

AIRCRAFT: **Hurricane P3661**

Poor weather night patrol that ended in sea tragedy

The first operational loss of 1941 for 79 Squadron came just before midnight on April 4. In poor weather conditions P.O. Robinson and Sgt. Parr were on a night patrol off Linney Head at approximately 15,000ft.

After giving out the wrong recognition signal P.O. Robinson's Hurricane was held in the beam of a searchlight. Dazzled and disorientated, Robinson lost control of his aircraft and at 23:57 hrs it crashed into the sea off the headland. Whether he was able to bail out, or whether he went down with his Hurricane is not known. His body was never found. His name is one of over 20,000 inscribed on the Air Forces Memorial commemorating missing airmen at Runnymede near Windsor.

APRIL 27 1941

AIRCRAFT: **Hurricane P3264**

Engine failure meant dip in the sea for two pilots

At the end of April, two 79 Squadron pilots had the misfortune of having to ditch in the cold waters off the South Wales coast. The sea temperature at this time of year is at its coldest, around 9 degrees Celsius, and survival time for a downed pilot without a dinghy, can be measured in minutes rather than hours.

While on a convoy patrol in the morning of April 27, P.O. W.R.A. Walters' Hurricane suffered an engine failure over the sea and was forced to ditch nine miles south west of Pembrey. After carrying out a textbook landing on the sea, he was last seen by his wingman swimming away from his sinking aircraft in his Mae West lifejacket. However, during the 90 minutes it took for the air-sea rescue launch to reach his location he had succumbed to the effects of exposure and died. He was buried at St Illtyd's churchyard.

During the inquiry which followed, the air-sea rescue service was severely criticised for its delay in reaching the pilot and as a matter of urgency 20 K-type, single-seat, survival dinghies were promptly delivered to the base. Two days later on 29 April, Sgt. Evans had a similar experience in Hurricane V7022 while patrolling off St Anne's Head. Luckily he was picked up by a fishing boat soon after the event.

MAY
8
1941

AIRCRAFT: **Hurricane Z2324**

Failed to pull up from ground target dive

A further accident at the air-to-ground firing range on Cefn Sidan beach occurred in the afternoon of May 8. In similar circumstances to that of the loss of Sgt. Venn two months earlier, P.O. Alexsander Kawczynski of 32 Squadron was diving at a ground target when he failed to pull-up in time. He is buried at St Illtyd's in a joint grave with another Polish pilot, P.O. Bohdan Anders. The reason for this joint grave, unusual when it comes to Allied airmen, remains a puzzle. It can only be assumed that they were good friends. The entry in the church register reads: 'buried by request in same grave.'

On June 2, 1941, while outbound from Pembrey to pick up a fellow squadron pilot from the Hurricane repair depot at Hanworth, Middlesex, adjacent to the modern-day airport at Heathrow, P.O. Bohdan Anders also lost his life. The tragedy occured when Magister, R1838, in which he was the sole occupant, flew into a barrage balloon cable anchored at Pen y Lan Farm on the outskirts of Newport. In poor weather conditions he had strayed off course, replicating the circumstances surrounding the loss of Wing Commander Hutchinson a few months previously. The crash site overlooks the M4 motorway near the Malpas interchange.

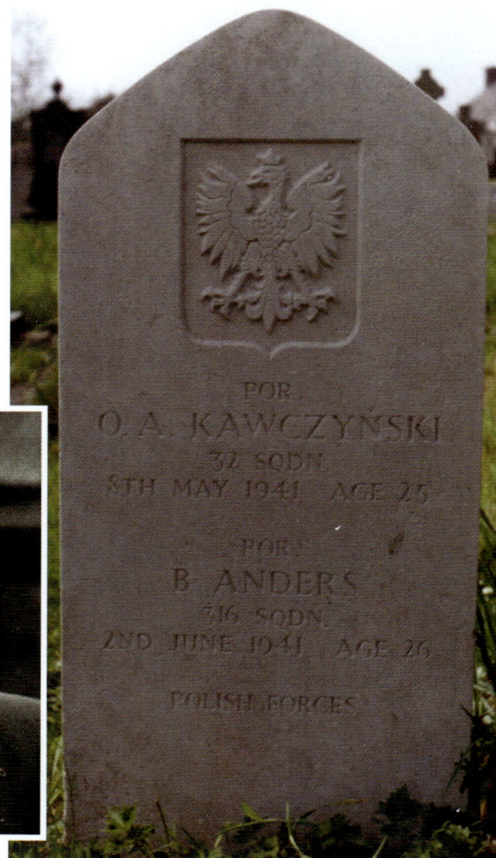

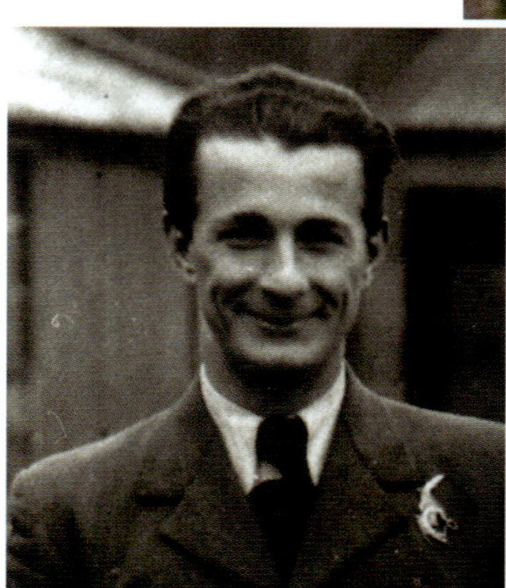

The headstone at St Illtyd's Churchyard Pembrey which marks the joint grave of Alexsander Kawczynski and INSET: Bohdan Anders.

Anders had the distinction of being credited with a 50 per cent claim in the shooting-down of 316 Squadron's first 'kill', a Heinkel 111 which force landed in County Wexford, Ireland on April 1, 1941. Both airmen were posthumously promoted to the rank of Flying Officer.

MAY 17 1941

AIRCRAFT: Hurricane W9231

Debris rained down from crippled shipping patrol

On February 15, 316 (Polish) Squadron was formed at Pembrey from former personnel of the 1st Warsaw Air Regiment. With the squadron code letters SZ on the sides of their Hurricanes they became known to their fellow countrymen as the shoe makers, a nickname derived from the Polish word SZewcy. One of the squadron's future Commanding Officers was Waclaw Wilczewski, who in May 1941 was a Flight Lieutenant at Pembrey.

During the afternoon of Saturday May 17, Flt. Lt. Wilczewski was airborne on a shipping patrol above the Bristol Channel when he noticed his Hurricane's Merlin engine vibrating strongly. While attempting to return to Pembrey airfield the vibration worsened, so he opted to force-land immediately in the nearest suitable field. Making landfall to the east of Llanelli and then heading west, his first choice of a landing area was the recreation ground at Pen y Fan on the side of Bigyn hill. This however was thwarted when he saw children playing in the vicinity. Passing low over Llanelli and concentrating on trying to find somewhere to put-down, Wilczewski failed to notice the web of high tension power cables which ran across his path near the cricket pitch at Stradey Park.

With a bright flash and loud bang his Hurricane clipped the cables, but miraculously, even after losing bits of its airframe, it flew on. Being a Saturday there was a cricket match in progress at the ground and both players and spectators were left in a state of shock as they came to terms with what they had just witnessed. Falling debris from the plane had even rained down onto the green.

Opening up the aircraft's throttle to gain precious altitude, Wilczewski kept the Hurricane airborne for a further mile or so before it lost its fight with gravity and crash landed on waste ground near the foreshore at Pwll. The area where the Hurricane touched down was at that time made up of uneven industrial spoil scattered among small fields – not an ideal spot for the force landing of an aircraft. With a limited amount of space available Wilczewski selected one of the fields and skilfully slewed the Hurricane onto one wing, enabling him to bring the aircraft to rest in a shorter distance. He emerged from the battered aircraft unhurt and was allegedly seen by bystanders kicking the side of the fuselage in a frantic 'John Cleese' fashion. The remaining few miles back to Pembrey airfield were made in a jeep sent out from the camp.

In August Waclaw Wilczewski became 316 Squadron's Commanding Officer until he was shot down over northern France on November 8. Following his capture he remained a prisoner-of-war until the end of hostilities. In 1945 he returned to Britain for a short time before emigrating to Venezuela.

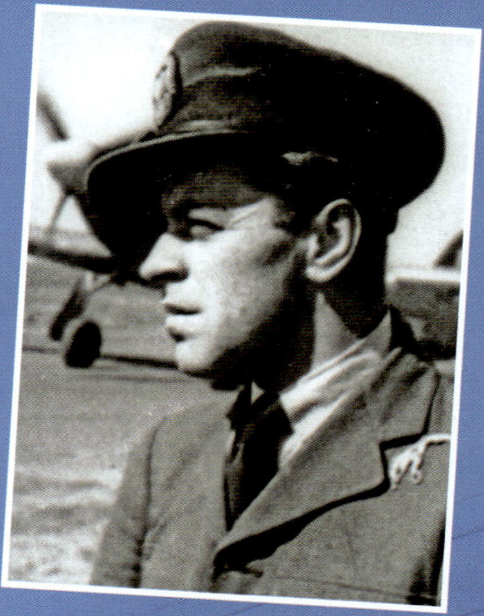

The power cables adjacent to the cricket pitch at Stradey Park, home of Llanelli Cricket Club, are still evident, though the waste ground at Pwll where Hurricane W9231 ended its days has been transformed into a sports field. The crash site was just a few yards off Tramway Road. Three days after Flt. Lt. Wilczewski's lucky escape another 316 Squadron pilot cheated death over the Bristol Channel. Sgt. Wladyslaw Kiedrzynski was patrolling off St David's Head in Hurricane V6873 when his engine also gave him cause for concern. While heading for the coast a serious fire broke out in the engine compartment which

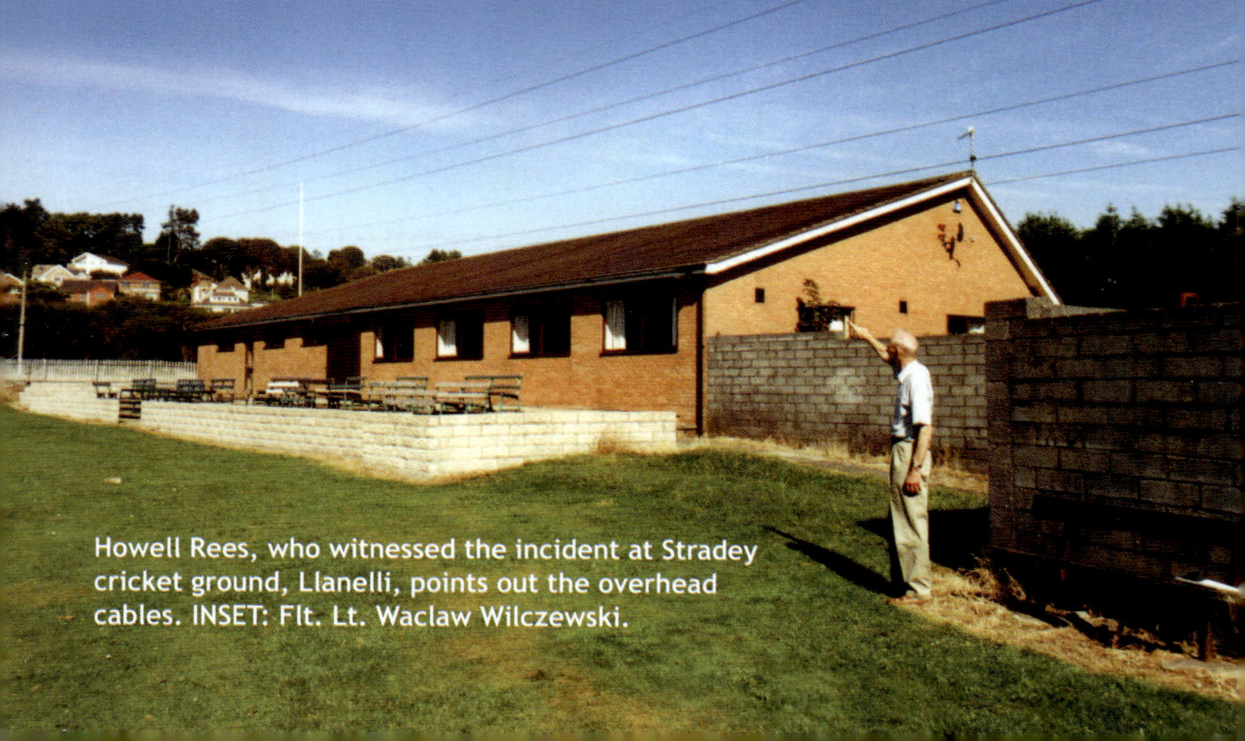

Howell Rees, who witnessed the incident at Stradey cricket ground, Llanelli, points out the overhead cables. INSET: Flt. Lt. Waclaw Wilczewski.

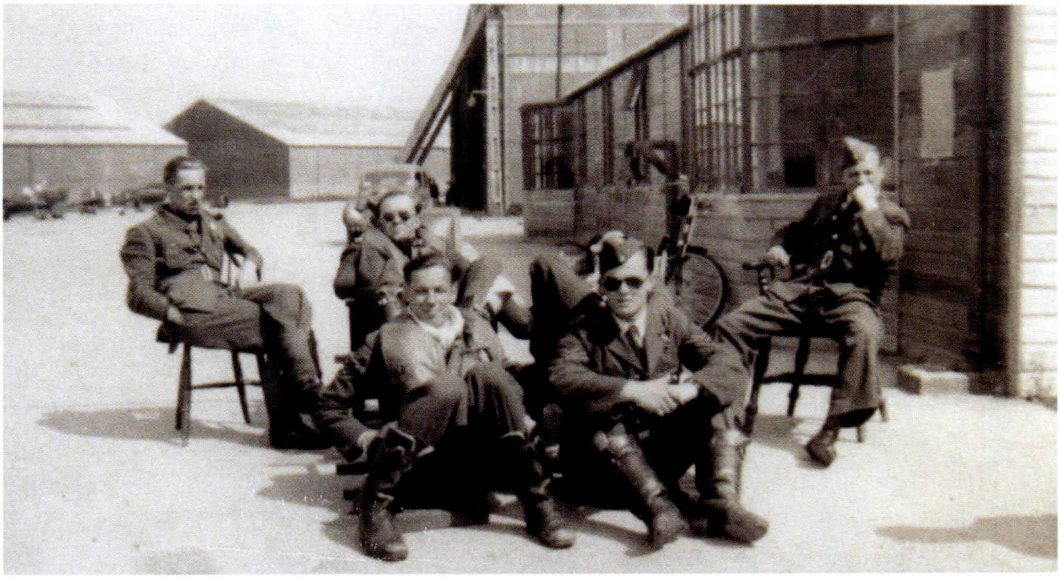

A group of 316 Squadron pilots at the ready outside the dispersal hut at Pembrey Airfield, in the spring of 1941.

spread into the cockpit forcing him to bail out near Ramsey Island. At a height of only 50ft above the sea his parachute opened and he fell into the icy water. The island farmer, Bertie Griffiths, had witnessed his descent and made his way over the rocky terrain towards the location of the downed pilot, who was not far from the shore.
After helping Sgt. Kiedrzynski out of the water, a rowing boat was then brought around by a farm labourer and both Bertie and the pilot were taken on board. Kiedrzynski was then transferred onto the St David's lifeboat to cross Ramsey Sound and taken to the mainland where his burn injuries were attended to at Haverfordwest Hospital.

Having survived the war Wladyslaw Kiedrzynski left the RAF with the rank of Flt. Lt. and emigrated to Canada.

In 1995 I located the wreckage of his Hurricane in the deep and turbulent waters of Ramsey Sound. One of the more interesting parts that I discovered was the aircraft's bullet-proof windscreen. The inner surface was heavily scorched, in itself a testament to the intense heat which forced the pilot to bail out.

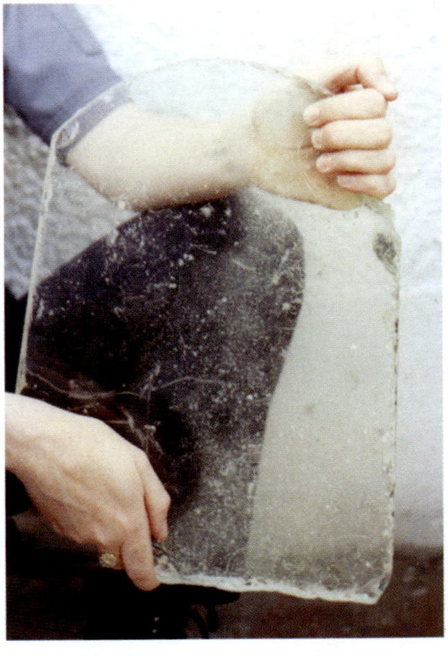

The bullet-proof windscreen from the wreck of Hurricane V6873. The inner surface was scorched by the engine fire.

Hurricane V6873's time with 316 Squadron was short-lived. Having arrived at Pembrey on 18 May from 257 Squadron at RAF Coltishall, possibly as a replacement for Waclaw Wilczewski's aircraft, it was first flown by 316 Squadron on the morning of May 20, before ending up in the sea off Pembrokeshire later the same day.

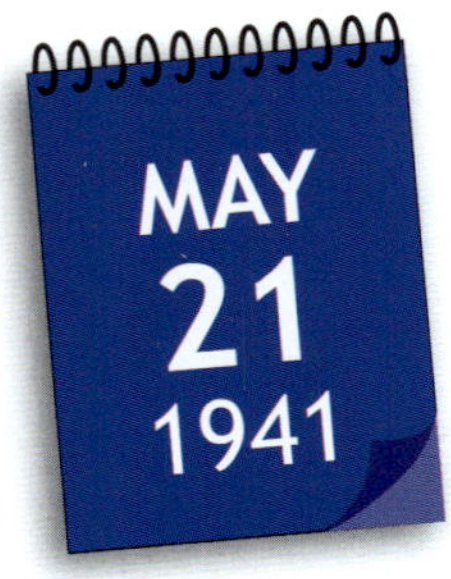

AIRCRAFT: **Lysander V9361**

Rescue Lizzie's mission ended in hillside inferno

As highlighted in the previous account, by 1941 the RAF had realised the need to have dedicated air-sea rescue aircraft stationed at strategic locations around the coastline of Britain. With so much aerial activity now taking place over the sea increasing numbers of aircrew were finding themselves in the 'drink' as such incidents were referred to. It was imperative to rescue these ditched airmen as quickly as possible before they succumbed to the effects of hypothermia. If immediate retrieval by either surface launch or amphibious aircraft proved impossible, then even an air drop of survival equipment and food rations could mean the difference between life or death for airmen in the open sea.

One type of aircraft used for these mercy missions was the Westland Lysander. A high-winged mainplane and low stalling speed made the 'Lizzie', as they were nicknamed, an ideal observation platform to search for downed crews.

At the beginning of April 1941 two Lysander aircraft arrived at Pembrey specifically for the role of air-sea rescue. One of them was V9361. This aircraft had a short career at Pembrey, for on May 21, just over six weeks after its arrival it was written-off in an accident.

The events which led to the aircraft's demise began in the early afternoon when a Tiger Moth, N6853, departed from Pembrey after an armament inspection of the camp. Later in the afternoon a telephone call was received at the base to inform them that the Tiger Moth was overdue at its intended destination and a search for it was to be carried out.

The Duty Pilot at Pembrey that day was F.O. Peter Lochnan, a Canadian on detachment from 400 Squadron based at RAF Odiham, Wiltshire. With Sgt. Cyril Cave as his wireless operator, he took off in V9361 and commenced a search for the missing Tiger Moth. During the sortie the weather started to deteriorate and with light, drizzly rain making visibility poor continuing the search seemed futile. At 18:20 hrs, while nearing the airfield, a tree-lined hilltop loomed up out of the mist. With no time to take evasive action the Lysander flew straight into the trees and caught fire.

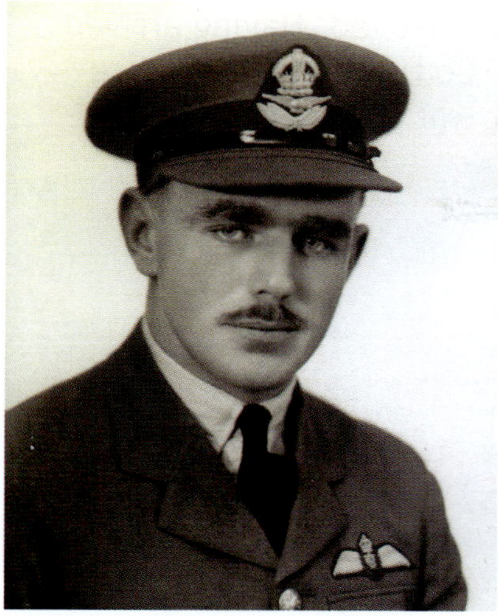

Trapped – F.O. Peter Lochnan.

At Coed Farm, Pinged, at the foot of Mynydd Pembrey, farmer William Howells had heard the Lysander crash and rushed up the steep hillside to help. Arriving at the summit he was confronted with a fierce blaze which had engulfed the whole aircraft. Exploding 303 rounds were flying everywhere. Despite these hazards he was able to pull Sgt. Cave clear of the inferno, but attempts to reach F.O. Lochnan, who was trapped inside the twisted cockpit, proved unsuccessful.

Later that night came news of the missing Tiger Moth, it had run out of fuel and crashed into the River Severn near Beachley at 17:40 hrs killing both crew members. An investigation into the crash came to the conclusion that the Tiger Moth had left Pembrey without refuelling and as a result had insufficient petrol in its tanks for its intended journey.

F.O. Peter Lochnan was a keen sportsman, at one time he was the northern Ontario slalom ski champion and excelled at many other sports including wrestling, football and tennis. Before joining the air force he studied medicine at Queen's University Kingston, Ontario. On the outbreak of the Second World War Peter Lochnan was already a P.O. in the RCAF and was posted overseas to the UK in the spring of 1940. During the Battle of Britain he served with 1 (Canadian) Squadron flying Hurricanes from RAF Northolt. Being based on the outskirts of London his tally of enemy aircraft destroyed rose steadily. He was himself shot down near Dover, but lived to tell the tale. In February 1941 he was posted to 400 Squadron, a Canadian, Army Co-Operation Unit based at Odiham. It was from here that he volunteered for air-sea rescue duties and arrived at Pembrey in mid-May, just days prior to the accident. A sad feature of his death was the fact that he was shortly due to return to Canada on leave. May 20, the day before the accident, marked his first wedding anniversary.

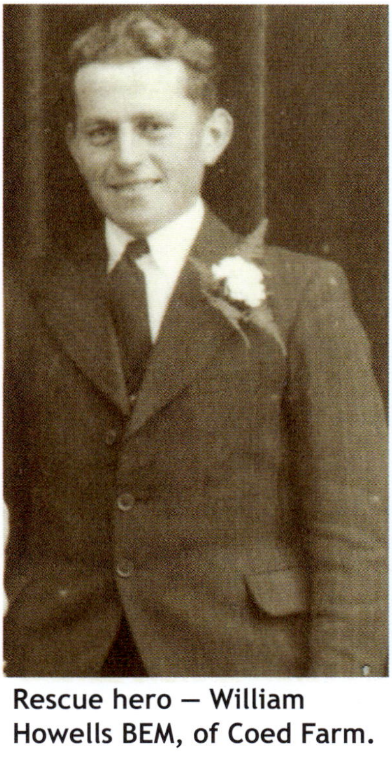

Rescue hero – William Howells BEM, of Coed Farm.

Sgt. Cyril Cave made a full recovery from his injuries and went on to serve with 276 Squadron (Air-Sea Rescue). On November 7, 1942 while searching for a downed Spitfire pilot off Dodman Point, Cornwall, the Defiant aircraft in which he was a wireless operator, crashed into the sea with no survivors. His name is recorded on the Runnymede Memorial at Windsor.

The downed Spitfire pilot he had been searching for was a Czech airman, F.O. Jan Doucha. Doucha's body was carried by sea currents around the Cornish coast and eventually washed ashore six weeks later at Freshwater West beach in Pembrokeshire. He is buried at Angle churchyard.

On May 22, the day following the accident on Mynydd Pembrey, a third incident connected with events of the previous day happened a few miles away on the Gower Peninsula. While attempting to reach Pembrey by air, a close friend of F.O. Lochnan crashed his Tomahawk aircraft in poor weather conditions and was killed. The pilot, Flt. Lt. William Rider, was a fellow

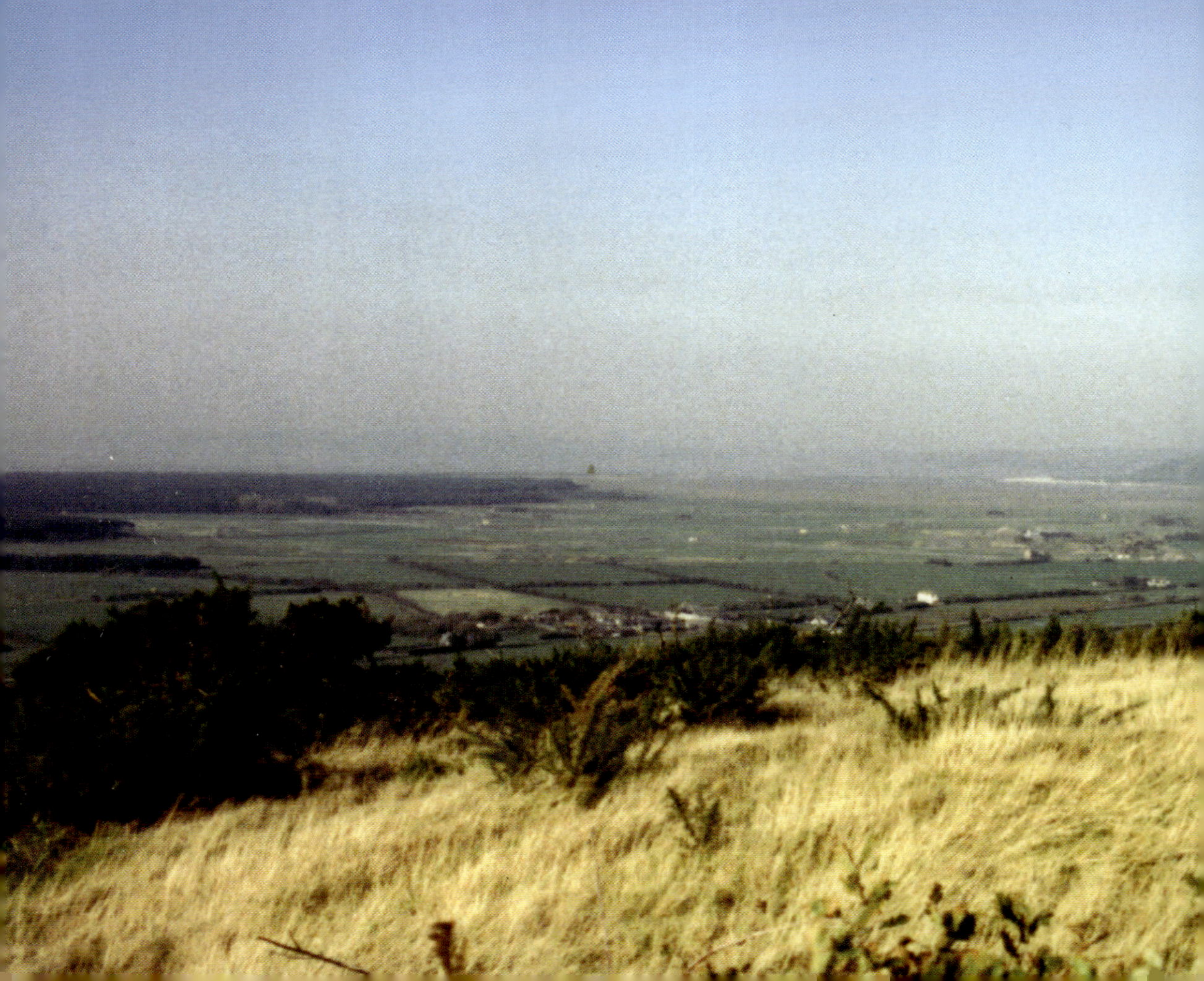

Lysander V9361 hit the trees on the right of this panoramic view. Pembrey airfield is just visible in the distance.

Canadian from 400 Squadron. Both Lochnan and Rider are buried side-by-side at Brookwood cemetery near Woking.

At Coed Farm life went on much the same as it had done before the events of May 21 with two exceptions – William Howells eventually received the British Empire Medal for his bravery on Mynydd Pembrey and he carried the scars from burn injuries to his hands for the rest of his life.

The hilltop into which Lysander V9361 crashed still holds evidence of the accident which happened nearly 75 years ago. Embedded in the trunk of one tree is a piece of aluminium while scattered amongst the undergrowth exploded 303 rounds lie in abundance.

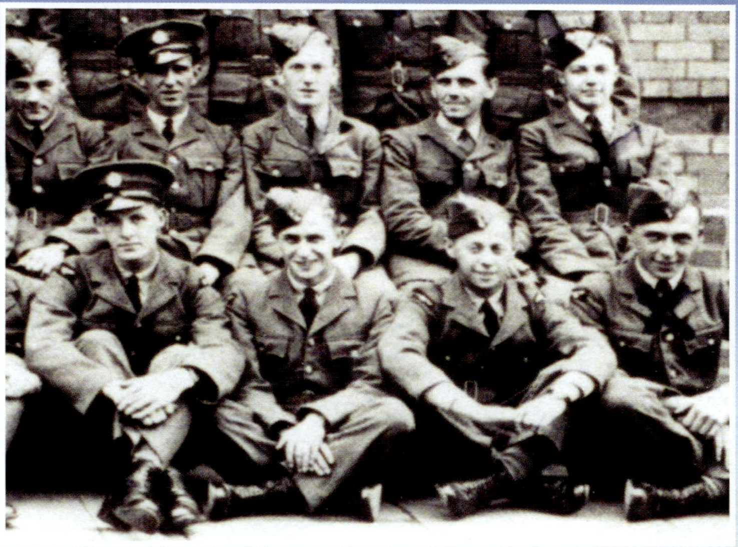

Sgt. Cyril Cave, is seated second from the right in the back row of this group.

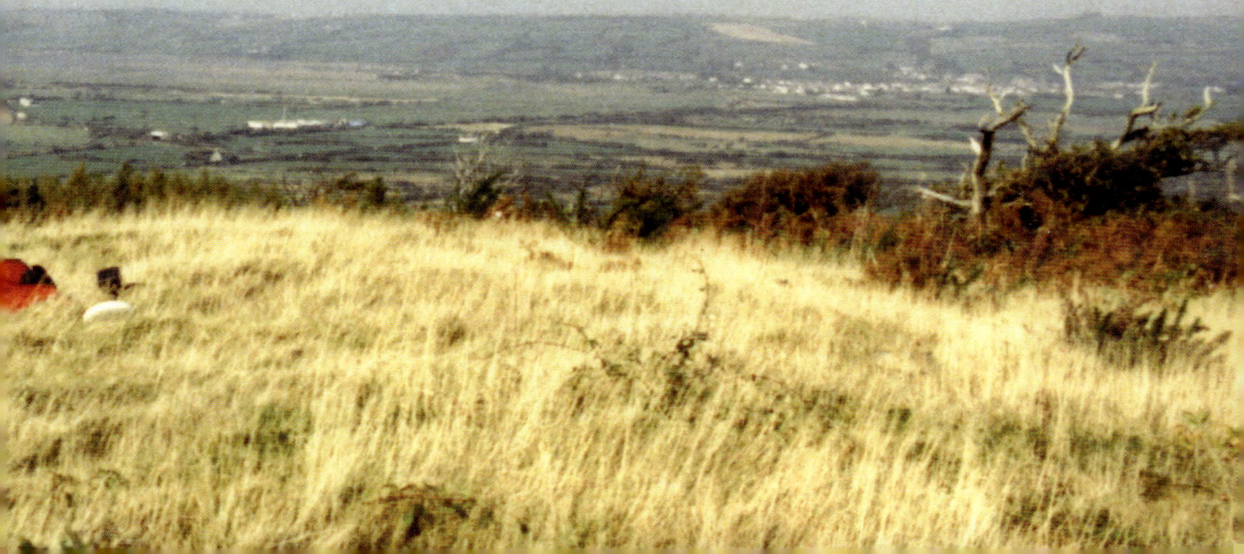

JUNE
13
1941

AIRCRAFT: Hurricanes Z2669/V6958/P7193

Unlucky day was no exception at Pembrey

To the superstitious Friday 13th is regarded as a day which brings with it bad luck. Friday June 13, 1941 was no exception at RAF Pembrey. By sunset on that day incredibly, the base had lost three of its Hurricanes.

The first victim was Z2669 of 79 Squadron. At around 09:00 hrs P.O. Thomas was engaged on a convoy patrol 10 miles west of the Smalls lighthouse with his section leader, Flt. Lt. Bryant-Fenn, when his Hurricane developed engine trouble. A short time later he successfully ditched the aircraft in the sea and was picked up by a passing destroyer.

Meanwhile, at midday four 316 Squadron aircraft were taking part in a training exercise. At 12:10 hrs, F.O. Jan Grzech, and his section leader, Sgt. Gottowt, were diving onto a target aircraft from 6,000ft when they collided. Grzech's Hurricane, V6958, went into a spin and, unable to regain control of the aircraft, he bailed out. Grzech made a safe parachute descent, but injured his foot when he landed at Wern Farm near Trimsaran. Sgt. Gottowt was able to nurse his damaged Hurricane back to Pembrey and

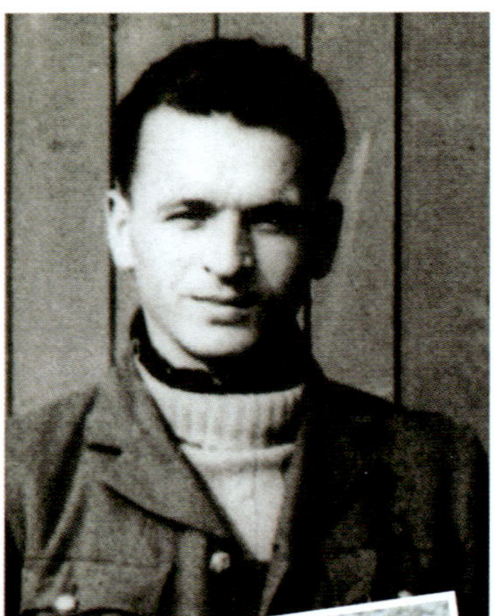

Flying officer Jan Grzech. BELOW: The Merlin engine of V6958 and alongside, the reflector gunsight recovered by the Green brothers in 1976.

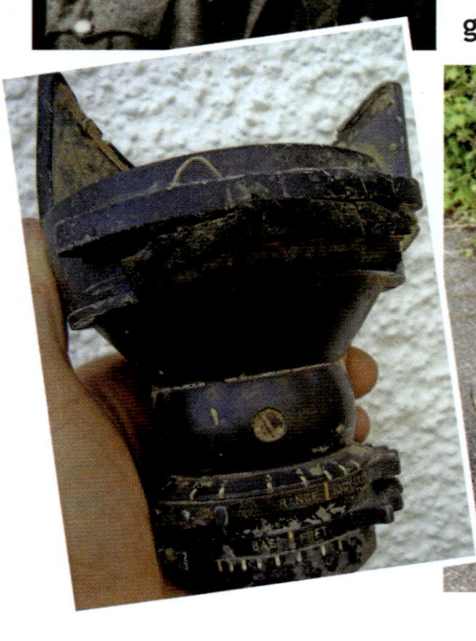

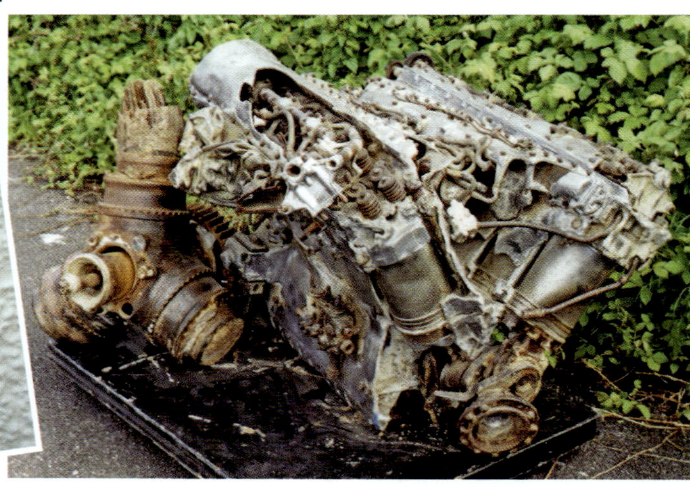

landed without incident. Less fortunate, V6958 crashed nose-down into boggy ground at Muddlescwm Farm on the outskirts of Kidwelly. So deeply buried was the wreckage that most of it was left where it fell.

In 1976 farmer Daniel Gravell was channelling a drainage ditch in the area where V6958 had crashed when the bucket of his JCB digger struck a hard object deep in the ground. Careful excavation of the earth around the drainage trench revealed a 12 cylinder Merlin aero engine in exceptionally good condition. The Merlin was later cleaned up and donated to the Abergavenny branch of the Air Training Corps who exhibited it at their crash site museum.

The museum closed in 2002, but thanks to the forward thinking of its curator, W.O. Danny Hickey, V6958's Merlin travelled back to Kidwelly where it can be seen on display at the town's Industrial Museum; less than a mile from where the Hurricane crashed.

Also on display at the Kidwelly museum are various other artefacts from Grzech's Hurricane kindly donated by Richard Green of Mynydd y Garreg. Richard, along with his brother, Alan, carried out a hurried excavation of the crash site before it was torn apart by mechanical diggers during the drainage work in 1976. Artefacts recovered by Richard and Alan include the reflector gun-sight, the firing button from the control column and a host of other interesting relics. Jan Grzech spent three weeks in hospital due to his injured foot, by which time his unit had moved to RAF Colerne near Bath. In September he was posted to 315 Squadron, another Polish unit, which flew Spitfires from RAF Northolt.

On November 23, 315 Squadron lost five pilots while escorting Hurri-bombers (Hurricane bombers) in the vicinity of Dunkirk; Jan Grzech was one of them. He is buried at Dunkirk Town cemetery alongside other Polish pilots lost on the same fateful mission.

On the evening of June 10, 1941 three Tomahawk aircraft from 26 Squadron, RAF Gatwick, touched down at Pembrey airfield. They were part of 26 Squadron, an Army Co-Operation Unit used primarily for spotting and recording potential artillery targets on the ground.

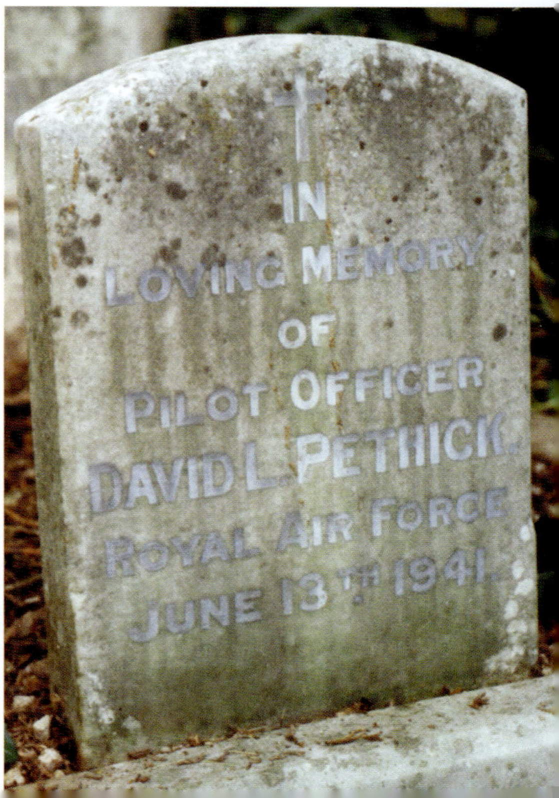

The private headstone of P.O. David Pethick at Efford Cemetery, Plymouth.

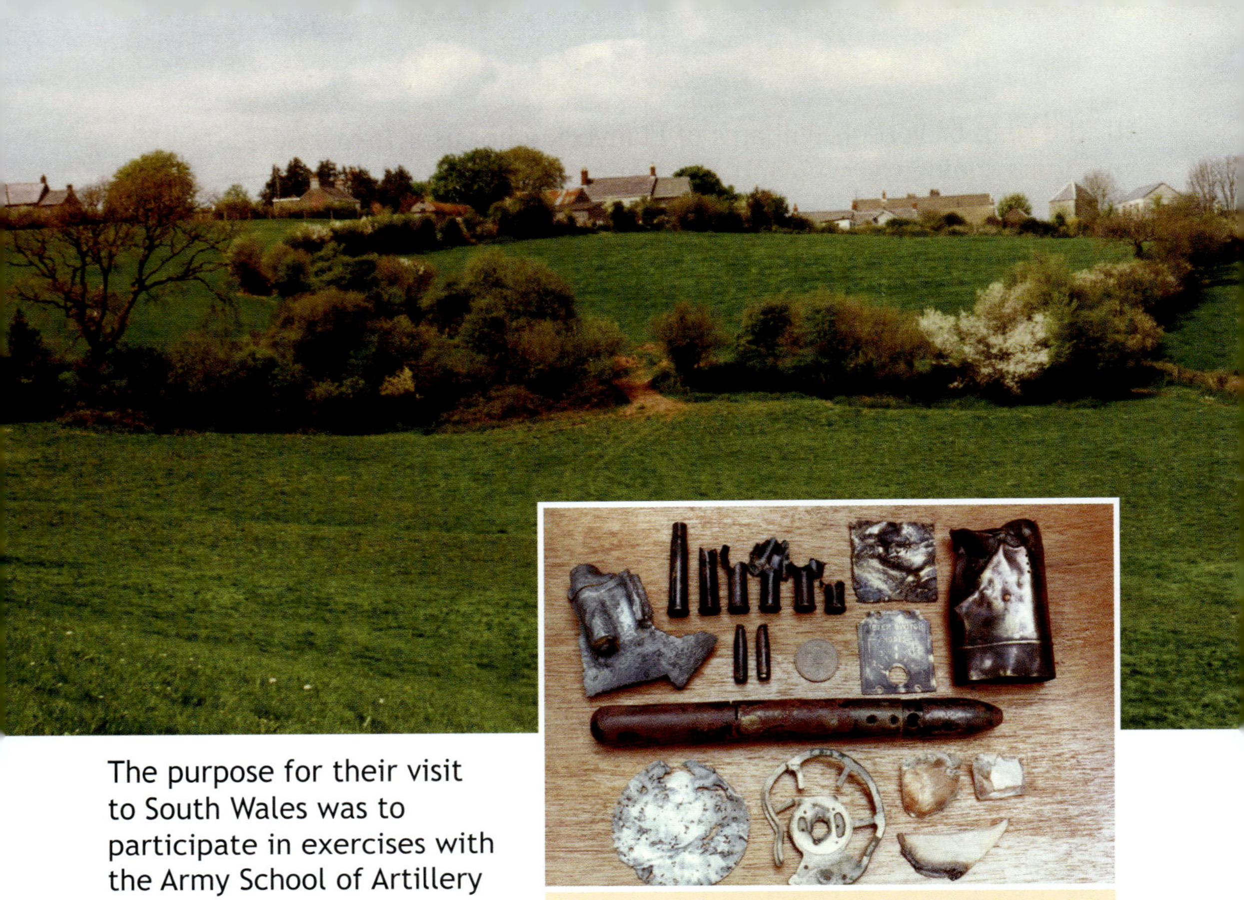

Hurricane P7193 came down below the tree on the bottom left of this view. INSET: Artefacts found after a metal detector search of the area. The cigar-shaped object in the centre is the aircraft's pitot tube. Located on the under surface of the wing, it measured air speed. The 'cooked' 303 rounds (top-centre) and melted plexi-glass (bottom right) indicate that there was a small fire after the crash. None of the other items recovered show signs of fire damage.

The purpose for their visit to South Wales was to participate in exercises with the Army School of Artillery at the Sennybridge firing ranges near Brecon.

On the afternoon of June 13, their third day at Pembrey, one of the Tomahawk pilots, P.O. David Pethick, was gaining some experience in a borrowed 79 Squadron Hurricane; P7193.
At 16:00 hrs while flying near Llanstephan the Hurricane's Merlin engine was heard to cut out. On trying to restart it the aircraft entered a stall and at 2,000ft started to spin. P.O. Pethick managed to temporarily regain control, but on descending to 1,000ft the Hurricane entered a dive towards the ground. At an altitude of only 200ft the pilot was seen to abandon the aircraft and was killed when he struck the ground near the village of Llanybri.

David Pethick obtained his 'wings' in November 1940 and had flown a total of 353 hours airtime, none of which were on Hurricanes. He is buried in the Pethick family plot under a private headstone at Efford cemetery, Plymouth.

With the help of Verdun Williams of Llanybri, who, as a 16-year old, remembers seeing the wrecked Hurricane after the crash, I was able to identify the field into which both P.O. Pethick and his aircraft fell. A metal detector sweep of the field, just below Dan y Capel, uncovered a number of artefacts left behind by the recovery crew. These included the Hurricane's pitot tube, 303 ammunition, a fuel gauge instrument face and pieces of airframe stamped G5. The latter indicating that the Hurricane was a Gloster-built aircraft.

On June 15, 1941, a year after it was handed over to Fighter Command, Pembrey ceased to be an operational station and was handed back to Flying Training Command. Its primary function for the remainder of the Second World War was to be the training of air gunners through the newly formed 1 Air Gunners' School.

JULY
5
1941

AIRCRAFT: **Hurricane Z2689**

Lucky drop for pilot who was downed twice

Even though 79 Squadron had relocated to RAF Fairwood Common near Swansea when Pembrey became non-operational, in early July it was unfortunate enough to lose yet another Hurricane over the Carmarthenshire countryside.

In the small hours of July 5, F.O. George Nelson-Edwards, a descendant of Admiral Horatio Nelson, was patrolling on a line from Swansea to Pembroke Dock when he was vectored to intercept a 'bandit' in the Llanelli area. Arriving at the co-ordinates he quickly homed-in on an enemy bomber caught in the cone of a searchlight, but on getting closer to the bomber the searchlights were suddenly doused. Losing contact with the enemy aircraft Nelson-Edwards resumed his patrol line along the coast. Minutes later he saw flames issuing from underneath the Hurricane's engine cowling which quickly spread to the floor of the cockpit; he had no choice but to bail out.

Descending in the inky darkness of the night's sky he was deeply concerned for his well-being as he was unsure of whether he was over the sea, or the Welsh countryside.

Ten months earlier, on September 29, 1940, the birthday of his famous ancestor, he had cheated death after having been shot down into the sea off southern Ireland by return gunfire from a Heinkel 111. Luckily on that occasion the crew of a passing merchant ship had seen his Hurricane falling out of the sky and plucked him from certain death. Now entering the same predicament at night nobody would be able to witness his demise.

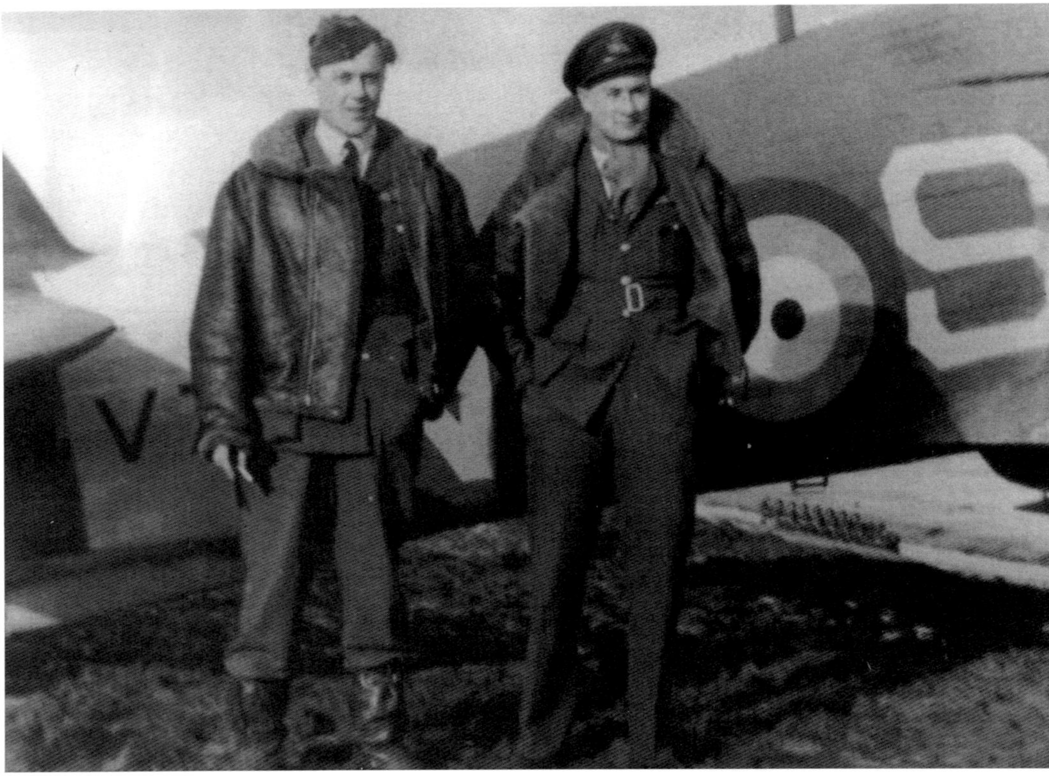

George Nelson-Edwards, left, with fellow 79 Squadron pilot Douglas Clift beside Hurricane V7013 (NV-S). Pembrey 1941. F.O. Nelson-Edwards had the distinction of being the first pilot to officially land an aircraft at the newly opened RAF Fairwood Common in June 1941.

To his relief as he neared the end of his parachute descent he could see and hear the sound of breaking waves below him on the coast, but an offshore breeze was carrying him seaward. Pulling downward on the lines of his parachute hastened his descent and in no time he landed safely on terra firma. Not having a clue as to his whereabouts he headed towards a small farmhouse. It was Pentre Wyman, the farmer inhabitant of which drove him to the searchlight and anti-aircraft battery headquarters at nearby Llwyn Du mansion, just outside the village of Llangain, south of Carmarthen.
From there F.O. Nelson-Edwards was taken back to Fairwood none the worse for his ordeal. His aircraft, Hurricane Z2689, had crashed only a few hundred yards from Llwyn Du mansion, in a field at Llwyn Farm. Its engine had impacted deep into the ground, but the wings and fuselage lay scattered on the surface.

George Nelson-Edwards survived the war and served as a Wing Commander in the post-war RAF. In 1960 he was demobbed from the air force and with his wife Pamela became a restaurateur, firstly at the Trewern Arms in Nevern, Cardiganshire, then in 1994 at the Swan Inn at Little Haven, Pembrokeshire. After briefly emigrating to Cyprus they returned to Narberth where one of their sons, Patrick, still lives. In 1996 I visited Llwyn Du mansion and was surprised to find the house still in the hands of its wartime owner, Mrs Myra Jones. Even more amazing was the fact that Mrs Jones was a good friend of the Nelson-Edwards family and through her I had the privilege of meeting Mrs Pamela Nelson-Edwards. Her late husband George having passed away only two years previously.

After locating the crash site and obtaining the appropriate excavation licence from the RAF, an archaeological dig was carried out at the site. During this exercise a number of engine related components were recovered, all in remarkably good condition. The climax of the excavation came when the Hurricane's propeller boss was located at a depth of five feet below ground level. It was hauled to the surface with the help of a front-loading tractor and can now be seen at the 1940s Swansea Bay Museum at Crymlyn Burrows, Swansea.

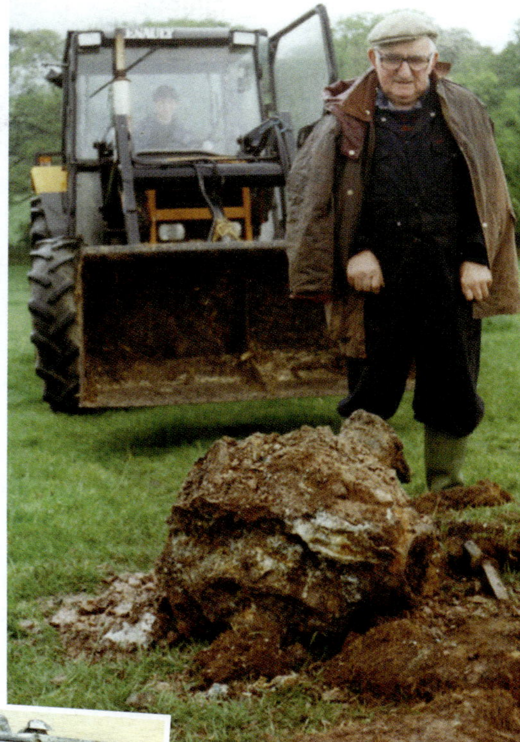

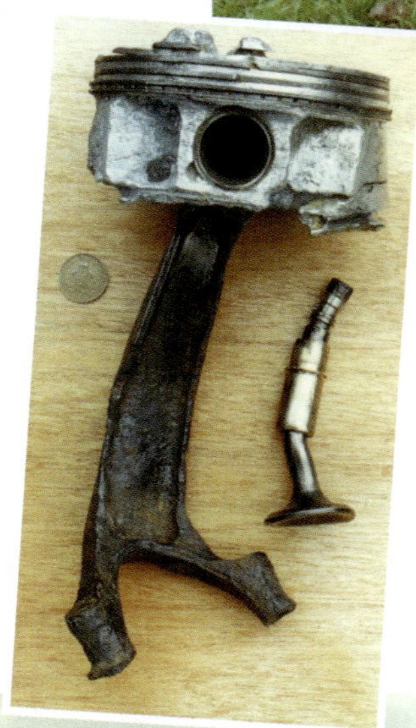

Vincent Davies of Llwyn Farm with the Hurricane's propeller boss, recovered from a depth of five feet. LEFT: a bent piston and engine valve unearthed during the excavation. BELOW: Llwyn Farm and, among the trees to the left, the mansion house. The arrow indicates where Hurricane Z2689 crashed.

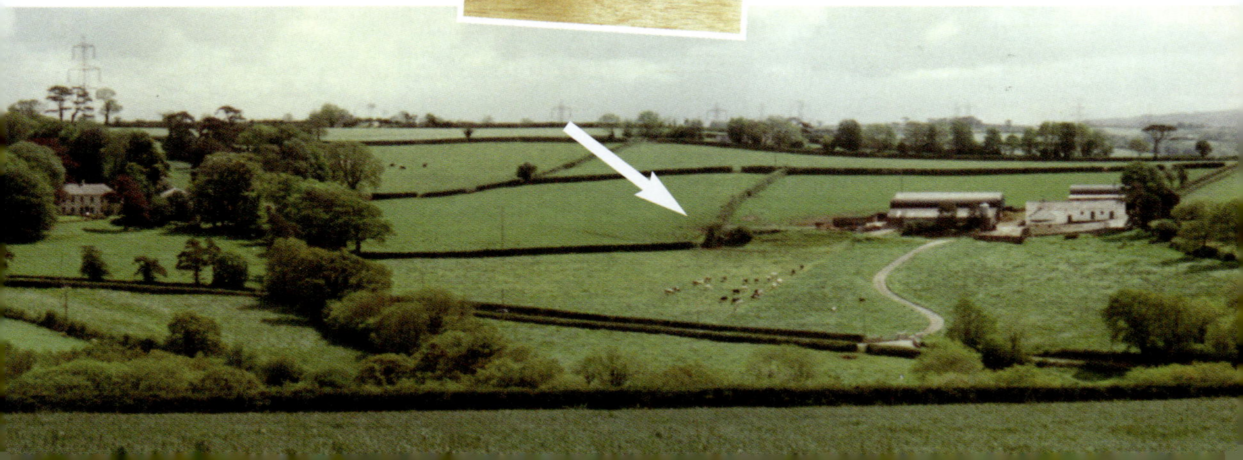

AUG 1 1941

AIRCRAFT: **Blenheim Z6242**

Training sorties increase along with casualties

On June 15, 1941 Pembrey was handed over to RAF Training Command and the station became home to 1 Air Gunners' School. Blenheim aircraft now filled the skies around the airfield. Training facilities were at first very basic, but as the need for replacement air gunners for Bomber Command's night offensive operations over Europe grew, so did the size and importance of the airfield.

With the number of training sorties on the increase, the casualty rate from flying accidents also grew. The first accident, involving a Blenheim from the gunnery school, happened in the early morning of Friday August 1,1941. Because of the fact that nobody survived the crash, the cause remained a mystery, though atmospheric conditions at the time may have been a contributory factor.

While on an air-to-air firing exercise over the sea Z6242 was heard by a Coastwatcher on Burry Holms crashing into the estuary one mile north of the island at around 07:30 hrs. The RAF Accident Report gives mention of sea fog shrouding the area at the time which extended from the surface up to 600ft. Rescue boats and aircraft were scrambled to the scene, but no survivors were found.The following day salvage work began on the wreckage which lay just off Broughton Bay on the north Gower coast at a depth of 20 feet at low water and the body of LAC Alexander MacKay, one of the trainee air gunners on board, was recovered. Further work over the next few days failed to find any trace of the other crew members. Their bodies had been washed away by the strong tides. One of the Blenheim's Mercury engines was raised and a small amount of wreckage washed ashore before the salvage operation was called off.

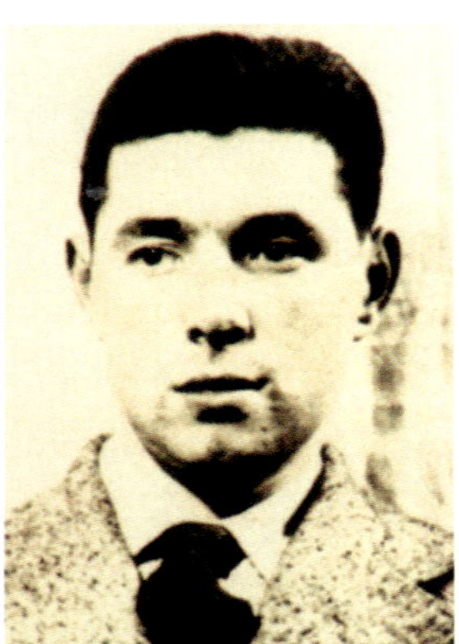

Sgt. Witold Bystrzynski, pilot of Blenheim Z6242.

On August 10, the body of another crew member, LAC Morris, was discovered on rocks at Butterslade Bay near Rhossili. An inquest into his death was held at Middleton Hall, Rhossili before he was laid to rest at St Illtyd's churchyard, Pembrey. The bodies of the other two crew, Sgt. Bystrzynski and LAC Lee were never found.

CREW LIST: Sgt. Bystrzynski W (Polish) Pilot; LAC Lee AE, Ag u/t; LAC Morris WL, Ag u/t; LAC MacKay A, Ag u/t.

Throughout the remainder of 1941 flying accidents still occurred, but due to the skill of the pilots involved there where no casualties. On August 8, Battle L5728, used for target-towing duties at Pembrey, suffered an engine failure while in the vicinity of Llangennith beach. Sgt. Marchewicz, the Polish pilot, carried out a forced-landing on the beach, thus saving the aircraft and his two crew. The Battle landed near Burry Holms.

AUG 10 1941

AIRCRAFT: Blenheim L8745

Highlight of a hot summer's afternoon

Two days later on Sunday August 10, P.O. Giedrys, another Pole carrying out target towing duties, was airborne in Blenheim L8745. During the flight the port engine failed and unable to make it back to the airfield on one engine, he put down in a field at Muddlescwm Farm on the outskirts of Kidwelly.

Dan Gravell recalls vividly the events of that hot summer's afternoon. He and his family had finished their Sunday lunch and had gone outside to enjoy the glorious sunshine. At 14:00 hrs the peace was shattered by the sound of an aircraft tearing up the ground a few hundred yards from the farmhouse. Luckily there was no fire following the belly-landing, enabling P.O. Giedrys and the two other crew, ACs Teasdale and Gray, to walk away from the wrecked Blenheim unharmed.

A short time later the emergency services from the base arrived at the farm and Dan remembers a senior officer escorting one of the crew members, who was 'shaking like a leaf', to a staff car. The officer insisted that the airman be taken back aloft before he lost his nerve for flying. Apparently it had been the airman's first flying experience!

SEP 3 1941

AIRCRAFT: Blenheim Z6259

Lucky crew walked away from crash unscathed

On the evening of September 3, two aircraft force landed within hours of each other. The first was another gunnery school Blenheim, Z6259, which crashed just short of the airfield in a boggy field. The aircraft's undercarriage had been lowered prior to landing and it somehow undershot. The pilot, Sgt. Millichamp, and his three trainee air gunners were fortunate and walked away from the incident unscathed.

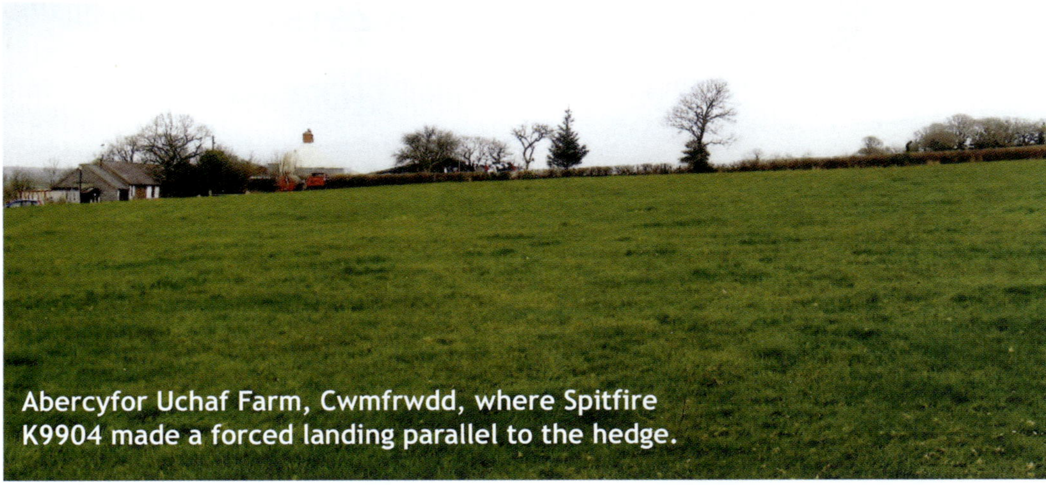

Abercyfor Uchaf Farm, Cwmfrwdd, where Spitfire K9904 made a forced landing parallel to the hedge.

SEP 3 1941

AIRCRAFT: Spitfire K9904

Narrow lanes proved a recovery headache

Later on the evening of September 3 at 20:30 hrs Spitfire K9904 from 53 OTU based at Llandow near Cowbridge, force landed at Abercyfor Uchaf Farm, Cwmfrwdd. Sgt. D. St John, a New Zealander, had been on a sector reconnaissance exercise when he became lost.

Unable to obtain a homing bearing through his unserviceable radio set, he opted to force land, wheels up, in the fading daylight. Although uninjured in the landing his Spitfire, a pre-war Mk. I, was deemed a write-off when it crashed on touching down just yards from the farmhouse. The recovery team from Bynea had considerable difficulty in manoeuvring their 60 foot long lorry through the narrow lane leading to the farm.

FEB 4 1942

AIRCRAFT: Blenheim V5965

Tarmac terror as fire engulfs crash crew

Just after midday on February 4, Blenheim V5965 overshot the runway while landing. After swinging off the tarmac it collided with a stationary Blenheim (V5891) causing both aircraft to catch fire. LAC Lacy M.G., a trainee air gunner, was killed instantly. The pilot, Sgt. Archie Hay, died of his injuries a few hours later. Two other airmen escaped unhurt.

FEB 16 1942

AIRCRAFT: **Blenheim Z6187**

Fishery protection patrol that ended in fireball

Stationed at RAF Carew, Blenheim Z6187 of 254 Squadron had taken off with another Blenheim at 14:54 hrs on the afternoon of February 16, on a fishery protection patrol of the Irish Sea. Arriving at the start of their patrol area at 15:30 hrs both aircraft monitored an area of water off the southern tip of Ireland for over two hours before setting course back to base at 18:10 hrs. During the return flight back to Carew visibility in the now dark night sky deteriorated even further and Z6187 was last seen entering a bank of fog near the coast at 19:19 hrs. The other Blenheim managed to find Carew and landed safely at 19:35 hrs.

P.O. John Tully, the pilot of Blenheim Z6187, became disorientated in the poor visibility, over-flew into Carmarthen Bay and became lost. However at 20:25 hrs, with the help of a radio-homing bearing, the crew were able to locate the runways at Pembrey and proceeded to land. In his haste to get the aircraft on the ground, possibly because of a dwindling fuel supply, P.O. Tully misjudged his approach to the airfield and decided on a 'go around' for a second attempt. The aircraft's throttles were opened-up, but the flaps were raised at too low an altitude. As a result the Blenheim lost height over the airfield, hit the ground and burst into flames.

All three crew were seriously injured in the crash and admitted to Llanelli Hospital. Flt. Sgt. Reginald Fenney, the Blenheim's observer, succumbed to his injuries two day's later. He is buried in his home town at Hoylake, near Liverpool.

During the investigation that followed John Tully was exonerated from any blame for the accident as the Blenheim's altimeter was found to have been defective.

In May 1942, on recovering from his injuries, the 28 year-old Australian from Quilpie, a remote town in the Queensland outback, was posted to 1 Photo Reconnaissance Unit based at RAF Benson in Oxfordshire. While flying from one of the unit's forward bases at RAF Wick in Scotland he failed to return from a photo reconnaissance mission over Norway on July 30. His Spitfire, AA800, was presumed to have come down in the North Sea.

CREW LIST: P.O. Tully JL, Pilot, injured;
Flt. Sgt. Fenney R, Observer, died from injuries;
Sgt. Carey H, Air Gunner, injured.

MAR
23
1942

AIRCRAFT: **Blenheim V5745**

Camera practice that was too close for comfort

Live firing exercises from RAF Pembrey were usually carried out over the vast expanses of Carmarthen Bay. However some training routines, such as camera gun manipulation for example, were undertaken over the sparsely populated countryside of rural Carmarthenshire.

At 14:30 hrs on March 23, Blenheim V5745 from Pembrey's gunnery school was airborne on such an exercise in the vicinity of Meidrim. Witnesses on the ground recall seeing smoke issuing from the aircraft while it was still in flight, possibly from one of the engines.

The Blenheim lost height and force landed in a field near Bryn Eglur Farm, just south of Trelech. On touching down the aircraft careered into a hedge and burst into flames, trapping all four crew inside.

The Blenheim had come to rest at a distance of only 100 yards from the front door of the farmhouse at Bryn Eglur and its owner, James Davies, was quickly at the scene. The fierce heat initially kept him away from the inferno and he assumed that no one had survived the crash.

On closer inspection he saw movement in the turret area of the fuselage and initiated a very brave rescue attempt. This resulted in LAC Olson, one of the trainee air gunners, being plucked to safety. Although seriously injured, Olson, a member of the Royal Norwegian Air force, was taken to Carmarthen Hospital and survived his ordeal.

Another local farmer, David Thomas of Pant y Coed and labourer, Alun Anthony, also helped in the rescue attempt, but all efforts to release the three remaining airmen failed.

James Davies, Alun Anthony and David Thomas were later honoured with bravery citations for their actions that day.

LAC Brynjolf Riise, another Norwegian Air Force trainee on board the aircraft, had been a keen amateur radio enthusiast with a passion for flying. Emulating over 3,000 of his fellow countrymen, he arrived in Britain via the 'Shetland bus' service, a network of undercover fishing boats which plied refugees and agents across the North Sea.

Brynjolf's journey in April 1941 was quite eventful. After first boarding a fishing boat from his home at Alesund, he sailed south to Leikanger in central Norway. A few days later embarking on the motor boat 'Statthav' with 25 other refugees bound for Lerwick in Shetland. The vessel encountered poor weather during its crossing and unaware of its true position, overshot Shetland. Heading out into the open Atlantic the 'Statthav' eventually ran out of fuel, but was spotted adrift by a passing trawler and towed to the Faroe Islands. On reaching mainland Britain Brynjolf undertook a Royal Navy radio operator's course before enlisting in the Royal Norwegian Air Force as an air gunner. Following the accident at Bryn Eglur Farm his body was buried in the Norwegian section at Greenwich Cemetery, London. In January 1947 his remains were repatriated back to his home town of Alesund.

In June 2012 my good friend Paul Liiv visited Alesund while on a motorcycle tour of Norway. On my behalf he left a small wooden, British Legion cross in front of Brynjolf Riise's headstone. Inscribed on the wooden cross were the words 'Cofio hwn' (Remember him in Welsh). On the reverse I had left my contact details should any of his family wish to contact me. Before Paul had arrived back from his adventure, a letter from Brynjolf's younger brother, Rolf, had made its way to my home at Cwmafan, Port Talbot. The following year I made a similar trip to Norway and had the privilege of meeting Rolf Riise and his wife

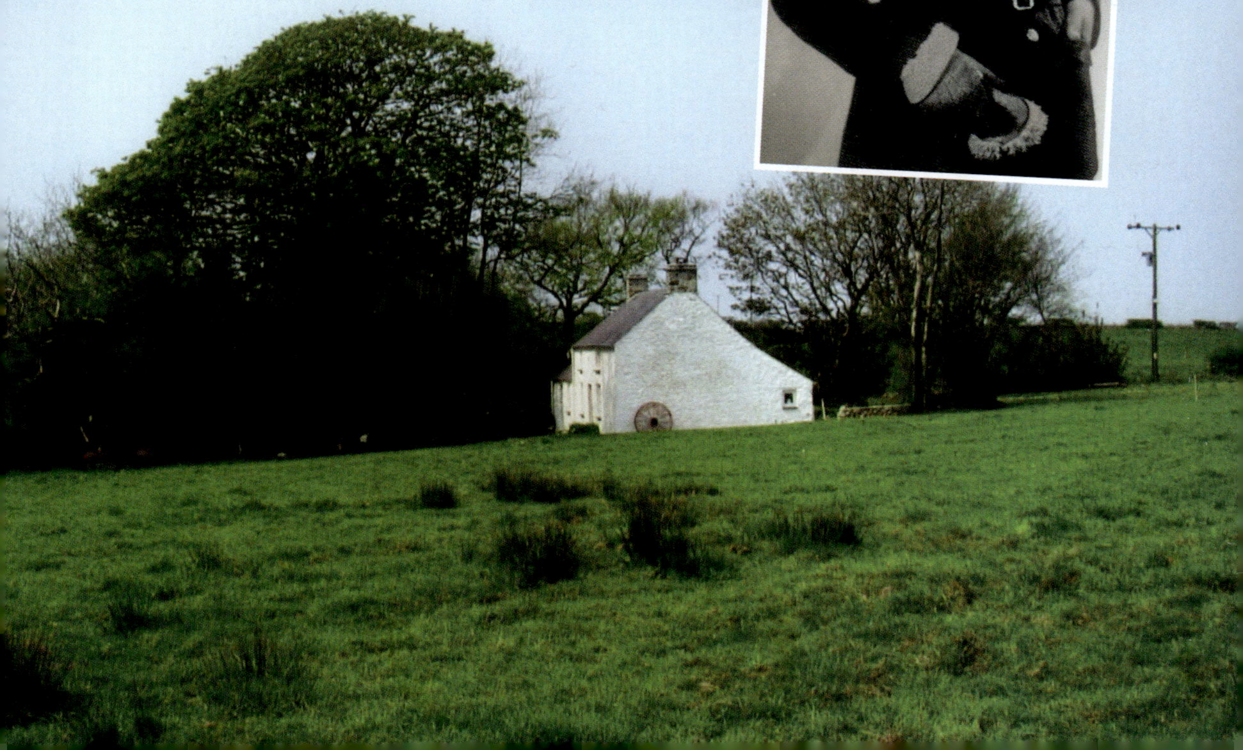

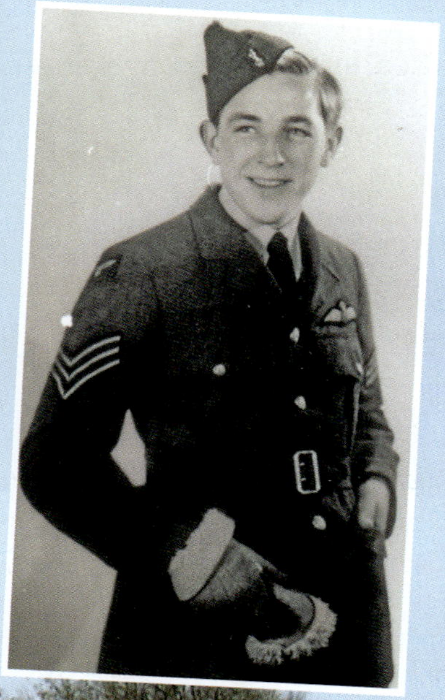

Bryn Eglur farmhouse, Meidrim. Blenheim V5745 force landed and burned-out in the foreground. INSET: Flt. Sgt. William 'Gully' Mason, its pilot.

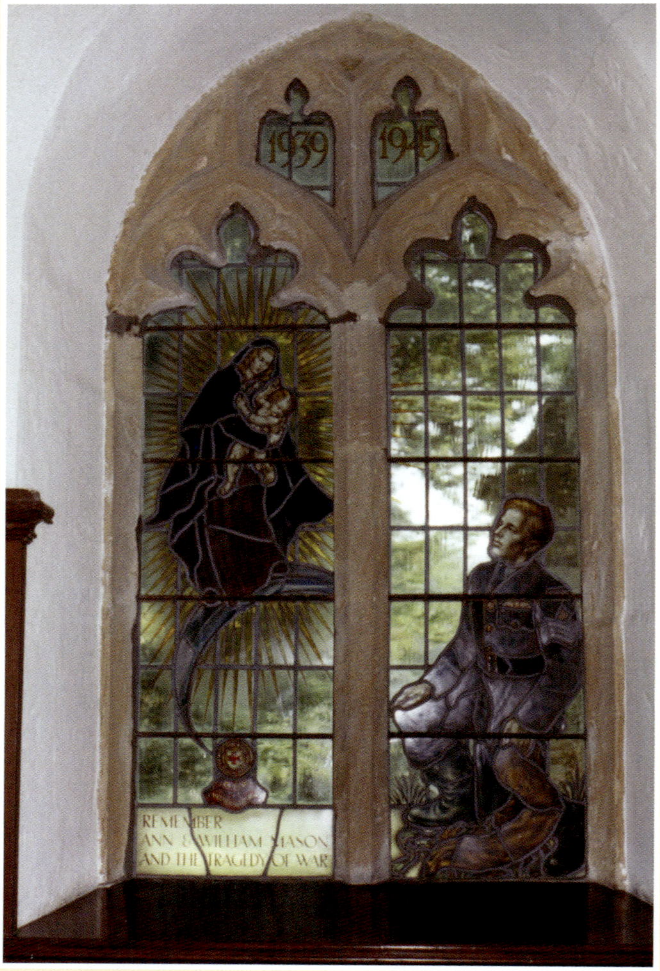

The stained glass window at St Mary's Church, Compton Pauncefoot commemorating William Mason and his sister, Ann, a nurse, who also died young. The inscription reads 'Remember Ann & William Mason and the tragedy of war'.

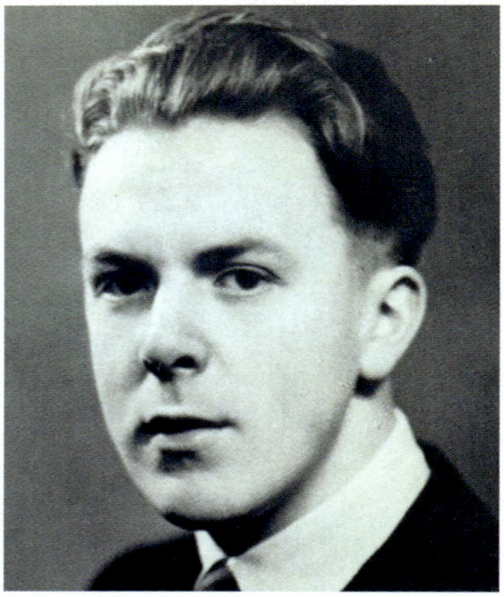

Brynjolf Riise prior to leaving Norway and below, Paul Liiv leaving the inscribed British Legion cross at his grave.

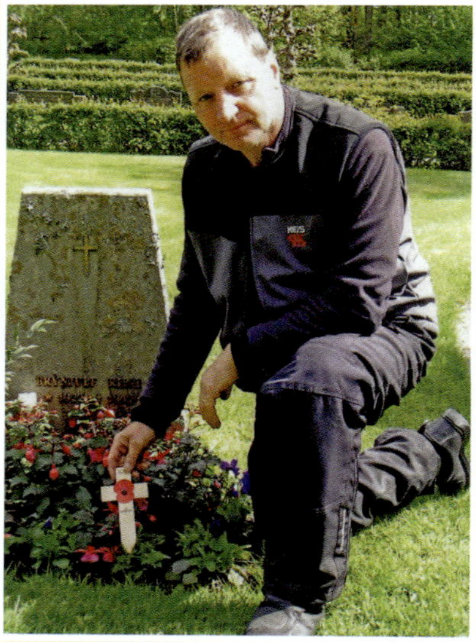

Kirsten. While in their company Rolf showed me a small pocket book which had once belonged to his brother. Written in pencil on the first page of the book were the names of the 25 people who had accompanied him on the 'Statthav' at the start of his adventure to Britain. One could not help but ponder over the fate which befell each one.

LAC Olson recovered from his burn injuries and survived the war. Despite research carried out by Rolf Riise over many years, little is known of what became of him after being demobbed from the RNAF. Rolf makes an interesting observation on the spelling of his surname; the Norwegian version being spelled: Olsen. Perhaps he was not a Norwegian national, possibly Swedish or even an American who may have had Norwegian ancestory. The search continues. The pilot of the 'Bryn Eglur' Blenheim Flt. Sgt. William 'Gully' Mason, was the eldest son of the MP for South Croydon, Keith Mason. William Mason turned his back on his opulent up-bringing and despite being an heir to the Blackford Estate at Compton Castle, near Yeovil, Somerset, decided to make his own way in life. One example of this was that on finishing his education at Eton he became a coal miner. His private headstone can be seen in the village church at Compton Pauncefoot. His epitaph reads: Happy, humorous, indefatigable.

In recent years the hedgerow where Blenheim V5745 burned-out has been up-rooted to increase the size of the surrounding fields. A metal detector search of the area uncovered many small fragments relating to the aircraft. Among these were melted aluminium, plexiglass, a gun port from the Blenheim's wing, 303 calibre rounds and amazingly, a strip of celluloid film from the aircraft's camera gun.

CREW LIST: Flt. Sgt. Mason WM, Pilot, killed;
AC2 Smith EJB, W.op u/t, killed;
LAC Riise BE (R.Nor.A.F.) Ag u/t, killed;
LAC Olson DO (R.Nor.A.F.) Ag u/t, injured;

MAY 24 1942

AIRCRAFT: **Blenheim L1218**

Percy saw tragedy unfold from passing bus window

Another camera gun exercise which ended in tragedy occurred two months later on May 24, when Blenheim L1218, also from the Air Gunnery School, crashed near the village of Pinged, just a mile or so to the east of Pembrey airfield.

Percy Jones of Trimsaran, who saw the fateful events unfold from a passing bus recalled the event clearly:

"It was about 7 pm as we approached Pinged Post Office. I and other passengers on the bus noticed through the windows that an aircraft overhead was in trouble. Distinctively, flames could be seen on the starboard side of the aircraft's fuselage; there was no doubt that the aircraft was in serious trouble. We then noticed that it had begun to descend rapidly and it became obvious to myself and the others that it was going to crash.

"By the time the bus arrived at Pinged the aircraft had crashed in flames, just missing the Post office, cutting a swathe through a thick hedge and finally coming to a halt against another hedge further along. One engine had detached itself and had careered on, finally coming to rest close to Tom Rogers house, Maes y Grove.

"Instead of remaining on the bus and continuing on to Pembrey, together with other passengers I quickly got off and hurried to the scene of the crash to render what help we could. With extreme heat coming from the burning aeroplane and ammunition exploding, it was a far from safe place to be. I then noticed that a crewman was lying underneath some of the outer wreckage. Not knowing if he was dead or alive I managed to get at him and removed him from the debris. It was a brave attempt, but sadly the man was found to be dead. A short time later RAF and civil rescue services arrived and we were ordered to clear away from the area."

All four crew were killed in the crash and an investigation into the cause of the accident proved inconclusive. Likewise, the outbreak of fire in the starboard engine was also unexplainable, though the Accident Report does mention the possibility of petrol seeping from a leaking fuel pipe being ignited by the hot exhaust.

CREW LIST: Sgt. Ramsdale K, Pilot; LAC Henry HG, Ag u/t; LAC Moore ECP, Ag u/t; LAC Layton GA, Ag u/t.

During excavation work to erect poultry sheds at the crash site in the 1970s, some aircraft parts were unearthed. The poultry sheds were demolished to make way for Brooklands House which has since been renamed Ty'r Nant. The graves of LACs Henry and Layton can be seen at St Illtyd's churchyard.

AUG 5 1942

AIRCRAFT: **Junkers 88 Werke No. 140715**

Secrets held deep on the ocean floor

Somewhere at the bottom of Carmarthen Bay lies the wreckage of a German Ju 88 bomber. In the early hours of August 5, it crashed into the sea for no apparent reason. Luftwaffe records show that Swansea Docks was attacked by a small force of bombers that night, four of which failed to return to their bases on the Continent. Two aircraft fell to the guns of 307 Squadron Beaufighters over Devon, while a third was brought down in the sea off Ilfracombe by 125 Squadron based at Fairwood Common. No unit lay claim to shooting down the Carmarthen Bay Junkers aircraft.

A week later, on August 12, the body of Unteroffizier (Corporal) Willy Krock, one of the JU 88's crew, was found washed ashore just below East House

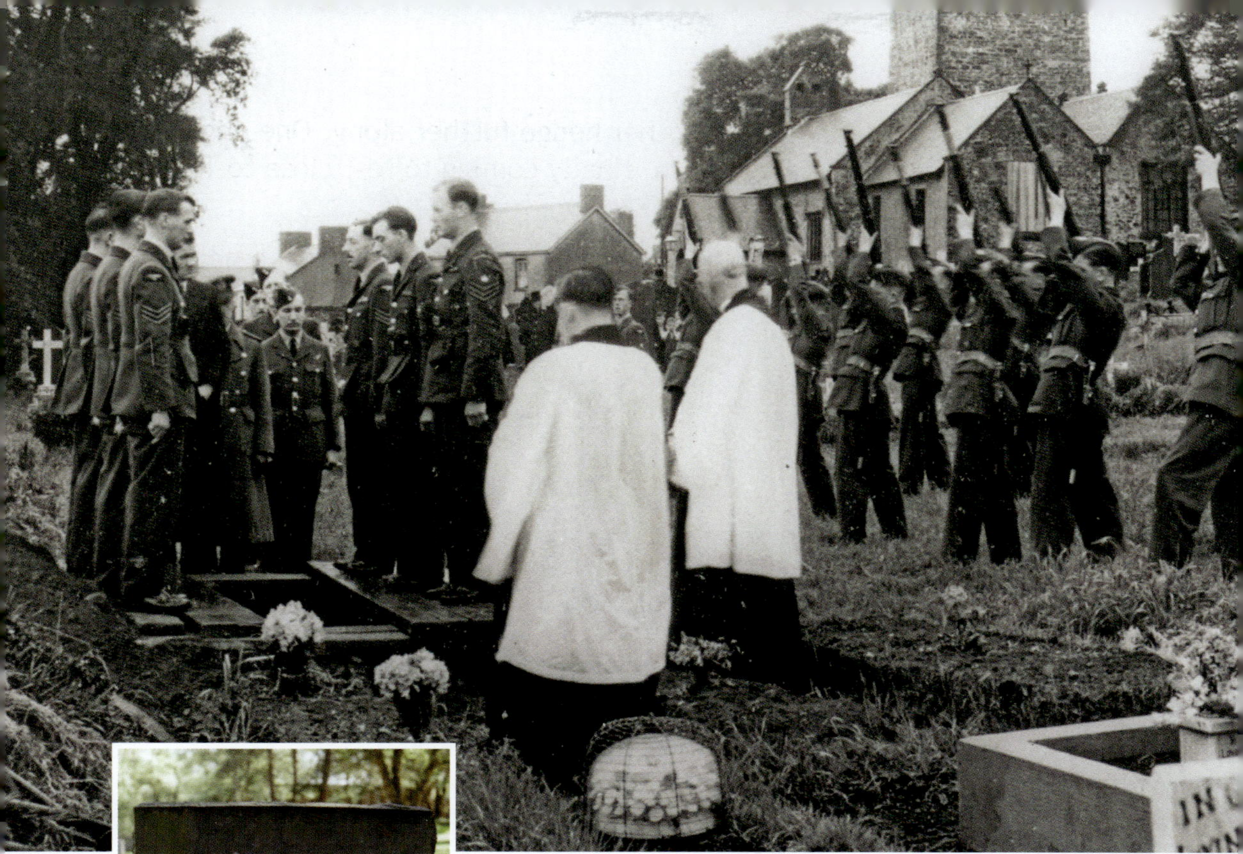

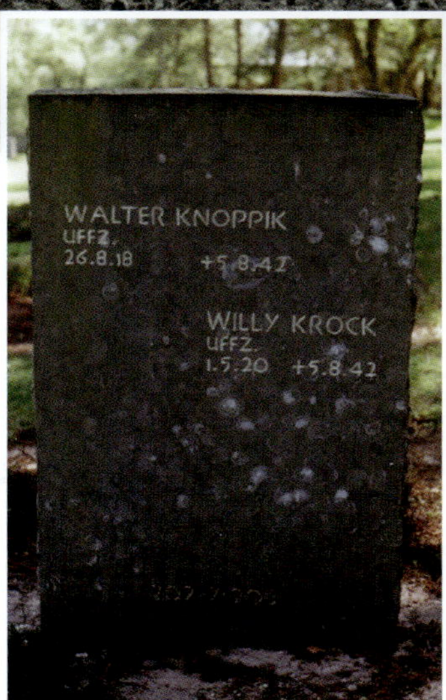

The military funeral of Uffz. Willy Krock at St Illtyd's Churchyard, Pembrey, August 15, 1942. INSET: The headstone of Uffz. Willy Krock at the Soldatenfriedhof, Cannock Chase. Buried in the same grave is Uffz. Walter Knoppik, lost on the same day in a Heinkel 111 shot down off Ilfracombe. His body was washed ashore near Porthcawl. It is standard practice at the Soldatenfriedhof for two airmen to be buried in each grave.

Farm on Laugharne Sands, near Pendine. His remains were brought to the mortuary at RAF Pembrey before being buried with full military honours at St Illtyd's churchyard on August 15. In the early 1960s, under guidelines drawn up by the German war graves authority, his remains were re-interred at the Soldatenfriedhof (Soldier's cemetery), Cannock Chase, Staffordshire.

Willy Krock was a member of 2 Staffel (flight), Kustenflieg Gruppe 106 (Squadron), a naval mine-laying unit attached to the Luftwaffe.

CREW LIST: Fw. Friedrich Grotsch, Missing; Uffz. Hermann Preymann, Missing; Uffz. Johann Endres, Missing; Uffz. Willy Krock, Killed.

NOV
14
1942

AIRCRAFT: **Blenheim Z6074**

Skilful pilot landed on the beach at Cefn Sidan

Pembrey's fifth and final Blenheim loss of 1942 occurred on November 14. Due to the skilful airmanship displayed by the pilot, W.O. McDaniel, the aircraft was force landed on the northern end of Cefn Sidan beach with little damage. One of its engines had failed. Six months later W.O. McDaniel was to lose his life in another Blenheim crash near Pant Teg Farm, Pinged.

DEC
7
1942

AIRCRAFT: **Lancaster ED322**

The ghost aircraft that came to a watery end

The target for one of Bomber Command's operations on the night of December 6, 1942 was the city of Mannheim in southern Germany. Among the attacking force of 272 aircraft was a Lancaster of 101 Squadron based at Holme-on-Spalding Moor, Yorkshire.

At 17:30 hrs on December 6, P.O. Howard Dabbs and his crew took off from Spalding Moor, disappeared into the dark night sky and joined the bomber stream routed towards Mannheim. Over the target area thick cloud obscured the city meaning that the Pathfinder aircraft, who flew ahead of the bombers to illuminate the city with target marking flares, could not do their job effectively. The bomber force dropped their bombs by dead-reckoning and set course for the long journey home.

It was during this journey home that ED322 strayed off track and just after midnight was plotted crossing the Bristol Channel on a northerly heading. For the next two hours the Lancaster flew an erratic course over the South Wales countryside attempting to seek out an airfield to land at. The weather at the time was windy, with 10/10ths cloud down to 300ft. The RAF were very much aware of the Lancaster's plight, but no radio contact could be made with the bomber. While circling overhead at both Talbenny and Carew airfields in Pembrokeshire the runway lights were illuminated and distress rockets fired to try to aid the aircraft's landing, but on each instance it flew away. At 02:00 hrs on December 7 it was plotted near Fairwood Common, again the airfield was lit-up, but again the Lancaster continued to roam the skies like a ghost. It then flew west and reappeared over Talbenny, before heading south and gaining altitude. At 02:50 hrs it faded from the plotting screens and was never seen again.

Later that morning at around 11:00 hrs, Aircraftman Len Hadman, stationed at Tenby as part of the target drone retrieval crew for the artillery range at Manorbier, saw a parachute billowing in the wind just off the Victoria Pier, between Tenby's North and South beaches. Rowing out to the parachute with a colleague he made a grizzly discovery. Submerged beneath the canopy was the body of Flt. Sgt. Robert Smith, the Lancaster's navigator.

The following day, December 8, the body of James Hughes, ED322's flight engineer, was located in the same area and on December 9, the body of Howard Dabbs was found on Amroth beach a few miles away to the north-east of Tenby.

A fourth body, that of Flt. Sgt. Robert Middleton, the Lancaster's wireless operator, was washed ashore at Lydstep on December 18. The three other crew members were never found and are officially listed as missing.

The cause of the loss of ED322 will never be fully explained, but the possible reason as to why the aircraft drifted off track on its return flight are recorded on the RAF's accident record card for the aircraft. It mentions that there was an unexpected change in wind direction and that in the western part of Britain coded navigation beacons were flashing identical letter codes to those on the intended route home for the bomber force over northern Britain. This would have given the navigator the impression that he was on course for a safe return to base.

Jim Dabbs, eldest brother of the pilot of ED322 and also a serving RAF officer in Britain during the war, interviewed a WAAF who was on duty in the squadron's operations room on the night of the accident soon after the event and has this theory to the chain of events:

"It's only conjecture on my part but, reading between the lines of the letter sent to my mother by the Commanding Officer of 101 Squadron and after talking to Cpl. Turner who was on duty in the communications room on December 7, I have concluded that the following probably happened. Their plane was caught in a cone of searchlights over or near the target area and was hit by anti-aircraft fire. At the same time they were attacked by night fighter aircraft. There was a lot of confusion and terrible sound over the airwaves from his aircraft and then, complete silence. I believe that my brother was killed and the radio put out of commission. I do not know who was the co-pilot, or, if he was alive. At any rate, there was no one able to fly the plane correctly. How it got back (to Britain) is a mystery, although the two who were found in the Channel (Tenby) could possibly have guided it in the general direction. Over Wales rockets and flares were sent up to guide this ‘ghost’ plane down as the ground was invisible because of fog. The plane flew erratically around Wales until it ran out of fuel and crashed into the sea, or, as one letter says, on the island (St Margaret’s, off Caldey). Had Howard been alive the two crew would not have jumped and he could have landed it OK with the help he would have been given from the ground.”

The Lancaster, unlike many earlier bombers, did not have a co-pilot position. Many operational pilots were however known to have unofficially trained their flight engineers in the basics of flying the aircraft in level flight. The flight engineer’s seat being the closest position to the pilot. It may well have been the case that Sgt. James Hughes was at the controls of the Lancaster as it strayed around the skies of South Wales. As Sgt. Hughes would only have had basic instruction on how to fly a Lancaster, this would tie-in with the reason as to why the aircraft did not attempt a landing at any of the airfields it visited. Flying an aircraft in level flight is relatively easy, landing on the other hand is a more skillful manoeuvre requiring much practice.

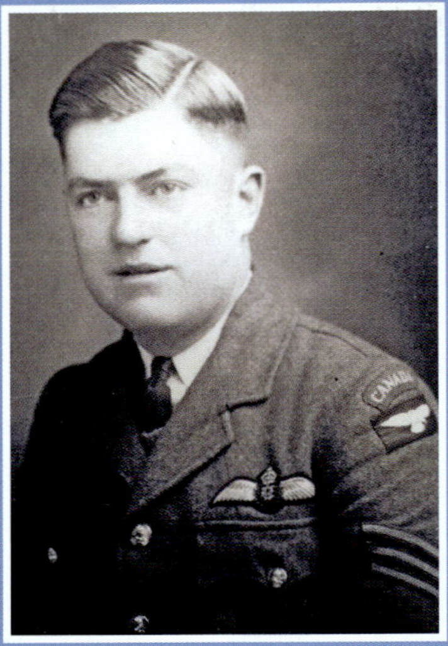

P.O. Howard Dabbs DFC.

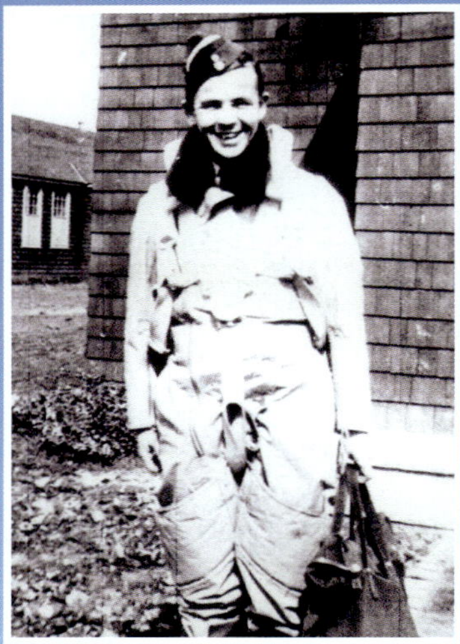

Flt. Sgt. Robert Smith.

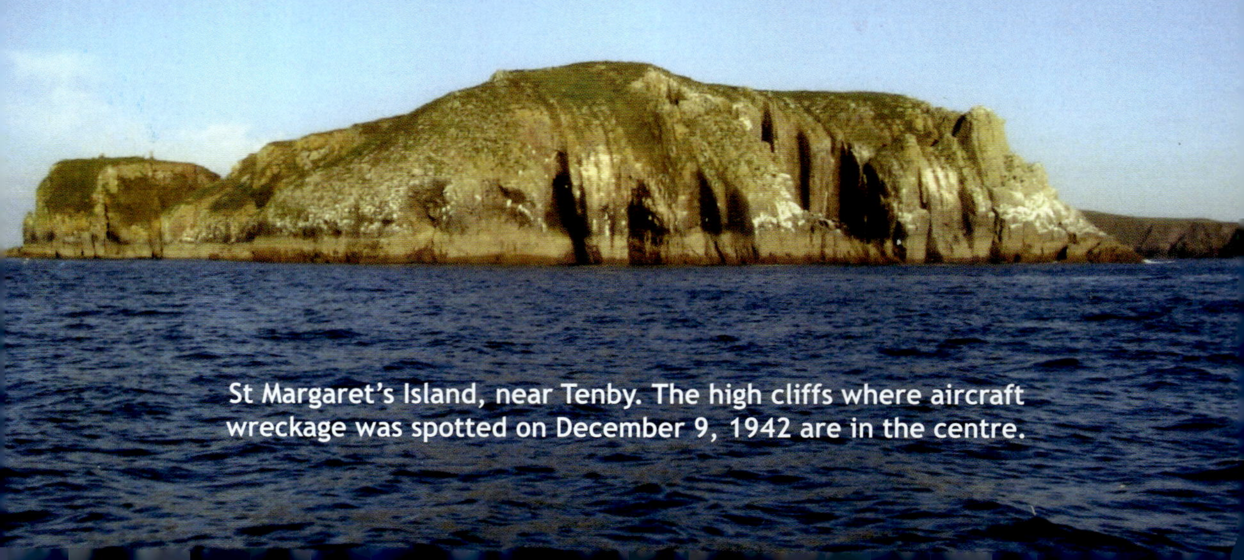

St Margaret’s Island, near Tenby. The high cliffs where aircraft wreckage was spotted on December 9, 1942 are in the centre.

The Operational Record Book for 48 Marine Craft Unit/Air Sea Rescue, Tenby, gives a tantalizing clue for anyone wishing to search for the missing Lancaster. On December 9, 1942 it records the following entry:

'A crashed aircraft was seen at the foot of a high cliff on the NW side of St Margaret's Island. Owing to rough seas no close inspection was possible. A search the following day failed to find any trace of the aircraft. It was assumed that the aircraft was pounded to pieces on the rocks. It appears that from papers found on the bodies that the aircraft was a Lancaster of 101 Squadron.'

Despite spending many hours of underwater searching for the wreckage of Lancaster ED322, I was unable to locate anything and nothing has yet come to light.

My personal theory is that the wreckage seen by the ASR crew was washed into that position by the tide. The near empty fuel tanks of the Lancaster would have acted like great flotation devices to some parts of the wreckage and drifted with the tide onto the rocks below St Margaret's Island. It is more likely that the main wreck site lies in deeper water somewhere off the island.

Lancaster ED233 was a new aircraft, having only flown 2 hrs 30 mins since it left the factory where it was made. The crew had taken the new aircraft after their usual Lancaster had been badly battle damaged on their previous mission to Frankfurt on the night of December 2/3. It was on this raid that Howard Dabbs earned the Distinguished Flying Cross.

While approaching the target his aircraft was held in a cone of searchlights and hit by anti-aircraft fire, resulting in the loss of one engine. Howard flew on, but over the target was unable to release the Lancaster's bomb load; probably due to the damage inflicted by the AA fire. With great skill he flew back to base and landed the bomb laden aircraft in poor visibility. His medal was awarded to him, posthumously, on December 9, the very day on which his body came ashore at Amroth.

Another consequence of the Frankfurt raid was that the crew's regular tail gunner, Sgt. Bradley, injured by gunfire on the raid, was unable to join the crew on their final flight. His place was taken by Sgt. Stefan Franchuk. Sgt. Bradley was lost on operations during August 1943.

CREW LIST: P.O. Howard Dabbs DFC (RCAF) Pilot, killed; Sgt. James Hughes, Flight Engineer, killed; Flt. Sgt. Robert Smith (RCAF) Navigator, killed; Flt. Sgt. Leonard Anderson (RCAF) Bomb aimer, missing; Flt. Sgt. Robert Middleton (RCAF) Wireless Op/Air Gunner, killed; Sgt. William Warren, Air Gunner, missing; Sgt. Stefan Franchuk (RCAF) Air Gunner, missing.

APRIL 24 1943

AIRCRAFT: Martinet HP365

Target-towing crew hit by fuel starvation problem

The new year was only three days old when the sight of a large four-engined B-24 Liberator bomber of the US 8th Air Force arrived low over the skies of Carmarthenshire.

Returning from a raid on the U-boat pens at St Nazaire in France, the aircraft, 41-23817, was one of a formation of eight Liberators of the 44th Bomb Group based at Shipdham in Norfolk. On the return leg of the mission the formation had strayed too far west across the Bay of Biscay and were running low on fuel. Nearing the Irish Sea they realised that reaching their base in Norfolk was now impossible. The airfields scattered around the south-west corner of Wales became their only hope of salvation.

Liberator 41-23817 managed to seek out Pembrey in the fading winter sunshine and landed safely. The rest of the formation, along with a number of B-17 Flying Fortresses, made emergency landings at bases in Pembrokeshire. Two Liberators ran out of fuel with disasterous consequences on the outskirts of Haverfordwest.

Another unusual aircraft that appeared in the skies over Pembrey at the beginning of March 1943 wasn't so lucky. It was the Miles Martinet. With its distinctive inverted gull wing profile the Martinet was the RAF's first purpose-built target towing aircraft and was used by the Air Gunnery School as a replacement for its ageing fleet of Lysanders.

Following the introduction of this type of aircraft at Pembrey airfield a number of fuel starvation-related engine problems started to emerge.

One such incident happened at around midday on April 24. Martinet HP365 was undertaking a routine target towing exercise over the sea when its engine suddenly cut out. The pilot, Sgt. Smith, immediately headed for the coast and managed a perfect wheels-up belly landing in a field on the high ground near Down Farm overlooking the Tywi Estuary. The aircraft would have perhaps been salvageable had it not ploughed through a hedge and into an adjoining field, finally coming to rest 200 yards in front of the farmhouse.

Farmer David Jones recalled that although the aircraft was wrecked, the radio equipment on board remained serviceable, enabling the crew to contact the control tower at Pembrey to inform them of their predicament. He also recalls that the target drogue was still trailing behind the Martinet when it landed.

A metal detector search of the area failed to reveal any trace of wreckage, but a small gap in the hedge, pointed out by Mr. Jones, serves as a lasting reminder of the event.

CREW LIST: Sgt. Smith, Pilot; LAC Jones, Tow Operator.

MAY 5 1943

AIRCRAFT: **Oxford T1321**

Surprise as St Clears dug deep for Wings appeal

During the first week of May 1943 Carmarthenshire hosted its annual Wings for Victory appeal. This was part of a campaign run nationally throughout the war years to raise funds for the RAF. The county's target in 1943 was to raise £350,000 which would enable it to pay for the much needed construction of five Stirling bombers and 30 Spitfires.

Throughout the week towns up and down Carmarthenshire held various events urging the general public to purchase War Bonds. In some cases the air force would help out by providing high-profile guest speakers at the events and even undertook the odd flypast to thrill the crowds. The slogan which accompanied the campaign was 'The plan is plain – planes.'

On the evening of Wednesday May 5, St Clears was 'doing its bit' by holding a school sports day in the fields adjoining the Afon Cynin near Pentre Farm. As part of the event two aircraft from 10 Radio School, RAF Carew, were scheduled to fly low over the town to bolster the 'Wings' appeal.

At 20:35 hrs the first of the two aircraft, a twin-engined Oxford, T1321, arrived on cue over St Clears. As it flew low over the town its pilot, Flt. Sgt. Holmes, perhaps a little too enthusiastic in wanting to please the crowds, clipped the overhead power cables which ran alongside the main road near the river bridge. As a consequence one of the Oxford's engines spluttered to a halt and losing height Flt. Sgt. Holmes was forced to put down in a nearby field. Luckily there was minimal damage to the aircraft and the only injuries sustained by the other two crew members on board were a bruised thigh and a cut lip.

By the end of the Wings for Victory week St Clears had raised the grand sum of £19,000; more than enough to pay for the repairs needed to Oxford T1321!

May Morgan of Pentre Farm witnessed the aircraft flying low over the town and recorded the event in her diary. Some 60 years on I was able to confirm the date under which she had noted the incident in the Operational Record Books for RAF Carew at the National Archives. May was also able to pinpoint the exact spot where the aircraft came down, though a metal detector sweep of the field failed to reveal any evidence of the crash.

MAY
11
1943

AIRCRAFT: **Blenheim Z6348**

Crew of four perished on featureless meadows

During 1943 Blenheims were still regarded as the workhorses of the Air Gunnery School at Pembrey and accidents involving this aircraft type continued to occur. Nearly a year after the fatal Blenheim crash near Pinged post office another crew perished not far away on the flat meadows near Pant Teg Farm.

At 10:50 hrs on the morning of May 11, Blenheim Z6348 was in the circuit preparing to land after a routine gunnery

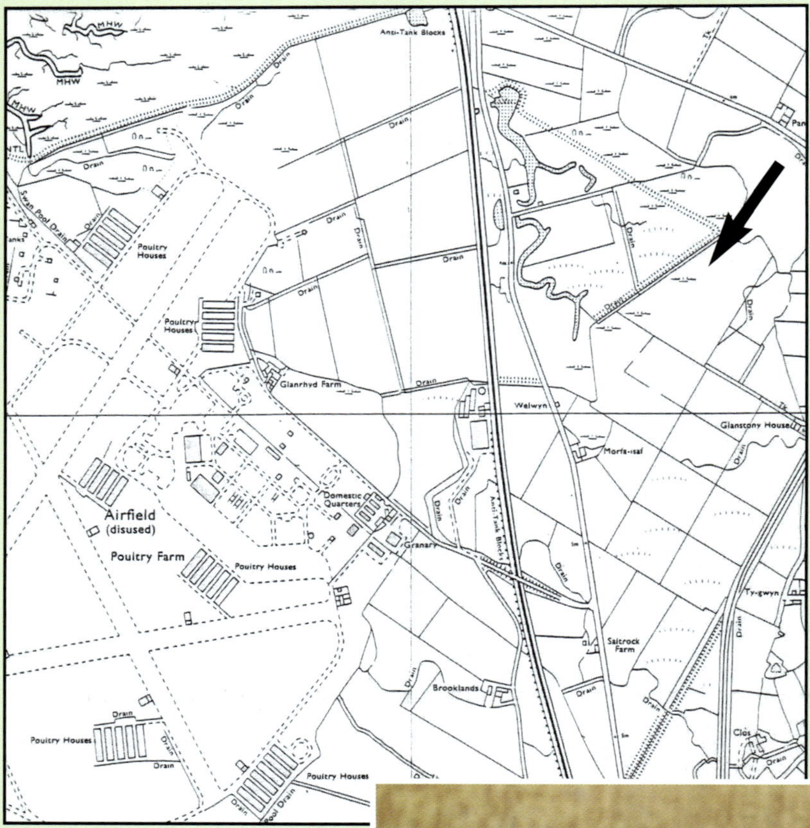

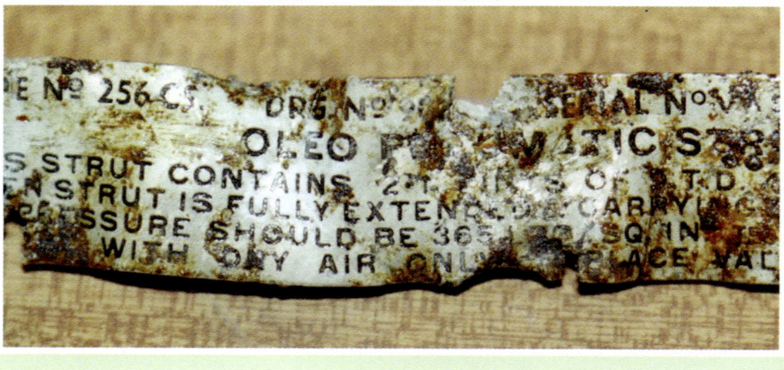

The crash site – marked by the arrow – of Blenheim Z6348, near Pant Teg Farm. INSET: An aluminium data plate found at the location.

exercise. When at about one mile to the east of the airfield it crashed to the ground killing all four crew. Today drainage ditches cut across the flat featureless meadows where the aircraft came down, but if you know where to look a few small pieces of the Blenheim can still be found.

CREW LIST: W.O. McDaniel FJ, Pilot; LAC Noble JC, Ag u/t; LAC Taylor K, Ag u/t; LAC Smythe R, Ag u/t.

MAY
23
1943

AIRCRAFT: **Wellington Z1147**

Farmer witnessed Czech crew's lucky escape

On the bright and sunny spring morning of May 23, Cliff Williams of Kidwelly was busy working at the hillside farm of Penlan Uchaf overlooking Pembrey airfield. At about 10:00 hrs his attention was drawn to a Wellington bomber flying spectacularly low over the surrounding fields. Had Cliff been able to observe the Wellington's port propeller he would have perhaps been able to understand why it was so low.

While on a ferry flight from its base at RAF Talbenny on the Pembrokeshire coast to Luton, the 311 (Czech) Squadron aircraft suffered an engine failure and was in the process of attempting an emergency landing at Pembrey when the remaining engine also cut out.

The aircraft brushed the tops of some trees in a nearby wood before slithering to a standstill in the middle of Cae Sgwar (square field), a 10 acre field between the two farms of Penlan Uchaf and Penlan Isaf. The forced landing had been fairly gentle, enabling the four Czech airmen on board to safely exit the Wellington before a small fire developed and destroyed the entire airframe.

When the crew sought help at Penlan Uchaf farmhouse there was great difficulty understanding each others language. Farmer Jack Evans and his family spoke predominantly Welsh, while the airmen all conversed in Czech.

Fred Lyne had a childhood recollection of the incident and remembers standing in a Kidwelly street watching the pall of thick black smoke rising high into the clear morning sky.

While metal detecting in the field during the 1990s Fred was able to locate the area in which the Wellington burned out. Among the items he found were a type of bomb shackle unique to this type of aircraft, some 303 rounds dated 1942 and an airframe modification plate inscribed with the prefix numbers 285.

The RAF Form 78, Aircraft Movement Card, shows that Wellington Z1147 was no stranger to mishaps; since its delivery to the RAF in November 1941 it had been involved in two previous accidents. The only crew member whose name is known, is that of pilot, F.O. Radina.

JUNE 4 1943

AIRCRAFT: Marauder 41-18252

Transatlantic trip that turned into a nightmare

To replenish its supply of combat crews and bomber aircraft in the air war over Europe the USAAF set up two Transatlantic ferry routes out of North America to Britain. The northern route was via Canada, Greenland and Iceland, terminating at RAF Prestwick in Scotland. While the southern route was through Brazil, Ascension Island, Dakar in West Africa and Morocco, ending at RAF St Eval in Cornwall.

In smaller aircraft such as the B-26 Marauder, crew numbers were reduced to four instead of the usual seven and non-essential equipment was removed in favour of better fuel consumption. When flying over vast expanses of ocean every effort was made to extend flight endurance times, this gave the crews a safety margin should they encounter bad weather or fly off track for any amount of time. Due to a combination of fatigue, poor weather and only rudimentary navigation aids, it was sometimes possible for American aircraft on the southern route to overshoot Cornwall and end up over South Wales.

On May 30, Lt. Jack Reiss and his replacement crew, from the 449th Bomb Squadron 322nd Bomb Group, arrived at Marrakesh airfield, Morocco, in Marauder 41-18252. They had all endured the hardship of flying for many hours at a time on their lengthy trip from MacDill Field in Florida along the southern ferry route and were looking forward to a few days rest before tackling the final leg of their flight to Britain.

Their journey across the Atlantic had not been without incident. While at Ascension Island their Commanding Officer, Major Ervin Berry, who up until that point had been piloting the Marauder, injured his back when he lost his footing and fell off the aircraft's wing; he had been watching other aircraft arriving and departing the island. The Marauder was Major Berry's personal aircraft and was named Mi'Laine in honour of his wife, Mira Elaine. With Major Berry unable to continue the journey because of his injured back a passenger, Lt. Earl Shoop, joined the crew for the final leg of their trip.

At 07:15 hrs on June 4, Mi'Laine took off from North Africa in the company of seven other replacement Marauders all bound for RAF St Eval. With only

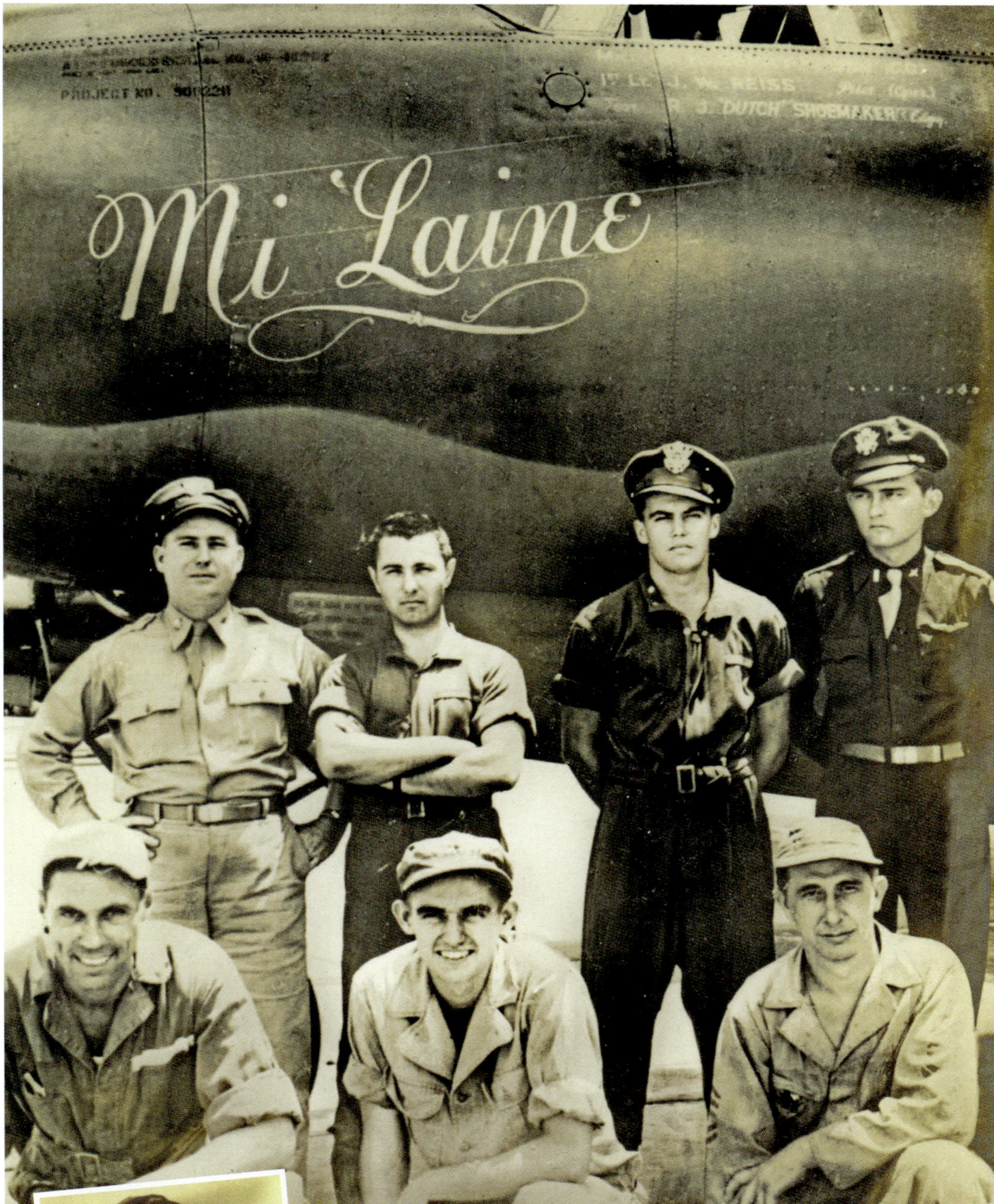

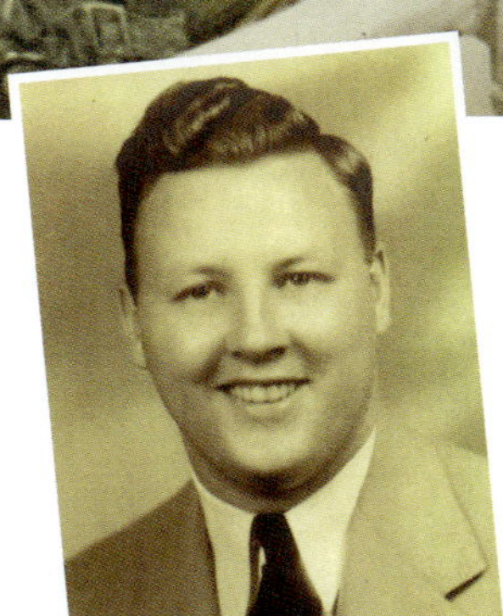

The crew of Mi'Laine at MacDill Field, Florida prior to their Transatlantic ferry flight. Only four of the seven were on the aircraft's fatal trip. The Mi'Laine lettering appears to be freshly painted. Standing, from left: Major Ervin Berry, C.O.; Lt. John Reiss, Pilot; Lt. Ken Reed, Lt. Eugene Carby, Navigator; Kneeling: Sgt. Dussing, Sgt. Fox, T. Sgt. Raymond Shoemaker, Flt. Engineer. INSET: Lt. Earl 'Bill' Shoop.

one radio set capable of contacting a ground station between the eight aircraft, they had good reason to stay in close visual contact with each other. In the clear skies of North Africa this was relatively easy, but as they progressed north along the 12th meridian the weather deteriorated; fog and heavy rain showers were affecting southern Britain.

By 14:00 hrs the inevitable happened, the formation had become scattered and it was a case of every man for himself. Through dead-reckoning the crew of Mi'Laine made landfall into Britain over South Wales, though they were having great difficulty in locating a suitable landing ground due to the inclement weather.

Just after 16:00 hrs at Penrhyn Farm, on the outskirts of Pwll near Llanelli, 16 year-old farmer's son, Hugh Bonnell, was helping out with the daily milking routine when he heard a low flying aircraft pass overhead flying in the direction of Kidwelly. This was not an unusual sound for him as Pembrey airfield was only three miles away to the north west. What did seem strange was the fact that someone should be up flying on a day when the fog was almost down to the ground.

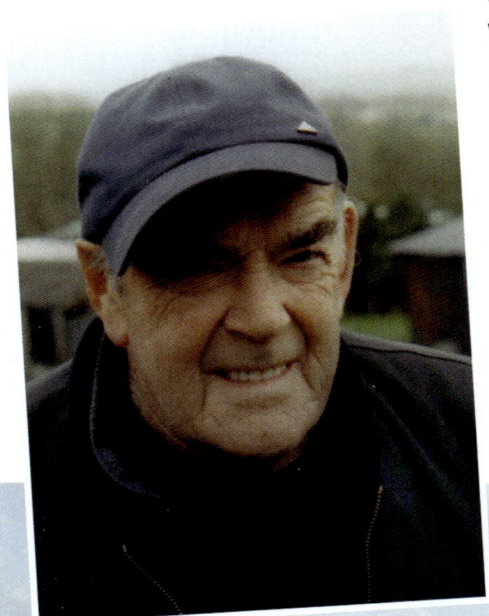

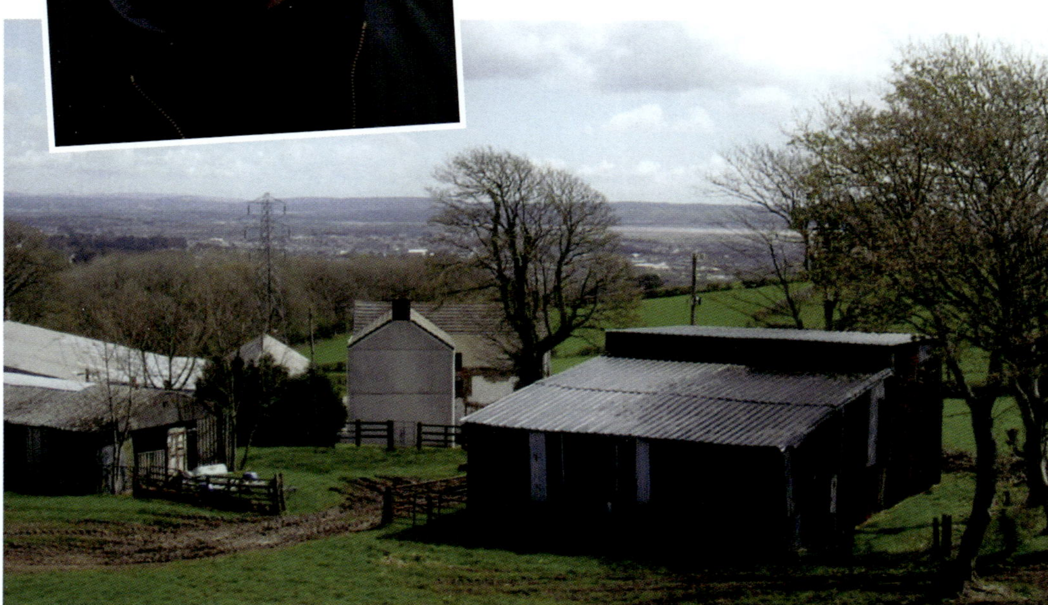

Penrhyn Farm showing the outbuildings where Hugh Bonnell sheltered, the farmhouse and the rebuilt corrugated barn. The tree which the Marauder first hit before continuing on through a number of fields to the right is in the centre. INSET: Hugh Bonnell on a visit to the Farm in 2004.

Hugh was about to collect some hay from the barn when he paused for a few minutes in the doorway of an outbuilding to shelter from a sudden downpour. He then heard the aircraft return on a reciprocal course towards Swansea. Minutes later the sound of the aircraft returned only this time it was frighteningly closer; so much so that Hugh, fearing for his life, dived into the outbuilding where he had been sheltering.

The aircraft skimmed across the farmyard, hit a tree near the house before impacting onto the hay barn where Hugh was headed. When Hugh emerged from the outbuilding he was confronted with a scene of utter devastation, the roof of the steel barn had been ripped off by the impact and the aircraft had totally disintegrated as it careered on into the fields behind the barn. One of its engines travelled a distance of 300 yards and came to rest near Pant Farm further up the hillside.

The crew of Mi'Laine were killed instantly. Three bodies were found that same day, while that of the fourth, Lt. Carby, the navigator, was found the following morning. News of the crash spread

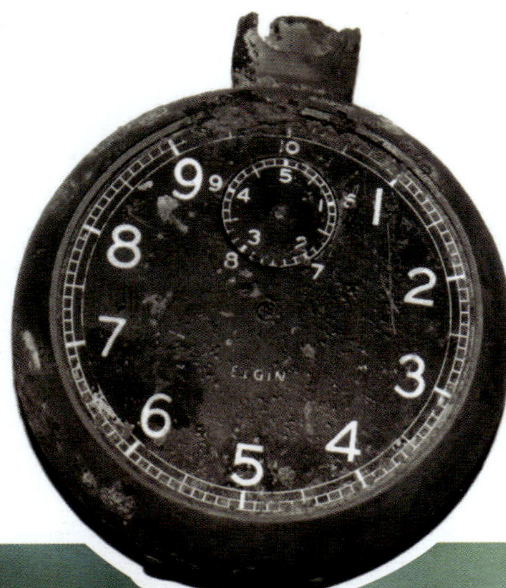

An Elgin bomb aimer's watch found by metal detectorist Fred Lyne. The watch was used for measuring speed across the ground. The analogue face only numbers up to 10. BELOW: Engine spark plugs, some of which were wrapped in wax paper, so would probably have been carried as spares in the crashed Marauder aircraft.

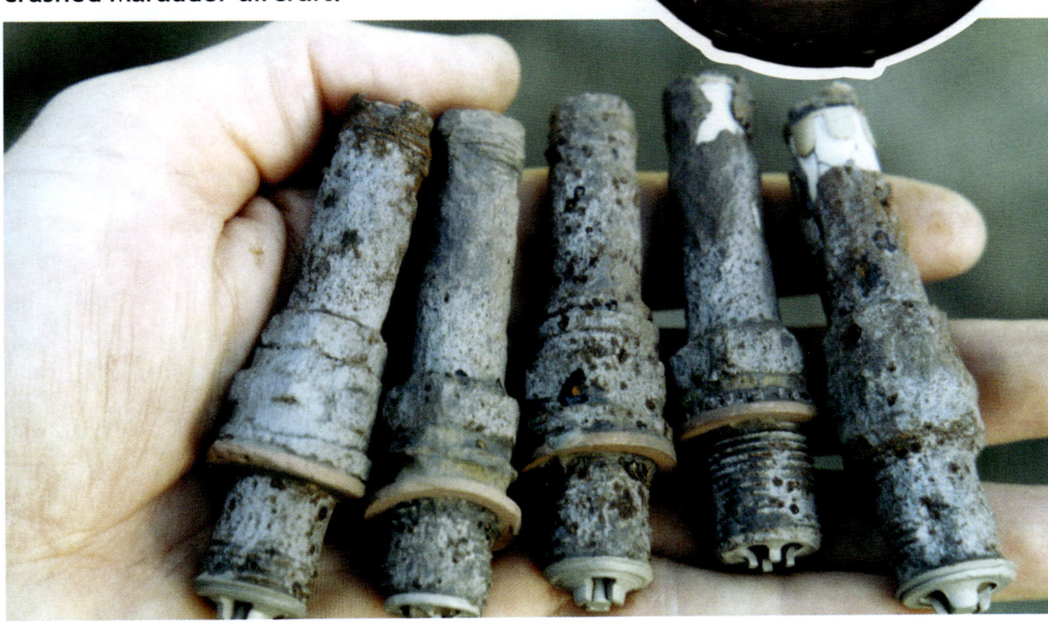

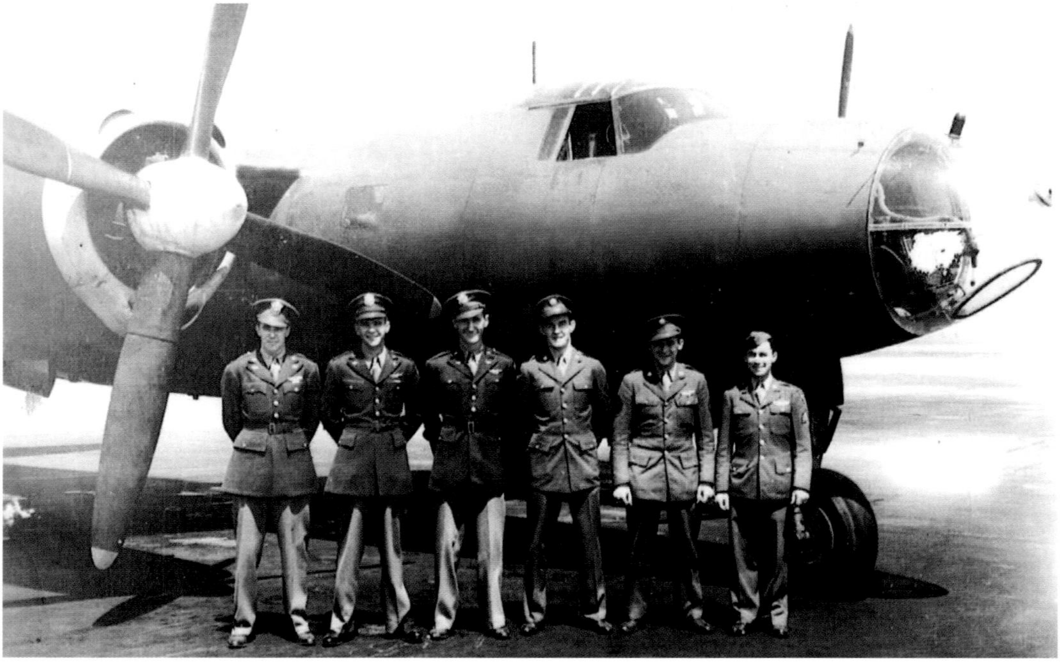

The crew of Marauder 41-34765, Lil'Lass, at Barksdale Field, Louisiana, April 1943. Only the four crew on the left were on board when the aircraft was ferried across the Atlantic. Sgts. Pramuk and O'Connell made the journey aboard a larger aircraft. The bomb sight in the nose of the aircraft has been discreetly censored.

quickly among the locals and it wasn't long before a large crowd gathered at Penrhyn to view the carnage. Littered across the fields were pieces of aircraft, personal luggage, ration packs and survival dinghies.

USAAF accident investigators arrived at the scene the next day, made observations and interviewed the Bonnell family as to what they had seen and heard. The investigators came to the conclusion that Mi'Laine had been in level flight and at normal cruising speed when it struck the tree and barn.

Criticism was raised as to why the crew were allowed to become airborne from North Africa before the issuing of the daily weather report at 07:30 hrs that morning; only 15 minutes after Lt. Reiss took off. Had the crew waited for this they would have been made aware of the bad weather which lay ahead of them and no doubt the mission would have been postponed.

Two other recommendations made by the accident investigation panel were that replacement crews departing North Africa bound for Britain should be issued with maps detailing new airfields around their intended destinations and that each aircraft should have on board a radio set and competent radio-operator when there is any doubt as to the weather conditions.

Of the seven other Marauders in the formation only the fate of four is known: 41-34765 Lil'Lass suffered a similar demise to Mi'Laine when it flew into Carn Llidi Mountain, just north of St David's, Pembrokeshire while trying to let down through the same foggy conditions. The accident report states the time of the crash as 16:15 hrs; exactly the same time as the Penrhyn tragedy. Again, all on board were killed. On June 4, 2005 relatives of the crew attended the dedication of a memorial at Whitesands Beach, at the foot of Carn Llidi. The centrepiece of the memorial is a propeller blade from the aircraft which stands as a lasting tribute to the four airmen.

Ridge Runner (41-34718) force landed on a remote beach at Termonfeckin, near Drogheda, Ireland, after running out of fuel. Its pilot, Lt. Seeley, made a wheels-up belly landing on the soft sand resulting in very little damage to the aircraft. However when the tide rose the Marauder became submerged and was later scrapped. This aircraft was the only Marauder in the formation to be fitted with a radio. When it was used in an attempt to obtain a position fix, it proved ineffective because of intense background interference.

Marauder 41-34722 overshot on landing at RAF Chivenor, North Devon, at 16:45 hrs. The crew walked away unharmed. Similarly the crew were unhurt when 41-34738 burst both main undercarriage tyres while landing at RAF Dalton, Yorkshire, at 17:50 hrs.

Lt. Reiss and the other three crew of Mi'Laine were initially buried side-by-side at Brookwood cemetery, Surrey, but in 1948 the remains of Lt. Carby and Technical Sgt. Shoemaker were repatriated to the United States at the request of their next of kin. Those of Lieutenants Reiss and Shoop were re-interred at the newly created United States military cemetery at Madingley, near Cambridge.

Penrhyn Farm is now farmed by Wyn Evans and the layout of the farm has changed little in the intervening years; even the rebuilt hay barn is of similar construction to the one destroyed in 1943.

CREW LIST: Marauder 41-18252 Mi'Laine 1st Lt. John Reiss, Pilot; 1st Lt. Eugene Carby, Navigator; 2nd Lt. Earl Shoop, Passenger (pilot); T. Sgt. Raymond Shoemaker, Flight Engineer.

CREW LIST: Marauder 41-34765 Lil'Lass 1st Lt. Robert Lawrence, Pilot; 2nd Lt. Hulbert Robertson, Navigator; Fl.O. James Jackson, Co-pilot; S. Sgt. William Brown, Flight Engineer.

JULY 22 1943

AIRCRAFT: **Blenheim V6514**

Overheating caused engine failure at take off

The most dangerous part of any flight is the take off. A mishap at this crucial point with a full fuel load can often spell disaster for the crew. At 12:25 hrs on 22 July Blenheim V6514 was in the process of taking off from Pembrey for a camera gun exercise when one of its engines failed. The aircraft overturned on hitting the ground, but luckily there was no fire. The cause of the engine failure was put down to a combination of an overheated engine prior to take off and the inexperience of the pilot, Sgt. Rushton.

The RAF Form 78, Aircraft Movement Card, shows that V6514 had accumulated nearly 400 hours of airtime prior to being written-off in the unfortunate accident.

CREW LIST: Sgt. Rushton PE, Pilot, Injured; Sgt. Chandler EP, Passenger; LAC Lester AT, Ag u/t; LAC McGregor W, Ag u/t, Injured; LAC Innis R, Ag u/t, Injured.

JULY 25 1943

AIRCRAFT: **Martinet HP380**

Mid-air collision crew perished near Caldey

Three days later, on the morning of July 25, Blenheim N3536 and Martinet HP380, both from the Air Gunnery School, were engaged on a target firing exercise over Carmarthen Bay. For reasons unknown, at 08:50 hrs the two aircraft collided near Caldey Island.

The pilot of the Blenheim, Sgt. Weiss, was able to fly his damaged aircraft back to base, but Martinet HP380 plummeted into the sea approximately one mile east of Caldey. The RAF air-sea rescue launch moored at Tenby was quickly on the scene, but neither of the Martinet's crew survived the crash.

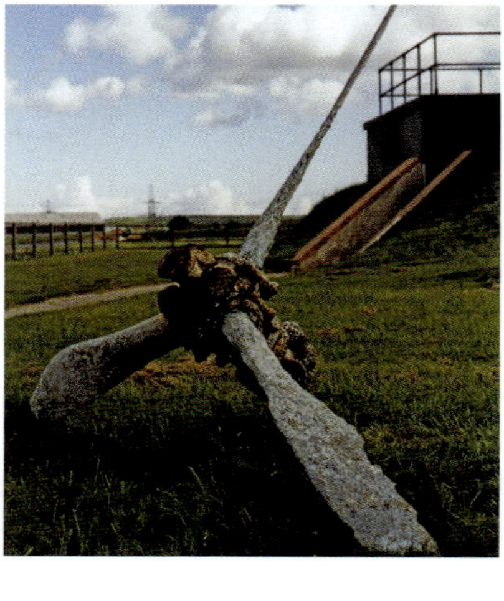

A propeller assembly trawled up off Caldey Island in 2002. The reduction gear indicates that it originated from a radial engine.

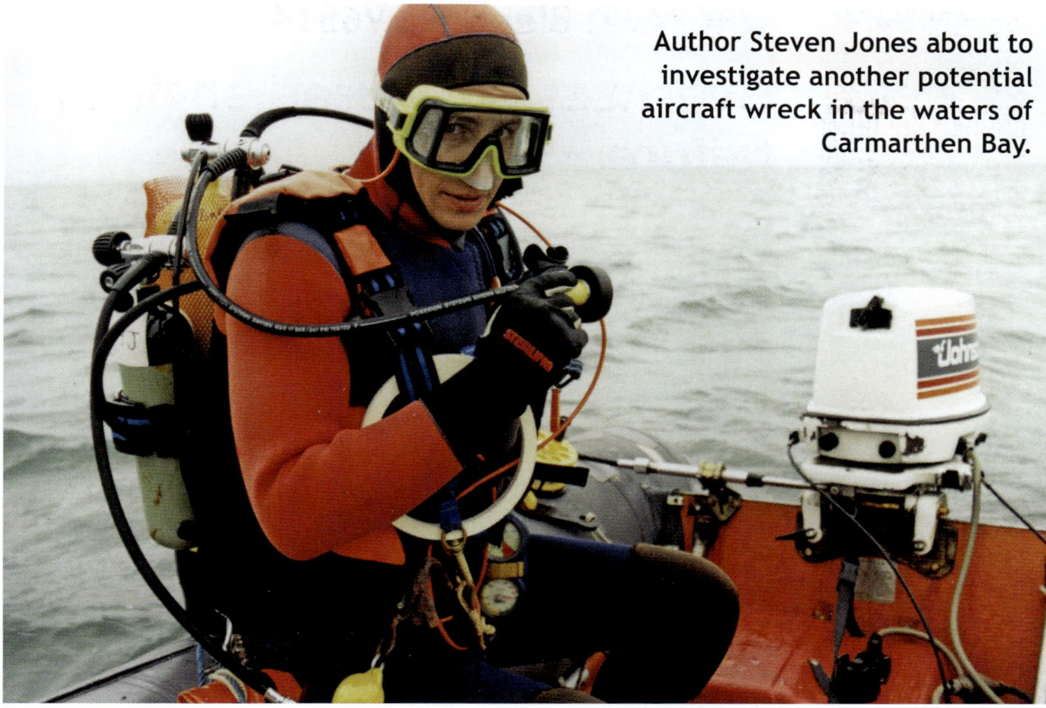

Author Steven Jones about to investigate another potential aircraft wreck in the waters of Carmarthen Bay.

The body of tow-operator, AC John Hendrick, was recovered by the rescue launch along with the Martinet's tail section. No trace of Sgt. Anthony Agar, the Canadian pilot, was found.

AUG 13 1943

AIRCRAFT: Blenheim V6518

Bodies of sea crash crew washed up on beach

Another Air Gunnery School aircraft lost in the vicinity of Caldey Island disappeared under the waves on the afternoon of 13 August. Blenheim V6518 failed to return from an air-to-sea firing session over Carmarthen Bay. A combined aerial and surface search was initiated, but nothing was found of either the aircraft or crew. The Blenheim was believed to have gone down in the Caldey to Amroth area between 12:40 hrs and 13:40 hrs. The cause of its disappearance is unknown.

A week later the bodies of the pilot, Sgt. Montgomery, and AC2 Pearson, one of the trainee air gunners, were found washed ashore on Marros beach.

CREW LIST: Sgt. Montgomery HG, Pilot, Killed; AC2 Pearson RS, Ag u/t, Killed; AC2 Clarke AJ, Ag u/t, Missing; AC Watson RB, Ag u/t, Missing.

In 2002 a complete propeller assembly from a British-built radial engine was accidentally snagged in the lines of a whelk fishing boat based at

Saundersfoot. When questioned the boat's skipper gave the location as being in deep water off the east coastline of Caldey Island. With both the Martinet and Blenheim using the same power plant, the Bristol Mercury radial engine, perhaps the recovered propeller may have originated from one of the two latter mentioned aircraft. The propeller unit can be seen as an exhibit at the restored Control Tower Museum at the former RAF airfield at Carew.

NOV 15 1943

AIRCRAFT: **Anson R9693**

Night time forced landing on riverside fields

The Avro Anson aircraft was in service with the RAF throughout the Second World War. Like the Blenheim it started off in operational roles, but as technology progressed it was relegated to use in Training Command.

The Staff Pilot Training Unit at RAF Cark on the northern shores of Morecambe Bay was one of the many units which utilised the Anson.

In the early morning of November 15, Anson R9693 was taking part in a night-time cross country training flight when the crew became lost. With the wireless-operator unable to use his radio set because of interference caused by the atrocious weather, and fuel running low, the pilot, Flt. Sgt. Lindsay, made the decision to force land on the flat fields which border the River Tywi near Towy Cot Farm, Golden Grove.

His landing would have been perfect had it not been for a lone hawthorn bush which loomed out of the early morning darkness at the last moment before touchdown. At a height of only six feet the aircraft struck the bush and crashed. No one on board was injured. The Anson was later salvaged and after some repairs flew again.

Owen Griffiths, who still lives nearby, recalls being woken early that morning to the sound of an aeroplane flying low over Towy Cot Farm and a short time later the arrival of the Anson's crew at the farmhouse. Over breakfast Flt. Sgt. Lindsay confessed that this was not the first instance that he had cause to force land an aircraft and was not relishing the thought of sitting before another court of inquiry.

A metal detector search of the area failed to reveal the exact spot where the Anson crashed, but the site can be viewed by walking approximately 300 yards along the former railway track below College Farm and looking towards the river. The Anson came to rest near a hollow in the field close to a line of mature oak trees.

NOV
20
1943

AIRCRAFT: **Martinet HP366**

Thud that indicated a mid-air collision

The skies above Ty Newydd Farm, just north of Burry Port, were often busy with the sound of aeroplanes during the war years. Being a sparsely inhabited area on top of Mynydd Pembrey lent itself to be an ideal location for simulated air gunnery practice. At 09:35 hrs on 20 November Glyn and Irfon Davies were at work on the farm under the supervision of their grandfather, Tom. High above them they could clearly hear the sound of two aircraft circling in close formation. Nothing seemed untoward until the distinctive thud of two aircraft colliding drew their attention skyward. Looking up they watched as one of the pair, Martinet HP366, entered a spin and started to fall to earth. Unable to regain control the aircraft crashed into the centre of a hedge near the farmhouse and caught fire. Tom, Glyn and Irfon ran to the burning wreckage and after warning his two grandsons to stay well clear, Tom attempted to break open the Martinet's canopy with a bill hook. With the fire now well established and being fanned by a freshening breeze, Tom was reluctantly forced to give up his valiant rescue attempt by the intense heat.

In a short time the emergency services arrived, but it was too late to save the two crew.

The stunted undergrowth at the spot where HP366 burned out can still be identified along an otherwise undamaged hedge. Pieces of molten aluminium can also be found.

CREW LIST: Sgt. Rigby RW, Pilot; LAC Egerton H, Tow Operator.

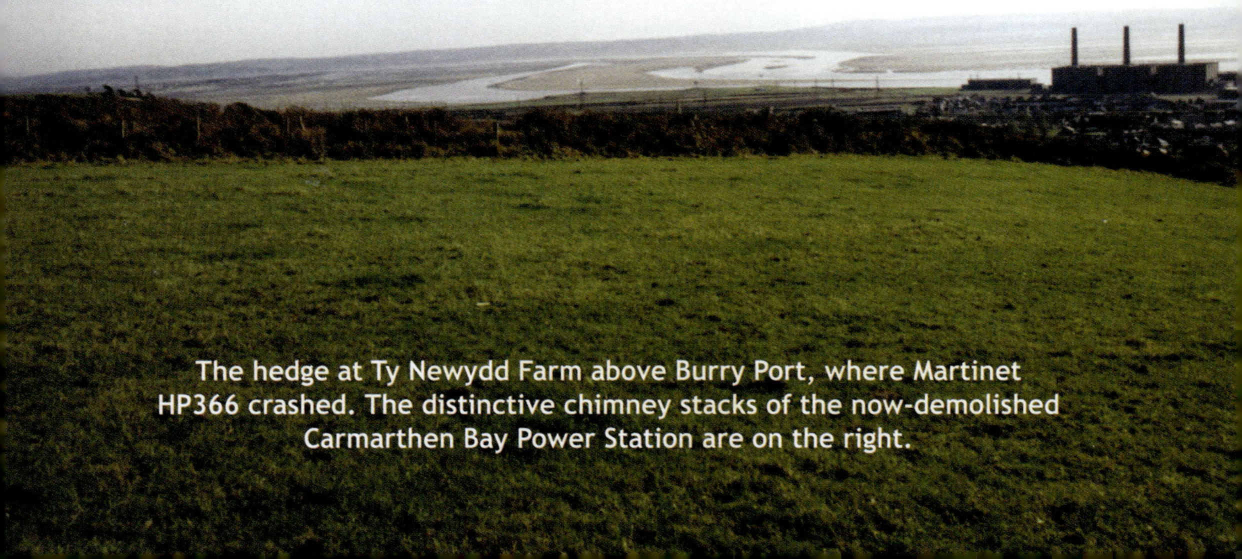

The hedge at Ty Newydd Farm above Burry Port, where Martinet HP366 crashed. The distinctive chimney stacks of the now-demolished Carmarthen Bay Power Station are on the right.

APRIL 21 1944

AIRCRAFT: **Marauder 42-96277**

Marrakesh flight was hit by bad weather

During 1944 the ageing Blenheim fleet at Pembrey's Air Gunnery School was gradually replaced by Anson aircraft, and later in the year the Ansons themselves were superseded by Wellingtons. This was reflected by a significant decrease in the number of flying accidents at the unit.

The first two mishaps of 1944 both involved American aircraft types which had recently arrived in the country, they also occurred within a day of each other. At 18:20 hrs on April 21, an unidentified aircraft was heard overhead at Pembrey airfield, but due to a cloud base of only 50ft that evening no visible contact could be made. In the base's communications centre a radio operator gave out directions on the distress channel 'Darky' which would enable the aircraft to land safely at the airfield; despite numerous attempts no reply was acknowledged from the crew.

The aircraft turned out to be an American B-26 Marauder, 42-96277, which was being ferried up from Marrakesh on the southern ferry route, bound for RAF St Mawgan, Cornwall.

On nearing St Mawgan the weather had deteriorated with a solid layer of cloud all the way down to sea level. As the aircraft had sufficient fuel in its tanks it was diverted to RAF Valley in North Wales; by then a common procedure when bad weather hampered Transatlantic flights arriving via the southern route.

Unable to contact Valley for a homing bearing to follow, the pilot, Lt. George Seipp, briefly sighted land through a small break in the cloud and let-down in an attempt to find a suitable airfield to land at. When clear of cloud another Marauder, 42-95861, also being ferried up from North Africa was spotted and as faint radio messages were intercepted by Seipp's crew it became apparent that the other Marauder was also in a similar predicament.

For a while both Marauders flew in close formation to each other, only to lose visual contact as the two aircraft again entered another blanket of cloud. By pure chance one of Lt. Seipp's crew momentarily glimpsed a fleeting view of Pembrey's runways, but lost sight of them almost immediately. Next a vast expanse of sand appeared in front of the aircraft and Seipp made the split-second decision to belly-land the Marauder.

Coming to rest with hardly any damage to the aircraft the crew scrambled out of the emergency hatches to find that they were at the eastern end of

Pendine beach, not far from the Proof and Experimental Establishment testing range. The Marauder was later raised onto its undercarriage, towed further up the beach and dismantled by the RAF.

Had Lt. Seipp's crew and the communications centre at Pembrey been able to make contact with each other there is no doubt that 42-96277 could have landed safely at the base. Excessive static over the airwaves seems to have been the root cause of the breakdown in communication. From the list below it is interesting to note that Marauder crews ferrying aircraft across the Atlantic now carried a fifth person, a dedicated radio-operator, a lesson learned from the tragedies at Penrhyn Farm and Carn Llidi the previous year.

CREW LIST: 2nd Lt. Seipp GA, Pilot; 2nd Lt. Render JR, Co-pilot; 2nd Lt. Arter JR, Navigator; S. Sgt. Vaughn WT, Flight Engineer; S. Sgt. Davies, Radio Operator.

Marauder 42-95861, the aircraft which Lt. Seipp had spotted after breaking clear of cloud, landed safely at RAF Carew further along the coast.

APRIL 22 1944

AIRCRAFT: **Cub 43-30212**

Piper's short take off drew an excited crowd

The arrival of Piper Cub 43-30212 in Britain was without doubt far less less dramatic than that of Lt. Seipp's Marauder; it was delivered by sea in a wooden shipping container which reached the UK on March 29, 1944.

Uncrated and reassembled at 3 Tactical Air Depot at Grove, near Abingdon in Berkshire, it was then destined for the US Army's 693rd Field Artillery Battalion airstrip at Kington near Hereford.

In the afternoon of 22 April the aircraft took off from Grove on its delivery flight to Kington. At the controls was 1st Lt. Howard Larsen with fellow pilot 2nd Lt. Merlin Black in the passenger seat. Some time after leaving Grove the Cub veered off course and was later seen circling above Upper Brynamman on the edge of the Black Mountain.

Unsure of their position Howard Larsen landed in a small hillside field below Bryn Farm on the outskirts of the town to inquire as to their whereabouts.

In no time at all a crowd of spectators had gathered to marvel at the Cub, among them were two local boys, John Thomas and Donald Evans. Both were to witness the aircraft's last moments.

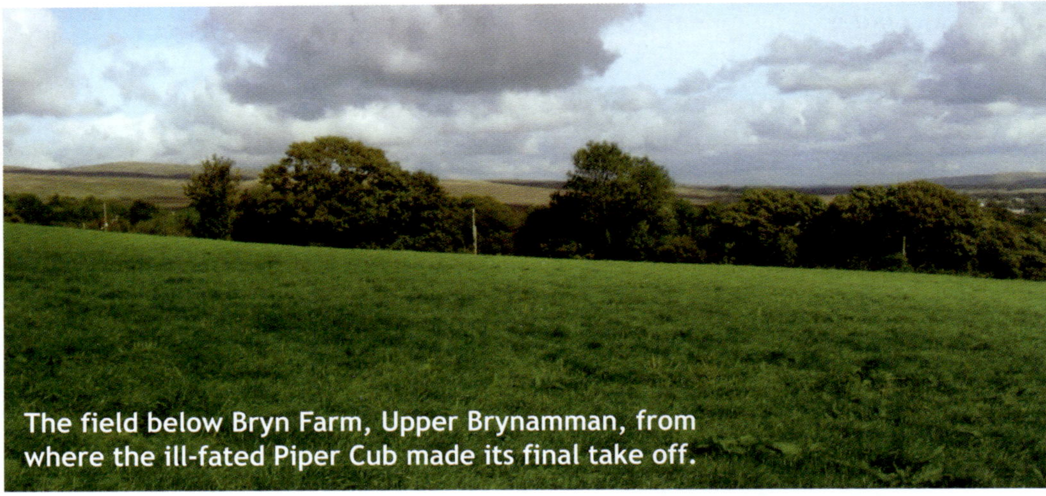
The field below Bryn Farm, Upper Brynamman, from where the ill-fated Piper Cub made its final take off.

The American airmen were given directions on how to reach Brecon which was marked on their air chart and at around 17:00 hrs Lt. Larsen taxied the Cub to the far end of the field in order to take advantage of every foot of ground to gain airspeed; even at its widest point the field was only 150 yards in length.

Unfortunately, due to a number of factors, the aircraft failed to gain sufficient height to clear the tops of the tall trees which fringed the slopes of the Nant Melyn gully, a former quarry which bordered the take off field. Once above the quarry the aircraft was seen to stall and crashed nose-down into the hedgerow of a field on the far-side of the gully. There was no fire, but Lt. Larsen had been killed while Lt. Black lay unconscious in the passenger seat.

Retired district nurse Lilian Moses was the first medically experienced person to arrive at the scene of the crash and immediately tended to Lt. Black who was slipping in and out of consciousness. An ambulance was summoned and he was taken to Morriston Hospital where his condition improved and he survived.

It is assumed that the combination of a short take off run with tall trees and overhead power lines in the flight path of the aircraft, coupled with the high ambient temperature which impaired the amount of power the Cub's engine was able to produce, all contributed to the crash.

Due to the low altitude at which the accident happened and the small size of the aircraft, no evidence of the crash exists today. If, after gaining permission, you stand in the field in which the Cub took off, it becomes apparent that Lt. Larsen didn't have much room for error when he attempted to take off. At nearby St Catherine's Church a small brass plaque mounted on one of the inside walls commemorates Lt. Larsen who came from Schiller Park, Illinois.

MAY 8 1944

AIRCRAFT: **Martinet HP361**

Crash ended flight to impress fiancee

Another accident involving an aircraft striking trees at low level occurred just before 10:00 hrs on May 8.

An hour previously Sgt. Jacek Kinel, a Polish staff pilot at Pembrey's Air Gunnery School, and his tow operator, LAC Stanley Hall, had taken off in Martinet HP361 on a routine target-towing flight. On completion of the exercise, and at the request of his tow operator, Jacek Kinel flew north to Cwrt Malle Farm, near Llangynog, where Stan Hall's fiancee, Joan Thomas, worked as a member of the Women's Land Army. At the time she was leading a horse through the narrow lanes to the east of the farm, around the Llangynog Road/Heol Smyrna area and guessed that the low-flying Martinet circling around her was indeed Stan's aircraft.

The smile which this brought to Joan's face soon turned to despair and disbelief however. As she stopped to watch the impromptu air display the Martinet disappeared from view for a few seconds before a dull thud echoed around the open countryside, followed by complete silence. At a height of only 30ft the Martinet had flown directly into a line of tall poplar trees, then dropped nose-first into a small stream killing both airmen.

The tragedy is still remembered by a number of local women who settled in the area after having served in the Land Army, some of whom knew Joan Thomas personally. After the war Joan married Stan's younger brother, Harry and settled in Stoke-on-Trent, the Hall family's home town and also where Stanley Hall is buried.

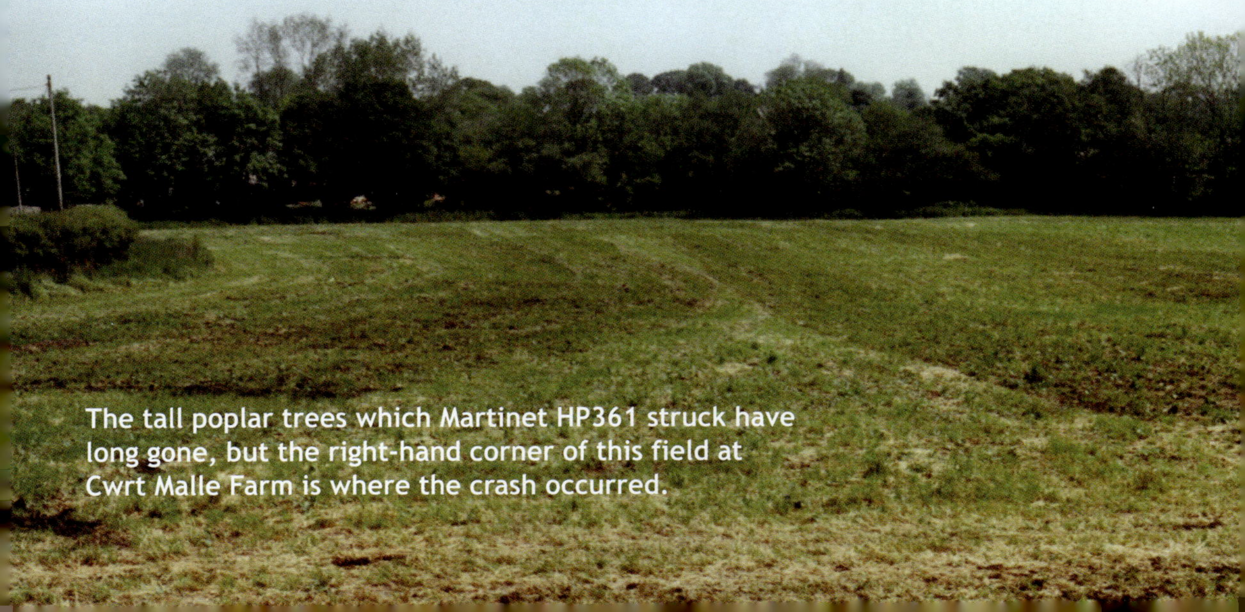

The tall poplar trees which Martinet HP361 struck have long gone, but the right-hand corner of this field at Cwrt Malle Farm is where the crash occurred.

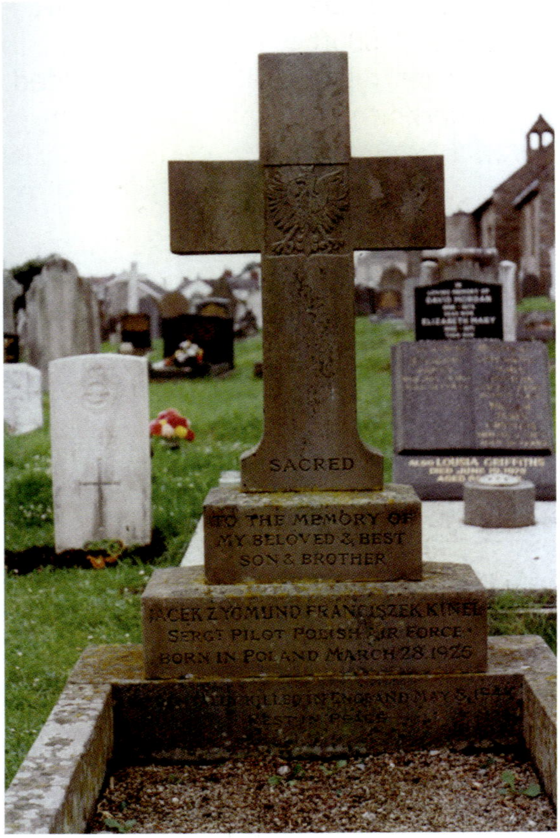

Sgt. Jacek Kinel came from the city of Bydgoszcz in Poland, and is buried at St Illtyd's Church, Pembrey. He has a private headstone.

The row of poplar trees into which the Martinet crashed have all been felled, yet a walk along the edge of the field at Cwrt Malle Farm, two miles south west of Carmarthen, will still reveal their stumps. At a spot about three quarters of the way along the field from the road bridge which crosses the stream below Cwrt Malle, a few small pieces of corroded aluminium also indicate where the aircraft fell.

The private headstone of Sgt. Jacek Kinel at St Illtyd's churchyard.

JUNE
4
1944

AIRCRAFT: Thunderbolt 42-26256

Weather conditions claim a further American victim

On the first anniversary of the loss of Marauder 41-18252 Mi'Laine near Llanelli another American aircraft crashed in the county in similar weather conditions. At 16:15 hrs on the afternoon of June 4, 1944, Captain James Wilkinson, Commanding Officer of the 82nd Fighter Squadron, left his base at Duxford in Thunderbolt 42-26256 on a flight to the air-to-ground firing range near the remote Pembrokeshire village of Rosebush in the Preseli hills.

Captain Wilkinson was due to give a demonstration on his technique of 'train busting' at the Rosebush range on June 8 and wanted to familiarise himself with the terrain prior to the exercise. Even after obtaining a weather report indicating the possibility of low cloud and rain showers over mid-Wales, he was reluctantly given clearance for the flight. However, while flying at cruising speed in cloud just east of Cynghordy near Llandovery, his aircraft struck the summit of Cefn Llwydlo at just over 1,000ft in level flight and plummeted down the steep slope into Glyn Saer, disintegrating as it skidded along the ground. Wreckage from the Thunderbolt was spread over a vast area and left a defined trail of debris from the summit all the way down the hillside to Nant Hirgwm on the valley floor, a distance of over half of a mile.

Due to the total destruction of the airframe and the remote location of the crash site, the Thunderbolt was not discovered until 10:00 hrs the following day, June 5. George Watkins, a farm labourer at Clyn Saer Farm, was walking to work along the footpath which leads down from his secluded cottage at Ffosgoy further up the Glyn Saer valley when he saw pieces of wreckage scattered on the hillside. George had passed this very spot the previous evening on his way home, but had failed to notice anything untoward in the fading light.

After realising that the pilot was beyond help, he made his way down to Cynghordy village to raise the alarm. Later that morning a small group of villagers returned to the scene with Sgt. McLaren, the local policeman from Llandovery.

Among that group was 14-year-old telegram boy, John Davies. John recalled the trek up Glyn Saer that morning with his uncle W.J. Davies, the village Post Master, Rhys Gibbins of Clyn Saer Farm, George Watkins and Sgt. McClaren. Arriving at the scene he encountered many pieces of twisted aluminium strewn across the ravine-like slope of the valley, the only recognisable part of the Thunderbolt being the burned-out cockpit section with the body of the pilot still strapped in. This grisly sight gave John nightmares for some time afterwards.

Captain Wilkinson had been classed as an 'ace', having destroyed a total of eight enemy aircraft; six in the air and two while ground strafing. His military service began on the outbreak of the Second World War when he decided to enlist as a pilot. After initially being rejected by the United States Army Air Corps due to an unfinished year in his studies at University, he crossed the border into Canada and enlisted in the Canadian Army, serving in the artillery. In October 1941 he transferred to the RAF, gained his wings and a year later joined the USAAF, formerly the USAAC.

On April 27, 1943, while with the 334th Fighter Squadron, he was injured in a training accident near Castle Camps in Essex. The tail unit of his Thunderbolt was sliced off as the result of a mid-air collision with another aircraft, forcing him to bail out. Unfortunately his parachute was torn and he landed heavily injuring his back. He was hospitalised for a number of weeks and in September 1943 transferred to the 82nd Fighter Squadron at Duxford. From here he shot down his first enemy aircraft on December 1, while on a bomber escort mission over Germany. In March 1944 he was promoted to the rank of Captain. As well as becoming an 'ace', in the months that followed James Wilkinson had become proficient in strafing rail transport. He contended that hits made in the right spot would render a steam locomotive unserviceable for months rather than weeks. It was this technique that he was to demonstrate at the Rosebush firing range. The crash site of Thunderbolt 42-26256 was lost in subsequent years under the forestry plantation which now exists in the Glyn Saer valley. In 2002 it was rediscovered by Abergavenny-based aviation archaeologists Gareth Jones and Glyn Morgan. After a long and arduous metal detector search of the area lasting many days, the pair meticulously followed a debris trail along the hillside to the main bury hole dug by the salvage crew. Of the many items found at this location perhaps the most poignant was the aircraft's time clock; its hands stopped at 17:12 hrs. Due to nobody having witnessed the crash, the accident investigation team in 1944 could only hazard a guess as to when the crash occurred; the official report estimating the time as being between 17:00 hrs and 19:00 hrs that evening. Over 60 years later, a more precise time was added to the history books.

In November 2005, as a result of writing a short story about the rediscovery of the crash location on the 82nd Fighter Squadron web site, I was contacted by Captain Wilkinson's son from his first marriage, James Wilkinson Jnr. It transpires that James Jnr. followed in his father's, and grandfather's, footsteps and also became an air force pilot, flying many missions in F-4 Phantoms during the conflict in Vietnam.

Below is an account by Major O.K. Jones, Staff Weather Officer for the 78th Fighter Group at Duxford, detailing how Captain Wilkinson was reluctantly given permission for his fateful flight:

"On June 4, there were no air operations scheduled for the 8th Fighter Command because of the bad weather. In fact, the whole of the 8th Air Force was stood down, bombers and all. Ceilings were on the deck, there was little or no wind and my forecast suggested no meaningful improvement for the rest of the day. Major General Kepner called me down to Combat Ops where he introduced me to Captain Wilkinson. Wilkinson was an RAF transferee to the 78th and had earned quite a reputation as a locomotive buster. During his time in England he had developed a phoney British accent and somewhat supercilious air. To be perfectly honest, I was a bit turned off.

"Anyway, he wanted General Kepner's permission to go on a sole locomotive busting sortie over NW Europe. I briefed them that the ceilings over there were OK, around 1,500ft, lowering over the hills, but the problem was finding an acceptable recovery base in England. The British weather was simply not going to improve sufficiently that a suitable recovery base would

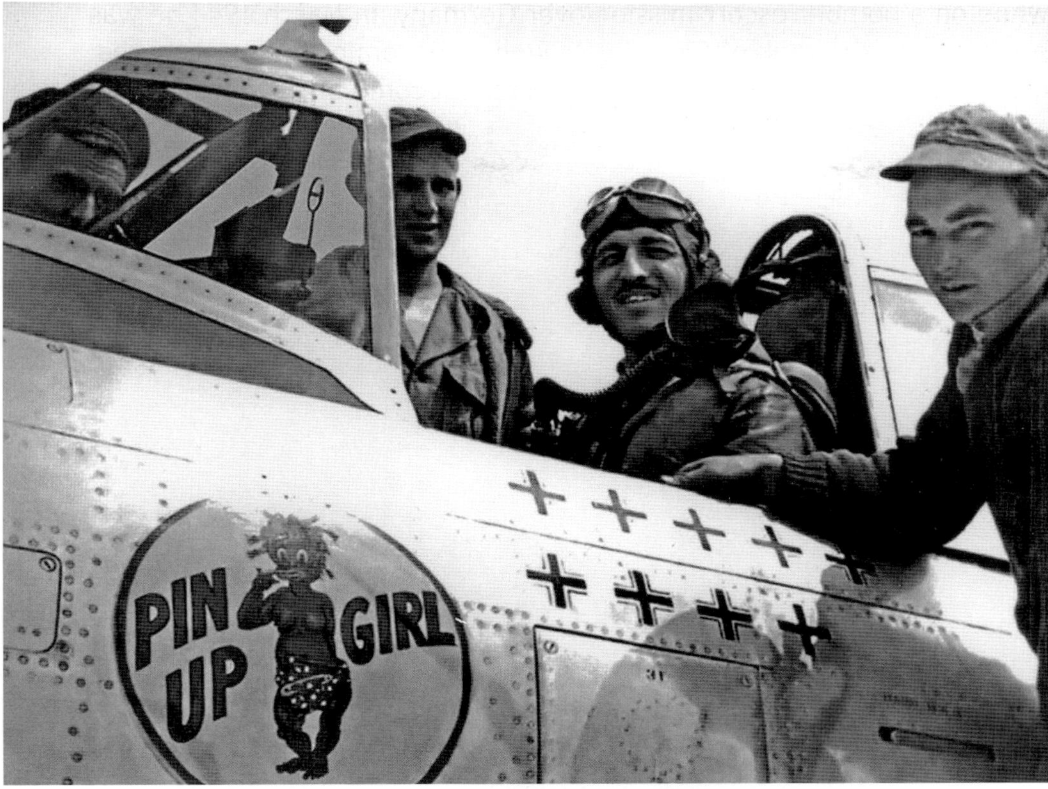

Captain James Wilkinson in the cockpit of Thunderbolt 42-7954, Pin-up Girl with, from left: Unknown; S. Sgt. Eugene Carter, assistant crew chief; Capt. James Wilkinson; Ismal Boase, crew chief.

be likely to be found upon Captain Wilkinson's return later in the day. Wilkinson looked down his nose at me – he was 6ft 1ins or more and I was 5ft 10ins – and said, 'Mayjah', 'ah've' been in this country for several 'yeahs' and 'ah' think 'ah' know quite a bit about this British 'weatha' and what it is going to do'. I responded to the effect that may well be, but I couldn't recommend a single base in all of the British Isles that would have even the minimal recovery weather upon his return later in the afternoon. General Kepner put the decision whether to fly or not up to Wilkinson who, as we know, elected to go. Later it emerged that he had tried to move a mountain in Wales."

Records show that instead of a train-busting sortie over the Continent Captain Wilkinson opted to fly west across Mid Wales to the Rosebush firing range, to recce the site prior to his display on June 8. In his account Major Jones also gives mention to the mystery surrounding the sudden death of Captain Wilkinson's second wife, Frieda, in January 1945. He continues: "Mrs. Wilkinson promptly moved in with the Commander of the 66th Fighter Wing at Hill House near Duxford, he needed that certain feminine touch I suppose. Some months later a story broke in the Daily Mirror that Mrs.

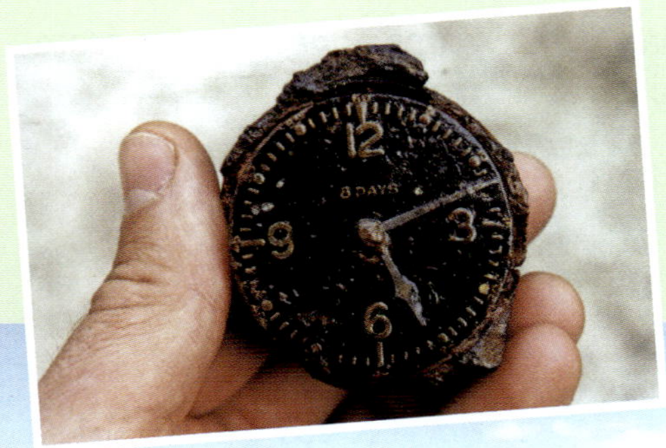

The Thunderbolt's time clock, stopped at 17:12 hrs. US Air Force crash investigators in 1944 had estimated the time of the accident as having taken place between 17:00 and 19:00 hrs.

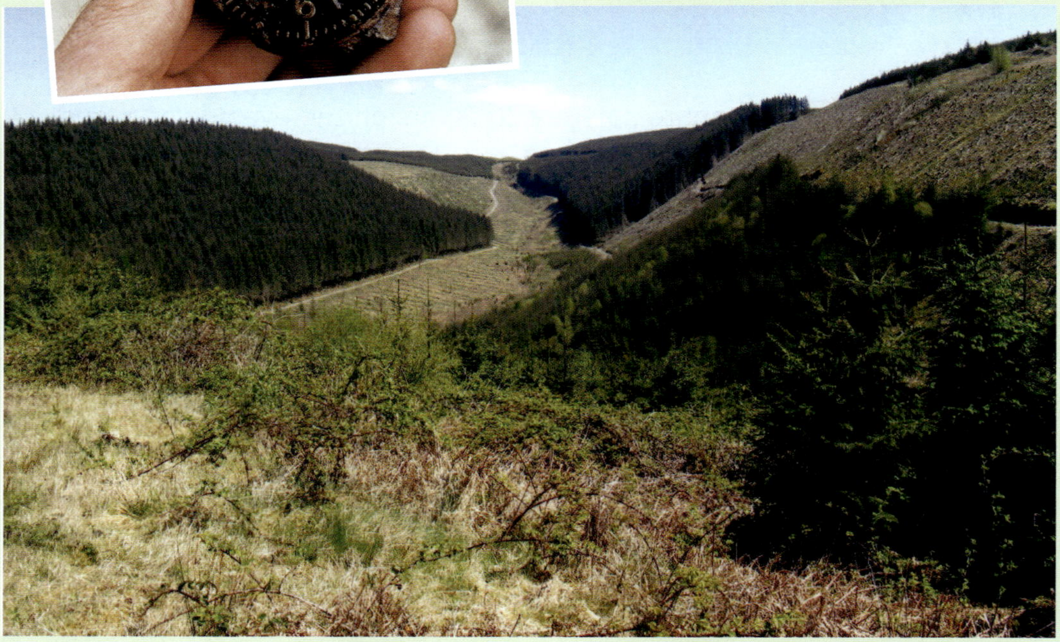

The Glyn Saer Valley, Cynghordy. Thunderbolt 42-26256 careered down the steep bank on the right, along the same route as the recently harvested trees, before coming to rest just below the tree-line on the left hand side of the valley. The footpath which led to George Watkins' home at Ffosgoy can be seen running along the base of the tree line on the left and up through the centre of this view.

Wilkinson's body had been found in her London flat, an apparent suicide. It seems that British Intelligence had been on her trail for some time and that she was a niece of Von Ribbentrop and was a German citizen who had been an active spy for some years."

Captain Wilkinson's assistant crew chief, Eugene Carter, cast light on 'Big Wilkie's' persevering character. A trait which inevitably cost him his life:

"It seems that for a time there were two 'Wilkinsons' in the 78th Fighter Group. Captain Wilkinson was known to the unit's ground crew as 'Big Wilkie', though not because of his tall stature. The other Wilkinson, 'Little Wilkie', had a habit of frequently finding something wrong, real or imagined, with his aircraft so that he could abort operations. To the contrary, Captain Wilkinson always had a strong desire to complete the mission in hand and for this reason was popular among the crew chiefs." James Wilkinson is buried at the American military cemetery at Madingley, Cambridge, not far from Duxford airfield the base he took off from on his final flight.

AUG
23
1944

AIRCRAFT: **Wellington JA453**

Final exercise claimed lives of four crewmen

At approximately 20:00 hrs on the evening of August 23, Wellington JA453, coded MZ-X, of 83 Operational Training Unit took off on a night cross-country training flight from its base at RAF Peplow in Shropshire. For pilot 'Mike' Emmanuel Hartstein and his crew this was to be their final exercise before being posted to an operational squadron. In the event four of the crew were destined not to return.

Leaving the Shropshire countryside P.O. Hartstein headed for the Irish Sea to carry out some air-to-sea firing practice for the air gunners and after dark, a night-time bomb dropping exercise for Sgt. Simons, the bomb aimer. Some time during the flight, while 40 miles off the coast of mid-Wales, the Wellington's starboard Hercules engine suddenly cut-out and moments later the port engine started to give cause for concern. A course was set to make an emergency landing at RAF Aberporth on the Cardiganshire coast and radio contact with the ground was sought via the distress channel 'Darky', but no response was gained. At this point the crew's navigator, Sgt. Rolfe Lindahl, a Norwegian, was unaware that Aberporth was only a day-time training airfield and had no runway lighting; air charts of that period indicated Aberporth as being a 24 hour flying station.

On reaching Aberporth the Wellington orbited the base at 2,000ft, but the airfield remained 'blacked-out' against the countryside below. Losing precious altitude with every minute that passed, P.O. Hartstein widened his circuit in the hope of finding the runway.

Shortly before midnight Wellington JA453 lost its battle to stay airborne and after first brushing the tops of trees on the outskirts of Cenarth, it plunged into the wooded-banks of the River Teifi a few yards downstream from the famous waterfalls. On impact the port wing was torn away from the fuselage and the aircraft's fuel tanks exploded, starting a major fire. Wellington aircraft were renowned for their structural strength by nature of the airframe's geodetic construction, but in a crash fire scenario this type of framework could easily become an inescapable twisted cage.

For wireless operator Sgt. Howard Hawkins, the tearing away of the port wing proved a miracle, as he was now able to exit the burning aircraft through a small hole which had formed close to his position near the radio compartment. The only other crew member to survive the crash was the rear gunner, Sgt. Johnnie Robertshaw.

As the drill for abandoning the aircraft via the rear turret had been well-rehearsed during training, the procedure became second nature to Sgt. Robertshaw, who vacated his position in seconds.

Sixty years on Johnnie Robertshaw recalled that in his haste to get out of the burning Wellington he forgot to disconnect his intercom cable, this led to an unpleasant jolt to his head as he jumped clear. Looking back at the aircraft through the trees he noticed that the base of the fire was burning extremely bright, possibly due to the magnesium-powdered practice bombs activating in the intense heat.

After spending the night in hospital at Newcastle Emlyn, the following day Johnnie and Howard were taken to Aberporth airfield where an inquiry was held to establish the cause of the crash. Two salient points which the investigation team queried were: (a) why the pilot did not ditch the aircraft near the coast as he had made landfall with insufficient altitude to clear any high ground and (b) the misleading manner at which Aberporth was depicted on air charts as having full airfield facilities. Down through the years Johnnie Robertshaw had often pondered over how the crash could have been averted. Even the very basic use of hand-held lanterns laid out in a 'T' shaped pattern on the ground, as used to guide down covert Lysander pilots in occupied France, would have helped P.O. Hartstein that night.

In the weeks that followed the accident Johnnie's arm became swollen and he was unable to continue his training as an air gunner for some time. 83 OTU was disbanded in October 1944, so Johnnie was

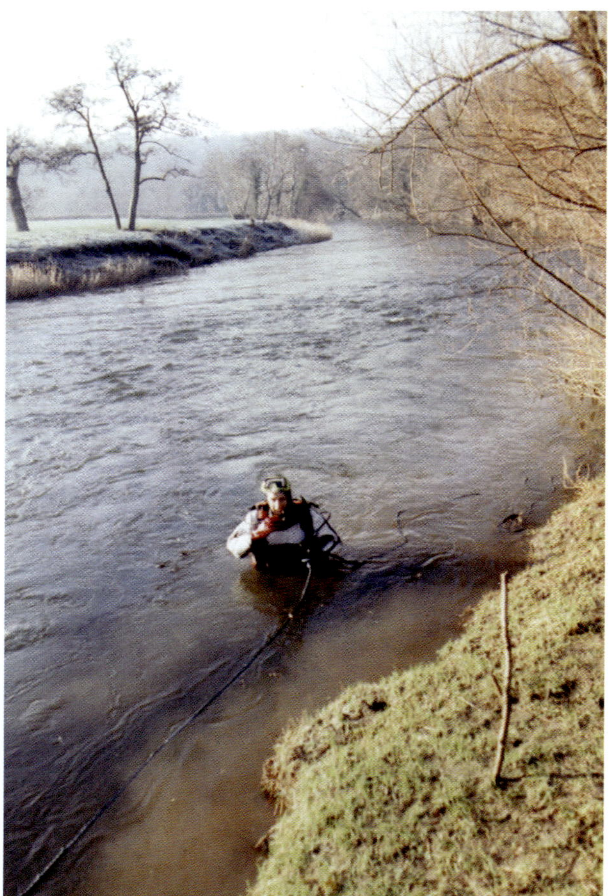

Author Steven Jones conducting an underwater search of the River Teifi close to where Wellington JA453 came to rest.

transferred to 30 OTU at nearby Hixon airfield where he finally passed out as an operational air gunner.

In September 1994 on the 50th anniversary of the crash, both Johnnie Robertshaw and Howard Hawkins returned to Cenarth as guests of honour at a memorial service held at St Llawddog's Church. Also among the congregation were close relatives of the other crew members. During the service a brass plaque commemorating the crew was unveiled at the village cenotaph.

Due to the crash site's close proximity to the main road, a stone's throw from the A484, most of the wreckage would have been easily cleared. Despite assuming this, on a frosty December morning in 1994, I conducted an underwater search of the river bed in the vicinity of the crash, but nothing was found. Making inquiries in the village I was told of how, some years previously, part of an undercarriage leg had been unearthed by a local resident while digging his riverside garden. The strut was subsequently displayed at Aberporth airfield, but has since disappeared.

CREW LIST: P.O. Hartstein E, Pilot, Killed; Sgt. Lindahl R, Navigator, Killed; Sgt. Simons F, Bomb aimer, Killed; Sgt. McKenna T, Ag, Killed; Sgt. Hawkins H, Wop/Ag, Injured; Sgt. Robertshaw J, Ag, Injured.

OCT 14 1944

AIRCRAFT: **Warwick HG342**

Pall of black smoke rose from crash wreckage

Similar in both shape and construction to the Wellington was the Vickers Warwick. Though never used for operational duties, it did serve an important role in both Air-Sea Rescue work and in research connected with engine development. In October Warwick HG342 found itself in trouble over Carmarthenshire and again it may well have been the case that the aircraft was intent on making an emergency landing at Aberporth.

Warwick HG342 is recorded as being utilised as a test-bed for the development of the powerful Bristol Centaurus radial engine. Based at the Centaurus Testing Flight at RAF Filton near Bristol, it took off in the afternoon of October 14 on an engine test flight. On board were the pilot, Flt. Lt. Leonard Crozier and a passenger, engine mechanic LAC Ron McAllen, who at the last minute, had volunteered to take the place of the co-pilot who had become unavailable. Not much is known as to the actual flight details as no Accident Record Card exists for the aircraft. However, a

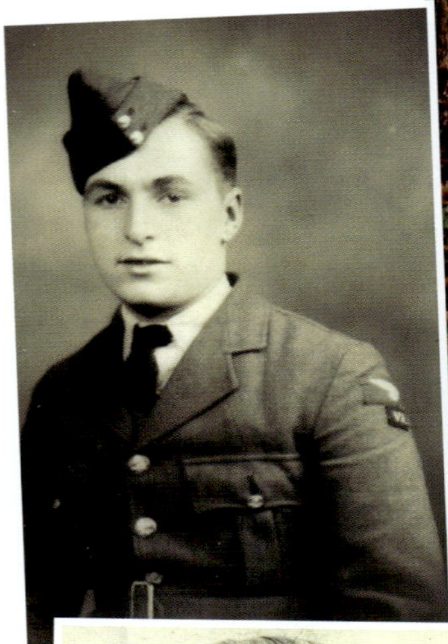

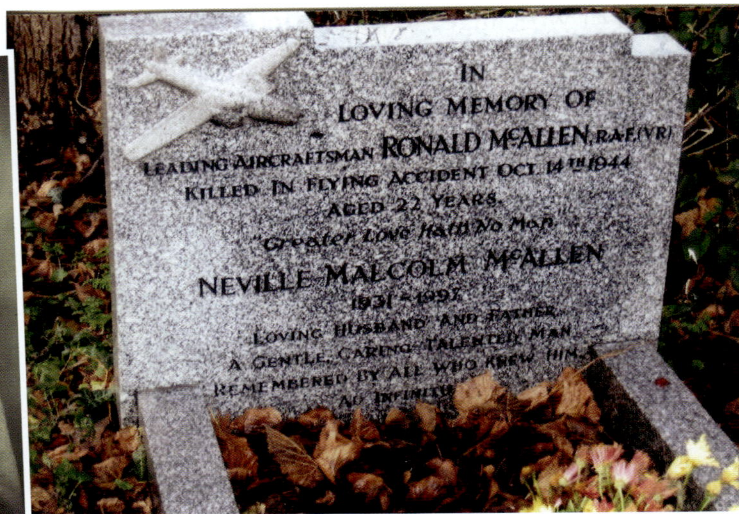

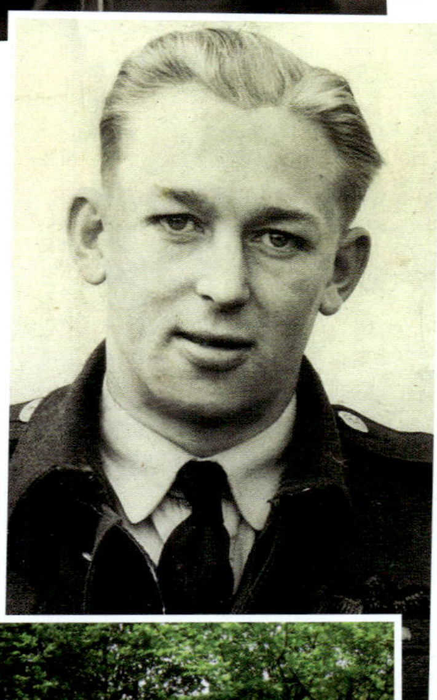

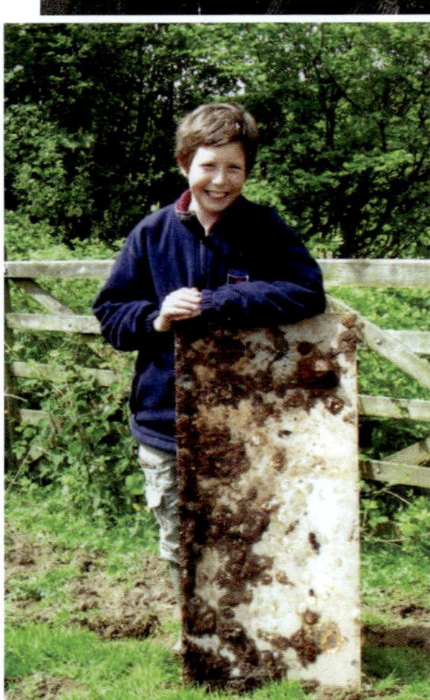

LAC Ron McAllen, left, the mechanic aboard Warwick HG342 and above, his private headstone at St Mary's churchyard, Humberstone, Leicestershire. CENTRE: Flt. Lt. Len Crozier, pilot of the aircraft and below, James Panayiotou can be seen holding an undercarriage door found in the hedgerow running along the Afon Mamog.

number of eye-witnesses on the ground that day near Gors Farm on the outskirts of Capel Iwan can confirm that the Warwick was flying at low-level, on a northwesterly heading and with one of its propellers in the 'feathered' position. The remaining healthy engine could also be heard labouring franticly trying to keep the aircraft aloft.

Elgan Jones, only seven years of age at the time, was cutting sugar beet with his father when the Warwick appeared from behind Moelfre hill. Their immediate concern was that the aircraft seemed to be on a collision course with Gors farmhouse where Mrs. Jones was inside attending to her daily chores. Both Elgan and his father watched in horror as the Warwick first hit a tree only yards from the farmhouse before disintegrating over the steeply-sloping field which leads down to the Afon Mamog. Immediately after the crash a pall of black smoke rose above the main area of wreckage. It wasn't long before people attending a farm sale at Penrhipyn Farm rushed to the scene to render help, but nothing could be done to save the two crew.

Leonard 'snowy' Crozier had trained as a fighter pilot with the RAF Volunteer Reserve in 1937. In the early months of 1940 he saw active service flying Hurricanes with 85 Squadron at Lille in northern France as part of the RAF's Advance Air Striking Force. He was credited with shooting down five enemy aircraft, three confirmed and two probables, during what became known as the Blitzkrieg. He was himself shot down in May 1940, sustaining burns in the process. Following his arrival back in Britain via Dunkirk, he spent six months convalescing from his injuries before becoming a flying instructor. For a short period in 1942 he took part in various aircraft experimental tests at the Royal Aircraft Establishment at Farnborough before becoming involved in Beam Approach training. In October 1943 he joined his brother Ivor, also a pilot, at the Centaurus Engine Testing Flight based at Filton.

Ron McAllen had enlisted in the Air Force in 1941 and trained as an engine mechanic. After qualifying in his trade in May 1942, he was posted to RAF Dumfries and also spent some time at the nearby seaplane base at Stranraer before joining the Centaurus Testing Flight in June 1944. The reason the usual co-pilot became unavailable for the flight in October 1944 remains a mystery.

Gors Farm is now a horse stud centre. A metal detector search of the field below the farmhouse uncovered many small pieces of the aircraft, some of which were stamped with the 285 prefix numbers relating to the Vickers Wellington and Warwick aircraft.

On July 14, 2012 Cenarth Community Council dedicated a memorial plaque commemorating the crew of Warwick HG342 in the centre of Capel Iwan. On a sunny day amidst the very wet summer weather of 2012, the plaque was unveiled by Melfydd Jones, who as a young boy out picking hazel nuts with his brother Hedydd, had witnessed the crash. Along with the residents attending the service were representatives of both the Crozier and McAllen families. It was a memorable day for all involved.

CREW LIST: Flt. Lt. Crozier LA, Pilot;
LAC McAllen RF, Engine mechanic.

JAN 6 1945

AIRCRAFT: **Wellington LN553**

County's worst disaster claimed lives of six

By 1945 Wellingtons were the primary training aircraft used by Pembrey's gunnery school. As the crew capacity for this type of aircraft was much larger than that of the Anson and Blenheim, any accident significantly increased the potential for greater loss of life. On January 6, 1945 Carmarthenshire's worst air disaster occurred on the mudflats just outside the boundary of Pembrey airfield when six airmen, four of whom were teenagers, lost their lives.

Events leading up to the loss of LN553 start at 13:55 hrs when the aircraft took off from Pembrey on a routine air firing exercise with a crew of seven. The exercise itself was uneventful and all five trainee gunners on board must have been keen to learn how well they had performed. Due to the north westerly breeze the pilot, F.O. Beverley Thomson, used the shorter NW/SE runway to make his landing. Touchdown was a little heavy and he was instructed by the control tower to overshoot and go around for a second attempt. The throttles were opened up, but while gaining height over the Gwendraeth Estuary the Wellington was seen to enter a nosedive from 300ft when turning across wind. It never recovered from the dive and crashed onto the marsh at 15:00 hrs.

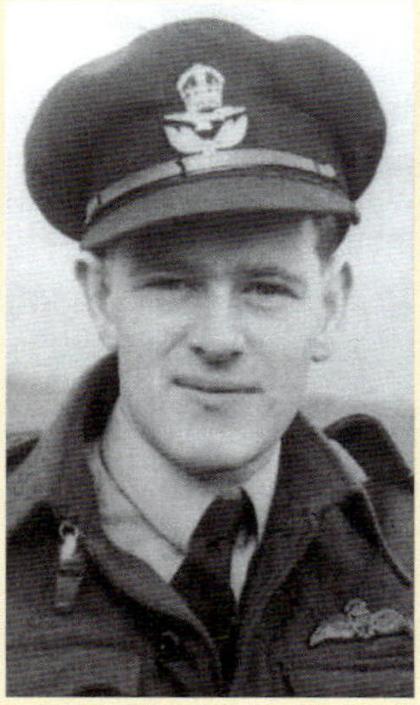

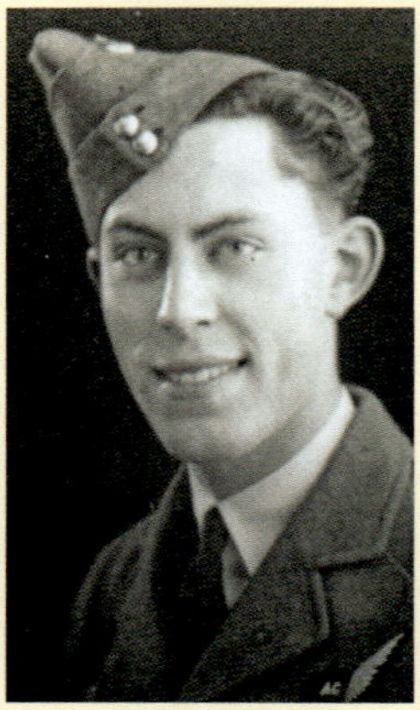

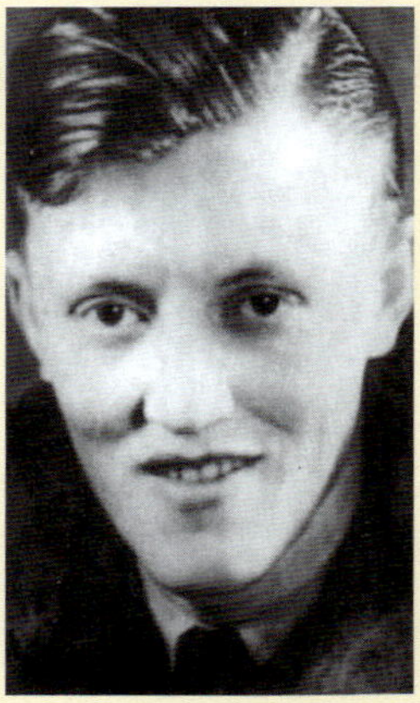

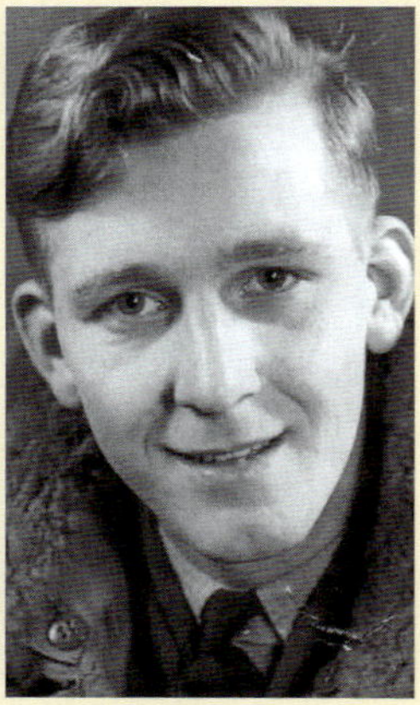

Four of the crew of Wellington LN553. From the left: F.O. Beverley Thomson, pilot of Wellington LN553. Thomson was from Sydney, Australia and married a local girl, Mary Harries of Pwll, only months before the accident which claimed his life. He is buried at St Illtyd's Churchyard, Pembrey; W.O. Gordon Dear, the gunnery instructor aboard the Wellington. Aged 23, he was the eldest of the crew and is buried at Hollybrook cemetery, Southampton. AC2 Barry Hay from Edinburgh and AC2 Frank Ford, sole survivor of the crash.

Dennis Rogers, a trainee air gunner at Pembrey, had just completed an air firing exercise himself that afternoon and witnessed the crash. Dennis recollects that somehow there was a delay in the crash rescue service being alerted. Fearing that no one had reported the accident he and a few others ran over to the control tower to raise the alarm. When the rescue service eventually responded they faced a gruelling one mile trek over the deep gullies and glutenous mud of the tidal estuary. Aircraft already airborne were diverted to the scene and circled the area in order to give the rescuers a reference point over the featureless marsh. From the air there was no sign of anyone having survived the crash. Dennis also recalls that the high security fence which ran along the curtilage of the base initially posed a problem for accessing the marsh. When the rescue team eventually arrived at the crash site they were exhausted from having to haul both themselves and all of their equipment over such difficult terrain. On discovering that six of the crew were already dead their morale sank further, but any sign of fatigue soon disappeared when it was discovered that one of the crew, AC2 Frank Ford, was still alive.

In the fading daylight AC2 Ford was freed from the wreckage and stretchered back over the rough ground to the station sick quarters; he was the sole survivor. Volunteers from the base worked throughout the night to recover the bodies of the remaining crew; four being extricated before sunrise the following day, while the last two were not brought out until after dark on the evening of the 7th. The cause of the crash remained obscure. It is thought that after landing, the Wellington's flaps were raised too quickly on the over-shoot, putting the aircraft into a stall from which it had insufficient altitude to recover.

CREW LIST: F.O. Thomson BJW, Pilot (RAAF); W.O. Dear CG, Ag Instructor; AC2 Hay BC, Ag u/t ;AC2 Bartholomew JF, Ag u/t; AC2 Field CM, Ag u/t; AC2 Cain PH, Ag u/t; AC2 Ford FR, Ag u/t.

Frank Ford recovered from his injuries and was later discharged from the air force. In April 1945 another tragedy befell the Ford family when Frank's brother, George, lost his life in a flying accident. The Tempest aircraft which he was flying hit a hillside shrouded in fog near RAF Milfield, Northumberland. In the late 1940s Frank became a police constable in the City of Glasgow Police Force where he served for 22 years. He passed away in 1970 at the rather premature age of 44.

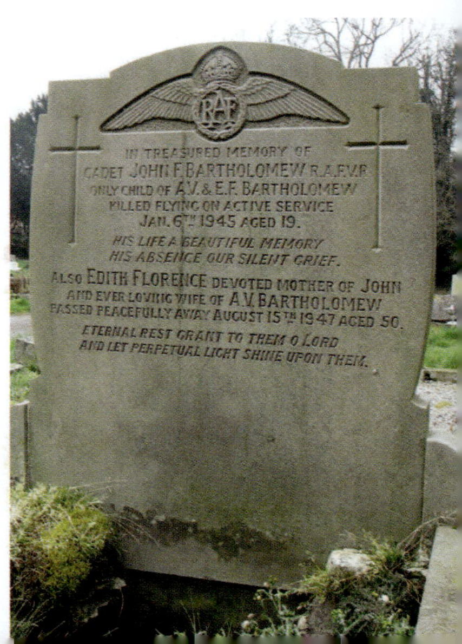

The private headstone of AC2 John Bartholomew at Devizes cemetery, one of the teenage, trainee air gunners aboard Wellington LN553.

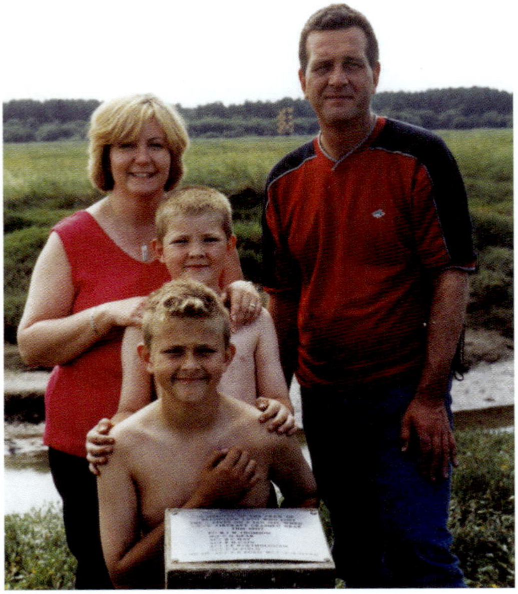

Frank Ford junior, his wife Julie, and sons, Frank and Calum, at the crash site in August 2002. In front of them is a plaque commemorating the crew.

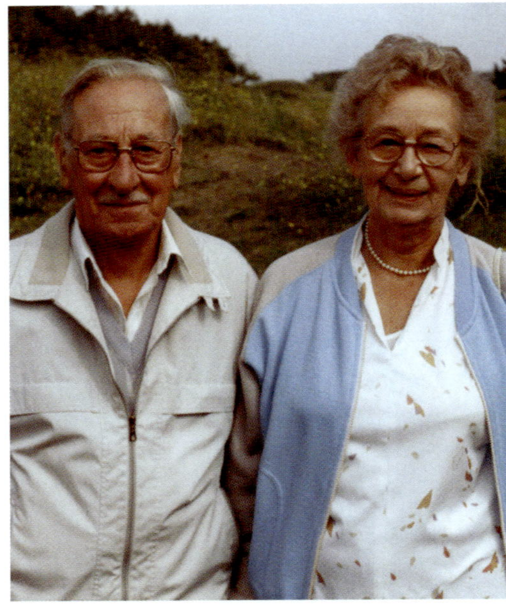

Donald Field, brother to AC2 Cecil Field, one of the trainee air gunners aboard LN553, with his wife Sheila, on a visit to Pembrey, July 1998.

In August 2002 his son, Frank junior, visited Pembrey with his family. After gaining permission to enter the RAF air-to-ground weapons range the author accompanied Frank and his family to the crash site of LN553.

Another visit to the site was made in August 2005, with Bruce Thomson, an 82-year-old ex-Wellington pilot and cousin to the pilot of LN553. Along with his wife Rene and other family members, including his daughter, named in his cousin's honour, Bruce had flown to the UK from Australia to pay his last respects to his long-lost cousin. Bruce had trained as a Wellington pilot in the UK during the closing stages of the war, and although he received the news of his cousin's accident, had not been able to locate his grave before being demobbed and returning home. A life-long quest had finally been fulfilled.

During the summer of 1995 work began on a project to raise the Hercules radial engines buried deep in the mud at the crash site of LN553. The project materialised as the result of a newspaper article written by Fred Lyne

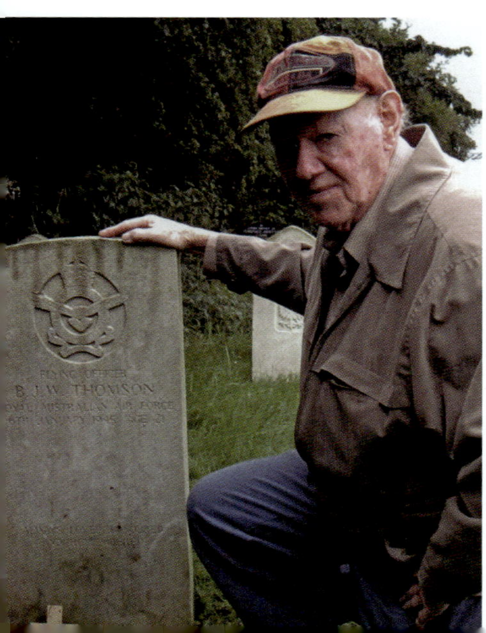

Bruce Thomson fulfils a lifetime quest to visit the grave of his fallen cousin at St Illtyd's Churchyard, Pembrey, July 2005.

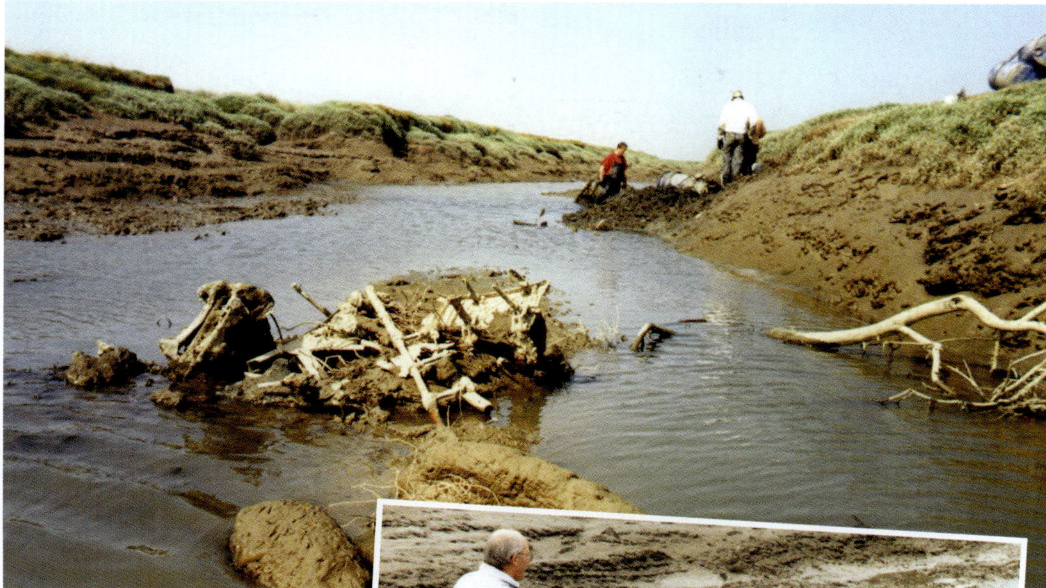

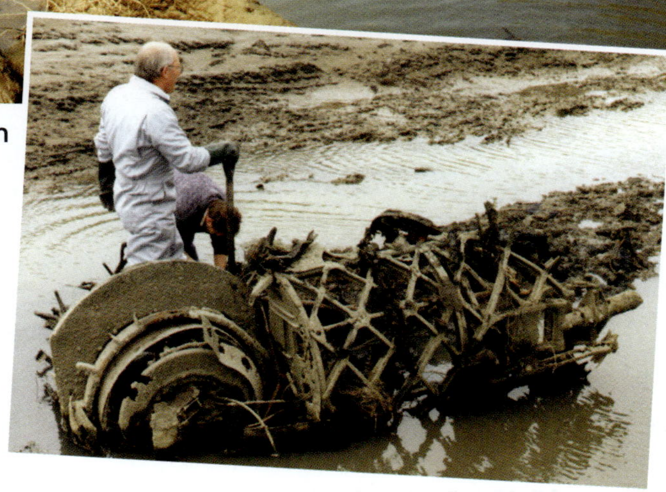

The crash site of Wellington LN553 in the tidal dyke. The port engine is being excavated in the distance. The starboard engine was later discovered near the blue oil drums, top right. INSET: The rear fuselage and tail turret in the middle of the dyke.

and initially appeared in the pages of the Llanelli Star newspaper on January 10 1986. Later that year, through channels unknown, the Air Crew Association published the story in their journal, Intercom. Here it caught the attention of members of the Northamptonshire Airfields and Aircraft Research Group (NAARG), in particular their chairman, Rob Allen. The group was interested in excavating an aircraft which had a link with their aviation museum at the former RAF base at Sywell. Wellington LN553 fitted that criteria in that it had been repaired there following a mishap in 1944.

Correspondence between Fred and Rob followed culminating in a preliminary dig at the crash site by NAARG members in April 1995.

Fred had known of the crash site's location for many years, sometimes even sheltering from the elements inside the fuselage while on wildfowling trips in his earlier years. He was very reluctant to reveal the exact position of the site to anyone as he knew that by doing so would expose the wreckage to unscrupulous souvenir hunters. An agreement was reached between Fred and

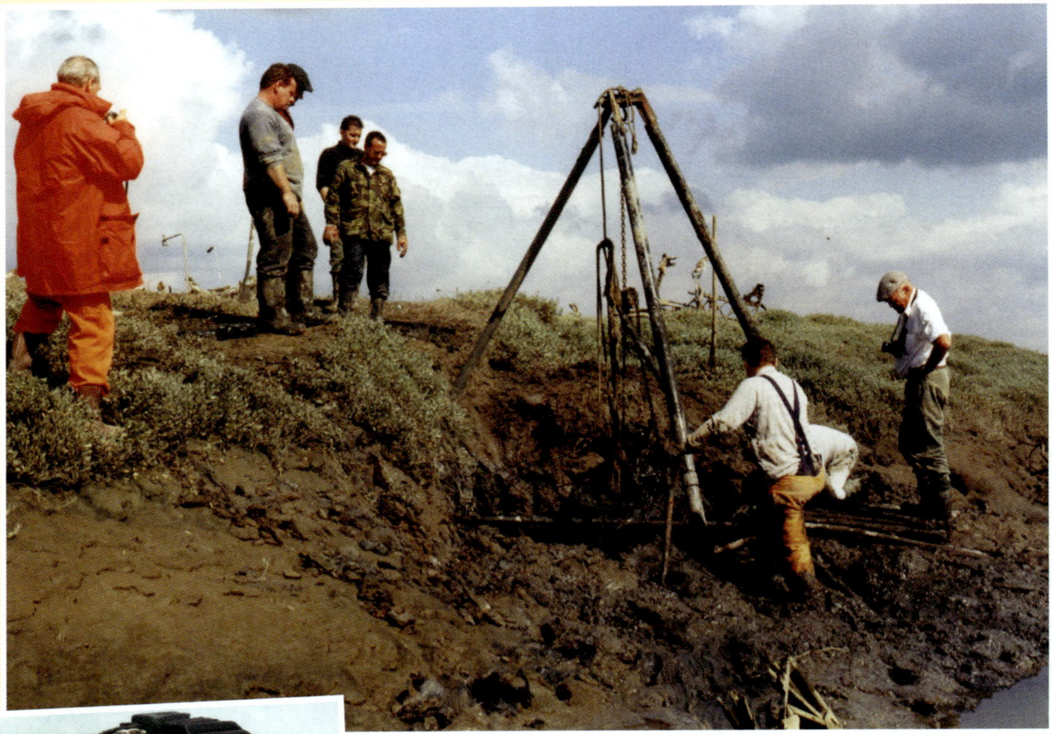

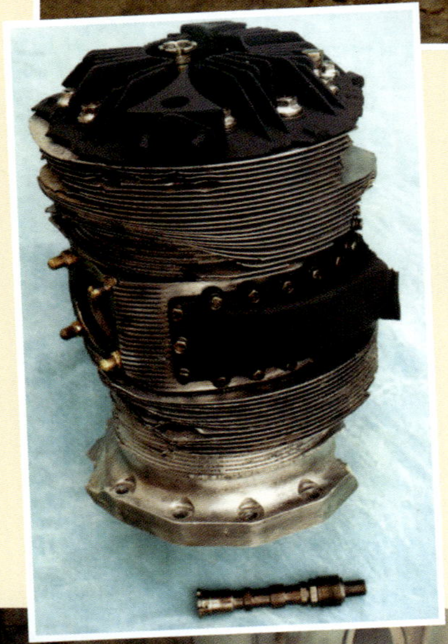

The glutinous mud of the Gwendraeth Estuary finally releases its grip on the port engine of Wellington LN553, September 1995.

NAARG on the understanding that at least one of the engines should remain locally and so the project began.

Initially work on uncovering the engines progressed well, with much hard manual labour exposing the complete port engine which lay at the bottom of a tidal dyke. The starboard engine was more elusive to locate, even though the nacelle to which it had once been attached lay close by. The starboard Hercules was eventually discovered by sheer luck one Sunday afternoon while the project's diggers were taking a well-earned rest.

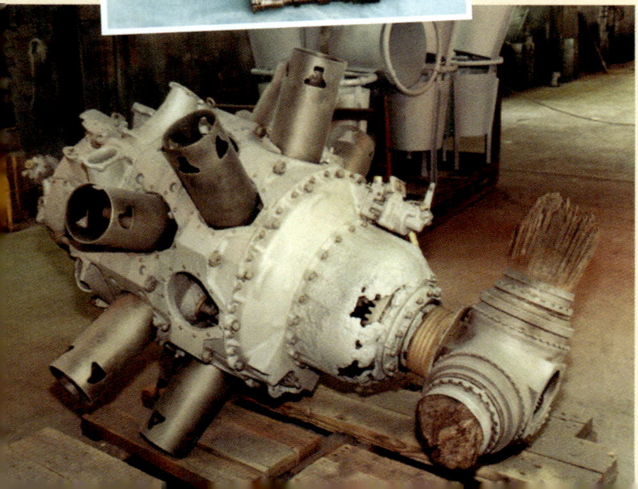

The port engine of Wellington LN553 after being shot blasted and above, a cylinder head from the starboard engine after cleaning.

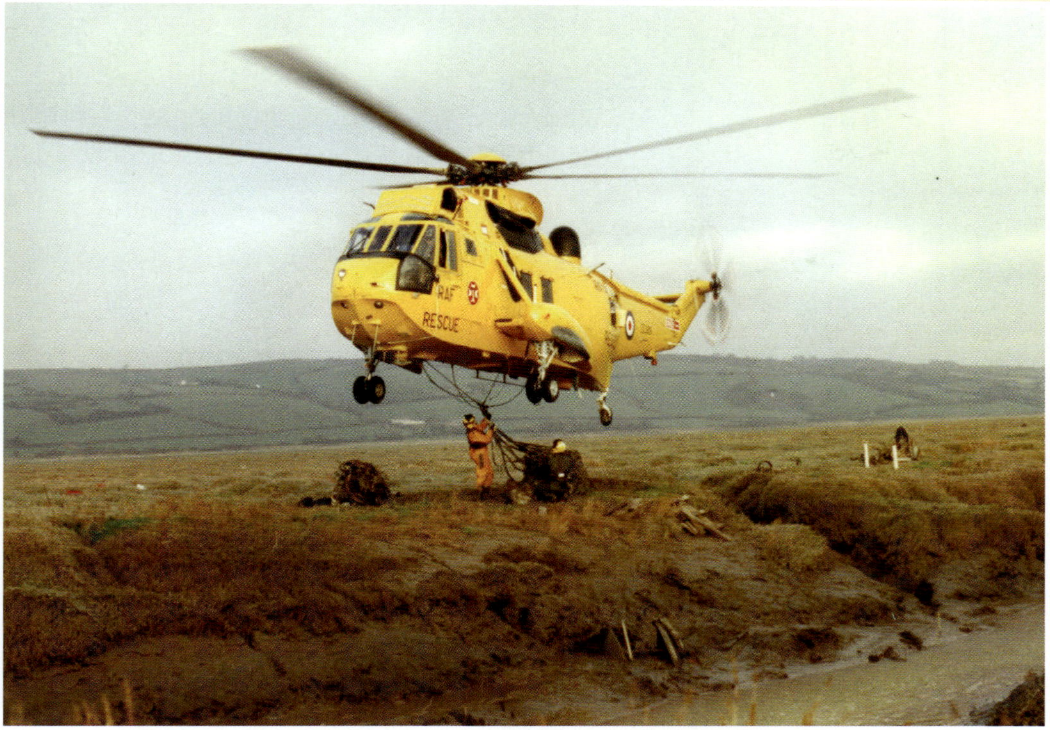

A Sea King helicopter from 22 Squadron, RAF Chivenor, prepares to lift the two recovered engines of Wellington LN553 off the marsh of the Gwendraeth Estuary, in December 1996.

The neap tide of the day had filled the main dyke with sea water and it was while waiting for the tide to recede that Ken May, one of the local members of the team, half-heartedly prodded a metal spike aimlessly into the ground on top of the marsh around where he was sitting. The sound of the spike striking a metal object buried just inches beneath him drew everyone's attention. A small hole was dug around the object which later turned out to be an engine cylinder. Further digging that afternoon unearthed the complete starboard engine. By September both Hercules engines had been extricated from the mud using a variety of homemade tripod designs and engine hoists. The next phase of the project was to move the engines, each weighing nearly one ton, onto firmer ground where they could be transported by road to a suitable workshop. This was an anxious stage in the project for as soon as the engines were removed from the mud, corrosion would begin to set in almost immediately.

In March 1996 the project suffered a set-back when Fred Lyne passed away suddenly at his Glanaber home. The months that followed were tinged with much sadness for myself. I had lost a good friend.

Work on removing the engines from the marsh did not restart until the following December when Rob Allen enlisted the help of 22 Squadron RAF

Air crash locator

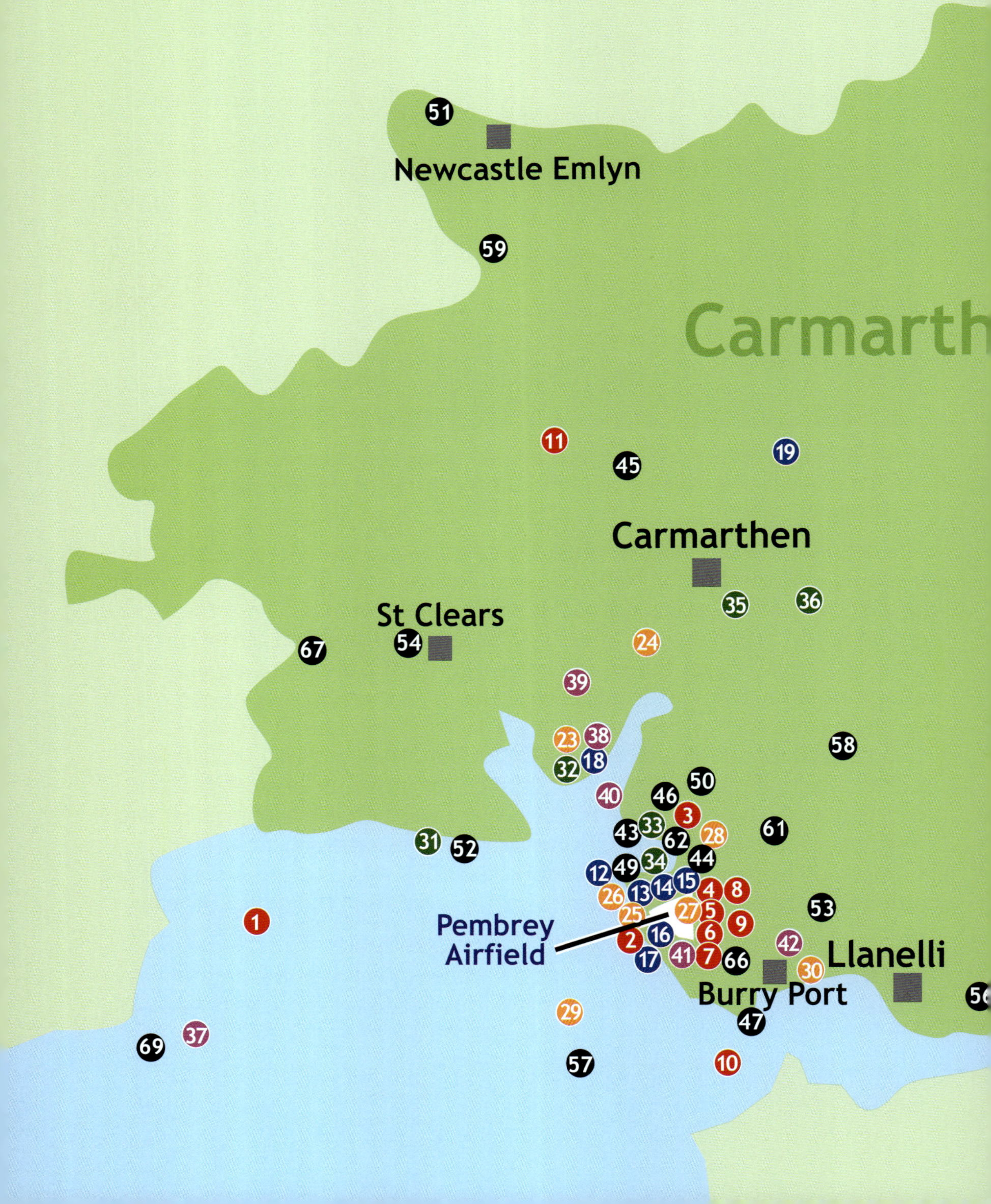

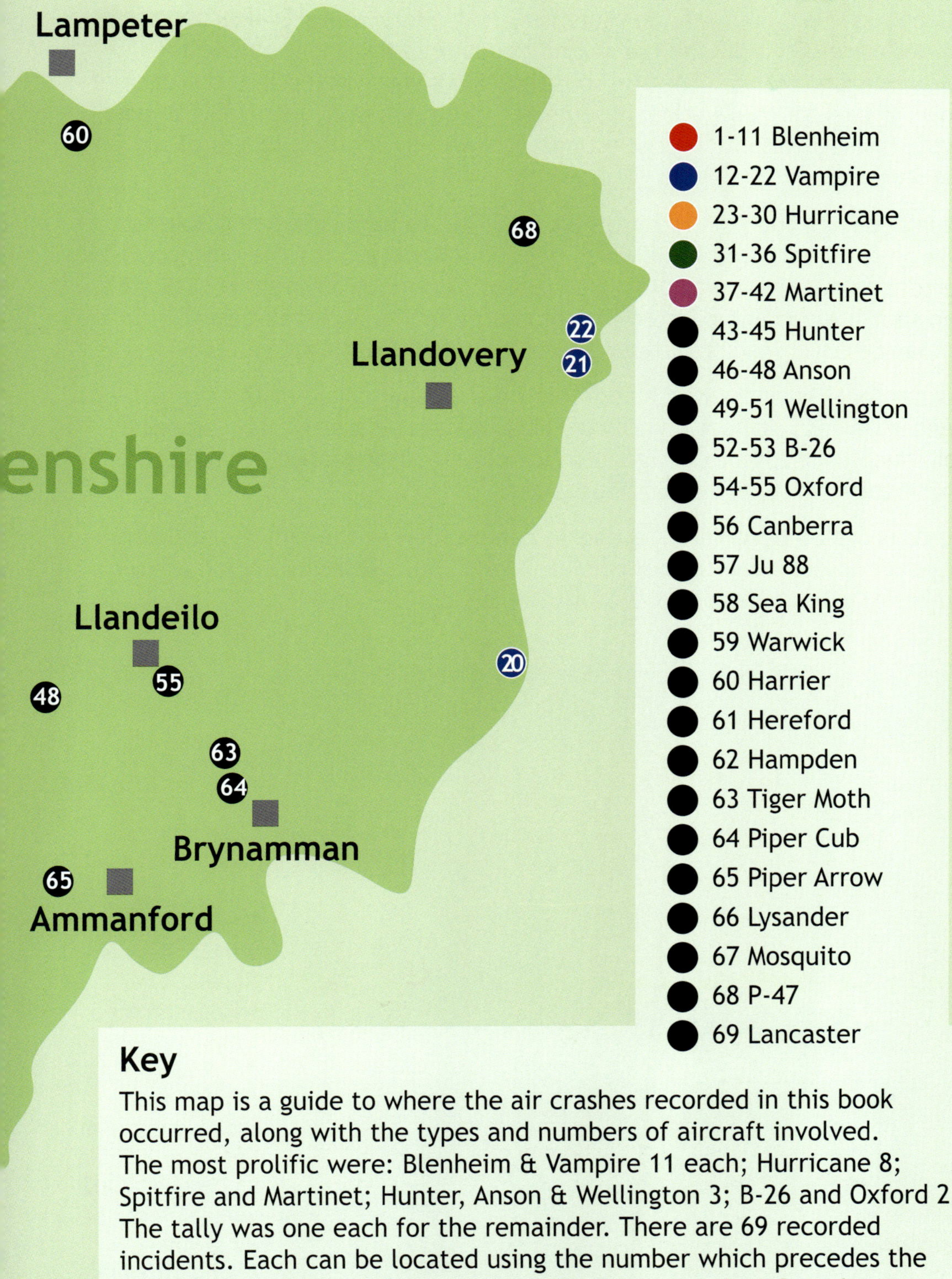

Key

This map is a guide to where the air crashes recorded in this book occurred, along with the types and numbers of aircraft involved. The most prolific were: Blenheim & Vampire 11 each; Hurricane 8; Spitfire and Martinet; Hunter, Anson & Wellington 3; B-26 and Oxford 2. The tally was one each for the remainder. There are 69 recorded incidents. Each can be located using the number which precedes the aircraft type. The numbers do not indicate date order of crashes.

Air-Sea Rescue based at Chivenor in North Devon. They kindly agreed to airlift the engines using cargo nets suspended from one of their Sea King helicopters. On a cold, and initially very foggy, mid-winter's afternoon both engines were lifted off the marsh and deposited at the heli-pad on the nearby weapons range. The starboard Hercules was hoisted into the back of a lorry bound for the NAARG museum at Sywell, while by nightfall the port engine lay secured in a Burry Port garage awaiting the first stages of its long restoration.

Actually having the port Hercules engine close to hand and being able to work on it regenerated some much needed enthusiasm for the project. Over the coming months it was pressure washed to remove 50 years of sediment, then shot-blasted and painted free of charge by the Swansea-based company, Hastie-Metspray, later Swansea Powder Coatings Limited.

Another local business which appreciated the significance of the project was Spencer Davies Engineering of Burry Port. A keen aviator himself, Spencer took much time to both design and fabricate a bespoke display stand to exhibit the engine, again, without charge.

The refurbished port Hercules engine can be seen at the Kidwelly Industrial Museum housed in the former tinplate works. Alongside the engine are a number of other aviation related artefacts from the area.

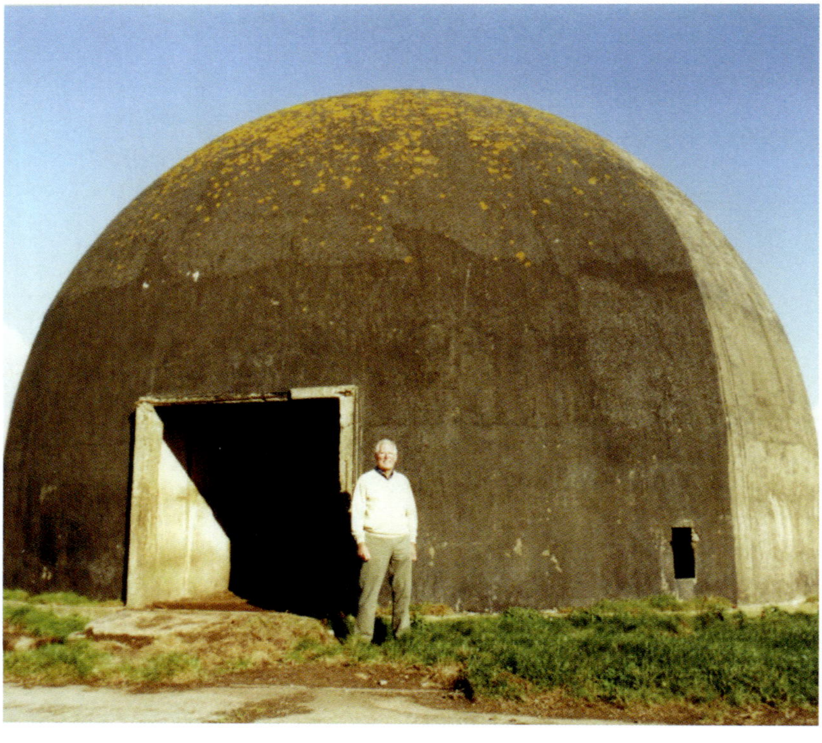

Former air gunner Dennis Rogers, who witnessed the final moments of LN553, outside the training dome at Pembrey airfield in October 2002 where he did his air gunnery course in 1945.

JAN
26
1945

AIRCRAFT: **Spitfire AR320**

Australian pilot hit by snow storm whiteout

Towards the end of the war Spitfires were in use by 1 Air Gunner's School for fighter affiliation exercises. Dummy attacks from differing angles by Spitfires gave trainee air gunners a sense of realism during practice sessions. In the first quarter of 1945 the unit lost three Spitfires during some of these.

At midday on January 26 (Australia Day), Australian pilot, W.O. Bernard Skelly, was undertaking some local flying in the Tenby area when he was caught out by a sudden snow flurry. Possibly blinded by 'white-out' conditions while flying at low level, his aircraft crashed into a field opposite St Anne's Church, New Hedges, not far from the main road leading to Tenby.

Local farmer Peter Brace remembers seeing the Spitfire flying extremely low on an easterly track, almost knocking off a chimney pot on a nearby house. The exact spot where the aircraft crashed is lost under tons of earth spoil deposited over the site when a road was constructed. W.O. Skelly, who lost his life in the crash, is buried at St Illtyd's Churchyard, Pembrey.

FEB
10
1945

AIRCRAFT: **Spitfire BL515**

Wheels up landing left pilot with injured back

On the morning of February 10, F.O. Robert Burnard was airborne on a training flight when his engine started to overheat. Unable to reach the airfield at Pembrey and not wanting to seize-up the Merlin he cut the engine and glided down from 1,500ft to make a wheels-up landing in a field at Groesasgwrn Farm north of Llangendeirne.

The aircraft was only slightly damaged in the forced landing, but F.O. Burnard sustained injuries to his back.

Farmer's daughter, Mair Thomas, aged 13 at the time, recalled that it was a Saturday as she was not in school. Due to the nature of the pilot's injuries he had to be helped by her father, John, and a neighbour, Percy Daniels, from the crashed Spitfire up to the farmhouse, where he was laid on the settee until the arrival of a doctor. He was later taken to Morriston Hospital, Swansea, by RAF ambulance.

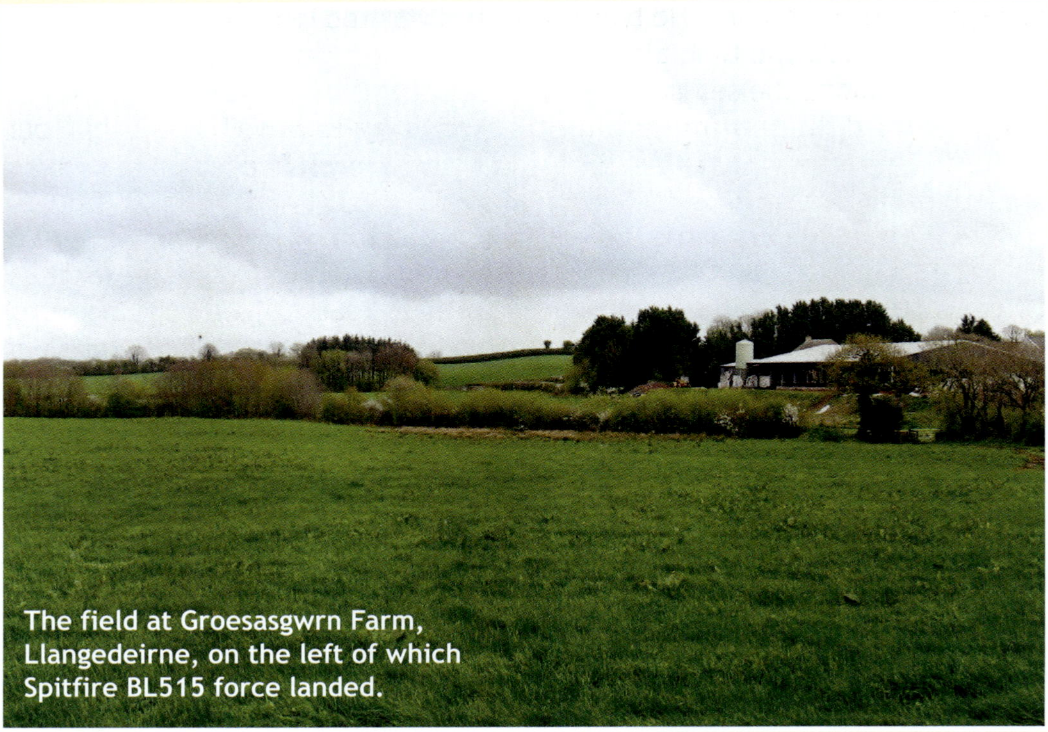

The field at Groesasgwrn Farm, Llangedeirne, on the left of which Spitfire BL515 force landed.

The Spitfire, which remained under guard in the field over the following days, became the centre of attention for crowds of local people; most never having seen an aircraft at such close quarters.

An engine strip down identified a coolant leak near one of the engine cylinders as the cause of the overheating and though only slightly damaged in the forced landing, the aircraft was later written off.

BL515 was no stranger to mishaps, since being commissioned by the RAF in 1941 the aircraft had been involved in a number of minor accidents before being handed over to the Air Gunners' School.

APR 25 1945

AIRCRAFT: Spitfire BM211

Flight schedule change proved a big mistake

On April 25, W.O. William Brown asked a fellow staff pilot if he could exchange a flight schedule with him in order that he could finish early for that day. It was a decision that was to cost him his life.

At 15:45 hrs Brown had just taken off from Pembrey in Spitfire BM211 and was flying over the salt marshes to the north of the airfield when his aircraft developed engine failure. He bailed out, but was too low for his parachute to fully deploy. At the time air gunner Ralph Gilbert was returning from Cefn Sidan beach along the sea defence embankment at the edge of the marsh when he heard the Spitfire's engine spluttering and saw W.O. Brown bail out. He reached the spot where the pilot had fallen only to find his lifeless body with his parachute wrapped almost shroud-like around him. A few yards away the wreckage of BM211 lay just visible above the muddy sediment of one of the tidal creeks which criss-cross the marsh. Due to the soft mud there had been no fire on impact and within the hour very little of the aircraft remained above surface level. It was never recovered and probably still lies entombed in the marsh.

The pilot with whom William Brown had exchanged flight schedules was W.O. Stan Kreciala (pronounced Kritchowa). A Pole, he married a local girl and made Llanelli his home. Stan who died in 2007, also had a close encounter while at the controls of aircraft 7, the fuselage code of BM211. One day while on a routine flight he became aware of a strong smell of aviation fuel around the cockpit area. He landed immediately to find that

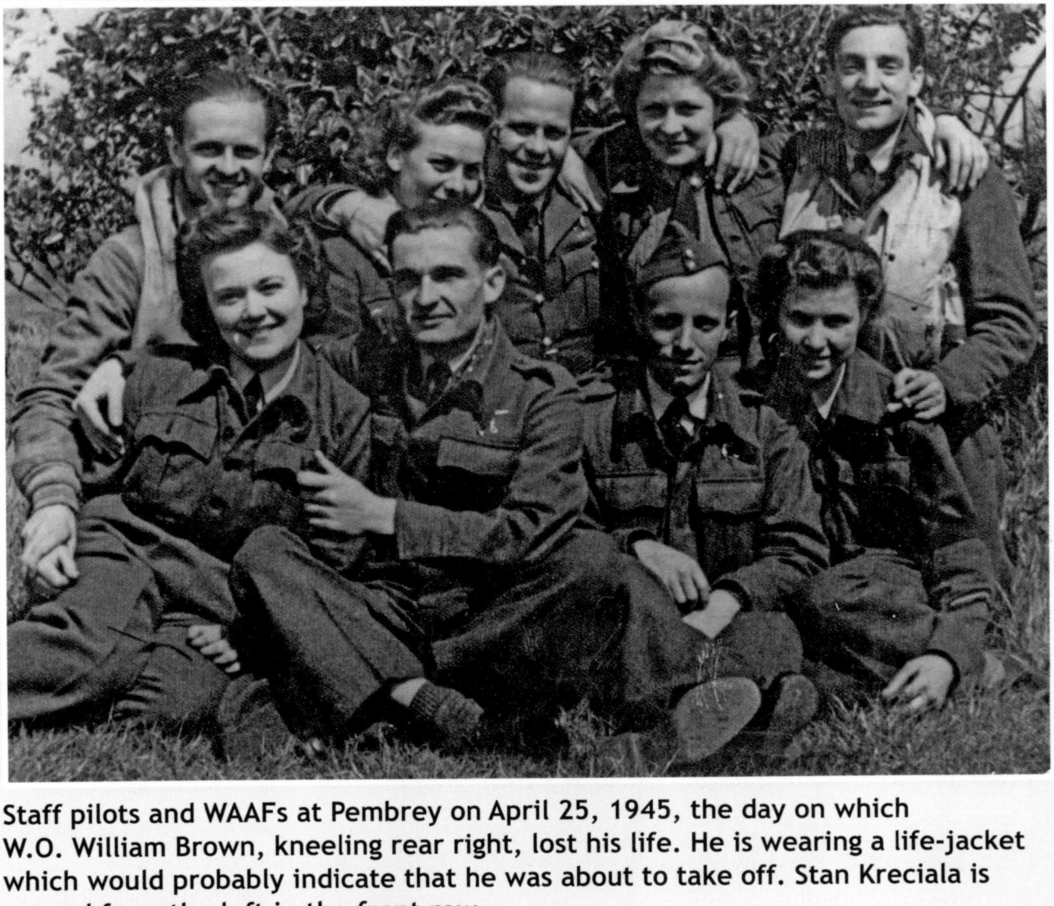

Staff pilots and WAAFs at Pembrey on April 25, 1945, the day on which W.O. William Brown, kneeling rear right, lost his life. He is wearing a life-jacket which would probably indicate that he was about to take off. Stan Kreciala is second from the left in the front row.

the fuel filler cap was missing and his aircraft was saturated with petrol. Stan attributed his survival as a pilot during Second World War to a four-leafed clover he picked up just prior to stepping into the cockpit of a Tiger Moth on his first flying lesson. It served him well not only during the war years, but on many overseas family holidays afterwards. In later years he had it encapsulated in plastic.

MAY
4
1945

AIRCRAFT: **Mosquito HR160**

Attack pilot watched his quarry plunge to earth

Another training establishment located in South Wales which incorporated Spitfires in its role was 8 (Coastal) Operational Training Unit based at Withybush airfield, Haverfordwest. The function of this unit was to train photo-reconnaissance crews prior to postings to operational squadrons. It utilised both Mosquito and Spitfire aircraft, the latter doubling up as the attacking aircraft in fighter affiliation exercises.

On May 4, 1945 the crew of Mosquito HR160, a Mk.VI fighter-bomber, were engaged in such an exercise. At 16:13 hrs while flying at 6,000ft the 'attacking' Spitfire pilot witnessed HR160 roll to the right after performing an evasive corkscrew manoeuvre, then spiral out of control to the ground. The aircraft exploded on impact in a field below Blaenfynnonau Farm on the outskirts of Whitland killing both crew

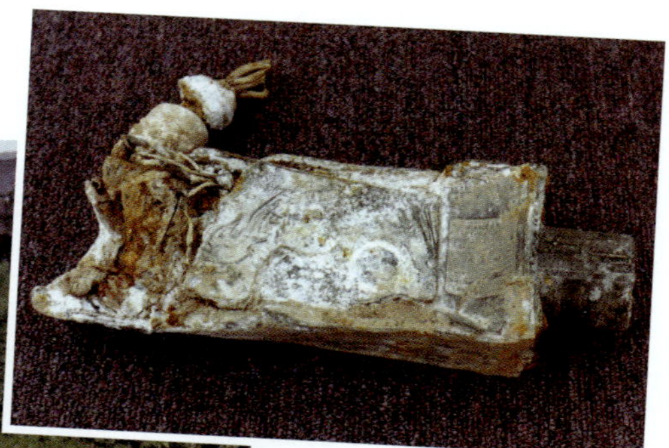

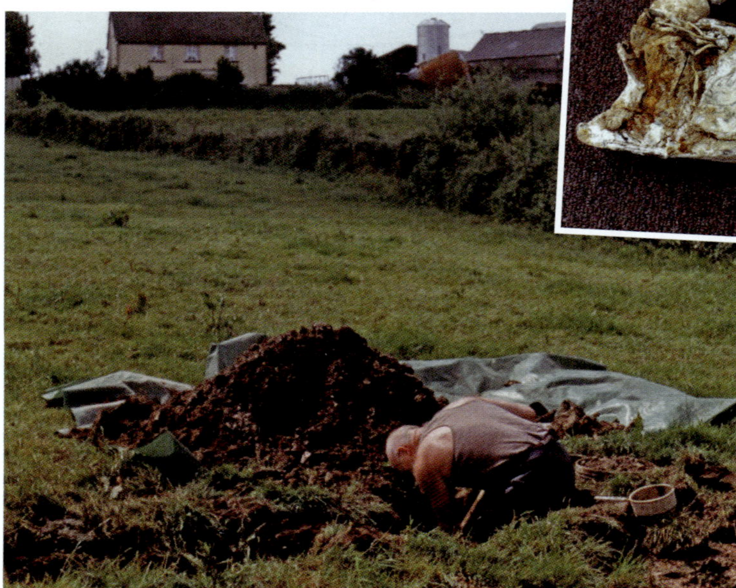

Aviation archaeologist Danny Hickey digging at the crash site of Mosquito HR160, in a field below Blaenfynnonau Farm. INSET: A gun camera found while excavating the site.

members instantly. Because of the total destruction of the Mosquito, the Air Accident Investigation Branch failed to establish the reason the aircraft spun to the ground in such an uncontrolled manner. In March 1998 I was shown the crash site by local resident, John Richards, who remembered the deep crater made by the impact. A metal detector sweep of the field to confirm the location exposed many 'cooked' 20 mm and 303 rounds as well as hundreds of the brass wood screws found at Mosquito crash sites.

CREW LIST: Flt. Sgt. Ross DLB, Pilot; Flt. Sgt. Sims AE, Navigator.

With the ending of hostilities in Europe on May 8 the need for replacement air gunners for Bomber Command ceased. As a direct consequence, on June 14, 1945, 1 Air Gunner's School was disbanded and the skies above Carmarthenshire fell silent. A total of 114 air gunnery training courses had passed through the gates of Pembrey in the school's four-year existence.

JAN 24 1947

AIRCRAFT: **Martinet RG896**

Jet age boosts aerial activity at Pembrey

The years following the end of the Second World War brought with them the advent of the jet age. This meant that after a period of relative inactivity, air traffic around Pembrey airfield began to increase again, initially with the arrival in October 1946 of 595 Squadron.

The unit moved to Pembrey from nearby Fairwood Common for two reasons. Firstly, the domestic facilities at Fairwood were falling into a state of disrepair, and secondly, the main runway at Pembrey was much longer, enabling the squadron's newly acquired Vampire jets to operate more safely. Pembrey also had the advantage of being slightly closer to the Army School of Artillery at Manorbier where 595 Squadron carried out most of its Army co-operation work. During 1947 the squadron lost two aircraft in accidents, which happened shortly after take off.

On January 24, that year South Wales suffered a day of bad weather though the afternoon had seen an improvement. At 14:45 hrs Flt. Lt. K.C. Saw and a passenger took off to air test Martinet RG896. They had been airborne for only 15 minutes when, at 800ft, the engine suddenly cut out. Unable to reach the runway, Flt. Lt. Saw made a wheels-up landing close to the airfield boundary with little damage to the aircraft. An inspection of the engine fuel filters showed that water had somehow contaminated the petrol, entered the carburettor and caused the engine to stop. Both crew members were unhurt.

JULY 22 1947

AIRCRAFT: **Vampire VF302**

Accident highlighted seriousness of defect

The Vampire, initially named the Spider Crab, entered service with he RAF in March 1946. As with de Haviland's previous success story, the Mosquito, its fuselage was constructed of laminated plywood, which although made the aircraft very light, also made it unable to withstand the sudden actuation of an ejector seat. A pilot wishing to leave this high-speed jet in a hurry had no choice but to do so manually, hopefully avoiding the horizontal tail unit in the process.

A negative trait which haunted many pilots who flew them in the early years was the unreliability of its Goblin jet engine, prone to self destruction caused by impeller disintegration. An accident in July highlighted the seriousness of this defect.

At 15:06 hrs on July 22, F.O. Geoffrey Robinson rolled down the runway at Pembrey in Vampire VF302 at the start of an aerobatic training flight. As he became airborne the impeller of his Goblin engine totally disintegrated causing it to lose power. Due to the Vampire's low altitude he was unable to return to the safety of the airfield and opted to attempt a forced landing on sand dunes behind Cefn Sidan beach. The aircraft overturned and with a full fuel load caught fire. Unable to escape Robinson perished in the inferno.

A check of the aircraft's service log showed that VF302 hadn't been subjected to the manufacturer's mandatory five-hourly impeller inspection and should have been grounded. As an immediate safety measure following the accident Goblin engines were inspected after every sortie.

APR 15 1948

AIRCRAFT: **Spitfire PT650**

Beach landing was caused by cooling system fault

Due to the fact that most of 595 Squadron's flights out of Pembrey were to the Army coastal range at Manorbier, any aircraft suffering engine failure to and from this location would more than likely have to put-down somewhere along the coast.

PII Claude Fryer had just arrived at 6,000ft above the sea off Manorbier in mid-afternoon on April 15, 1948 when he noticed the coolant temperature gauge on his Spitfire starting to rise. Postponing the Army co-operation

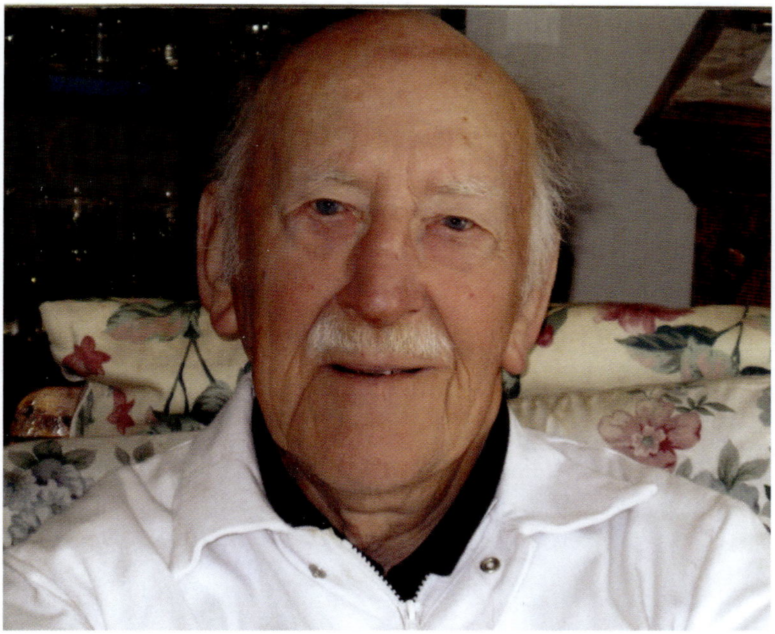

Claude Fryer, pilot of Spitfire PT650, at his home in Ferryside, September 2009. As a consequence of the Sandys report of 1957, which recommended that Fighter Command be significantly reduced in strength, he transferred to Coastal Command and flew Shackleton aircraft for the rest of his career in the Royal Air Force.

exercise he was about to begin, he headed east back to Pembrey to make a precautionary landing.

Nearing Pendine the coolant temperature rose still further which necessitated the engine to be shut down and made an emergency landing on the beach inevitable. Claude was aware that a Lancaster had once successfully landed on, and taken off from, Pendine Sands, to off-load supplies to the armament proofing range just beyond the dunes, so he was confident that a wheels-down landing on the sand was achievable. However, there was a more pressing reason for adopting a wheels-down, rather than a wheels-up, approach.

At 500ft Claude had insufficient height to turn back into wind, and to make matters worse, remembered that slung underneath his Spitfire was a fully-laden, 45 gallon 'slipper' auxiliary fuel tank. With the realisation that this tank might fracture and explode on impact, a wheels-down landing was now his only hope of survival. With the Merlin engine cut, the wind-milling propeller generated very little hydraulic power to operate the undercarriage. Unable to reach the emergency 'lock-down' cylinder, a compressed air cylinder used to charge the hydraulic system in such an emergency, because he had tightened his seat harness prior to landing, Claude could only hope that the wheels would lock into position by the time he touched down.

As luck would have it, when PT650 landed on the sand the undercarriage legs held and the aircraft ran for approximately 400 yards. However on coming to rest, the starboard leg which had not quite entered the fully locked position, collapsed.

With the aircraft tilted to one side Claude released his harness and was out of the cockpit in no time, initially standing well clear in case it caught fire.

A short time later a jeep arrived alongside the aircraft. The driver, Wing Commander Peveler, the RAF liaison officer at the Pendine proofing range, had seen Claude approaching from the west and came to offer his help. After allowing the Merlin to cool a little the pair removed the engine cowling and the cause of the rising coolant gauge became apparent – a large split could be seen in the rubber hose below the glycol header tank.

In the days that followed a team of RAF fitters carried out a complete engine and propeller change to PT650 on the beach. On April 23 the aircraft took off and was flown the short distance back to Pembrey.

The following month Spitfire PT650 was written off in a flying accident. On May 31 F.O. Cousens was taking off from Pembrey when the aircraft's engine failed and the Spitfire came back down to earth among the trees that stood at the end of the runway.

MAY
3
1948

AIRCRAFT: Martinet MS509

Mystery hitch brought sudden end to flight

On May 3, while returning to Pembrey after a three hour towing exercise off Manorbier, Martinet MS509 force landed with wheels-up on the beach at Ferryside after its engine cut at 16:10 hrs. Close examination failed to discover any technical fault concerning the engine and the theory was advanced that perhaps it had simply run out of fuel. The pilot, PII Eyers and his tow operator were unhurt.

There was a third 595 Squadron aircraft loss in the spring of 1948. In the afternoon of May 29 the unit's Commanding Officer, Sqn. Ldr. John Carey in TE443, was leading a formation of five other Spitfires, in-line astern at 1,000ft over Manorbier during an open day at the camp.

At 15:40 hrs his aircraft suffered an engine failure and he successfully force landed, wheels-up, in a field overlooking Stackpole Quay.

Claude Fryer, who was number four in the formation, recalled the frightful moment when the other members of the formation followed their leader down thinking that it was all part of the display. At the very last moment Flt. Lt. Wallace, who wasnumber two in the line, realised what had happened to Sqn. Ldr. Carey's Spitfire and yelled out the command 'break' over the radio.

JAN
31
1949

AIRCRAFT: **Spitfire SM348**

Black smoke caught farmworker's eye

Engine failure was once again to blame for the loss of another 595 Squadron Spitfire, SM348, on January 31,1949. At 11:00 hrs that morning farm labourer Evan Thomas paused from his work in the fields at Cwm Farm near Llangynog. His attention was drawn skyward to two Spitfires, one of which was trailing black smoke from its exhausts and losing height rapidly.

In an attempt to force land in fields at nearby Hendre Farm the aircraft struck a copse of trees and crashed to the ground. Luckily there was no fire and the pilot, PIII Frank Wareham, sustained only slight injuries. After freeing himself from the wrecked Spitfire he made his way down to Hendre farmhouse and was made comfortable by the Davies family who lived there before returning to Pembrey.

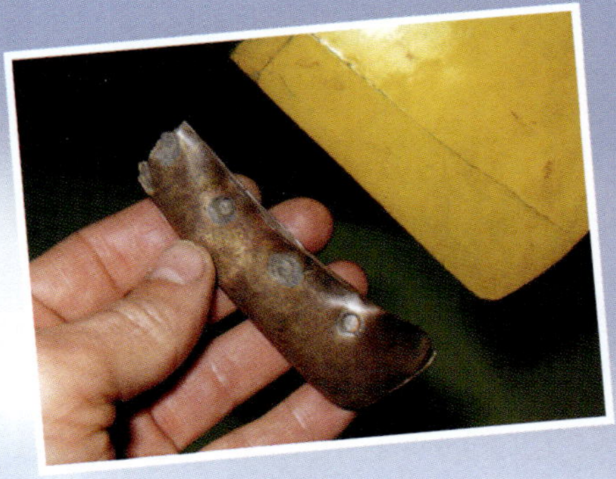

The copse which Spitfire SM348 struck before crash landing. INSET: A piece of copper propeller-sheathing found underneath the trees. The shape of the sheathing is compared to the tip of an undamaged propeller.

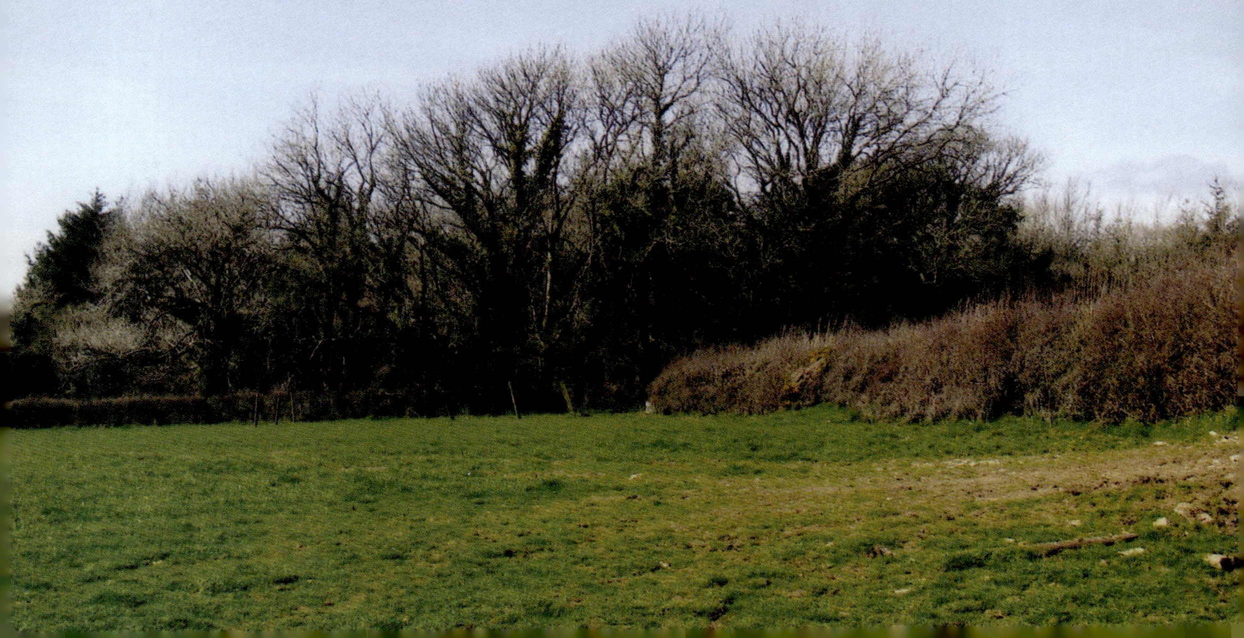

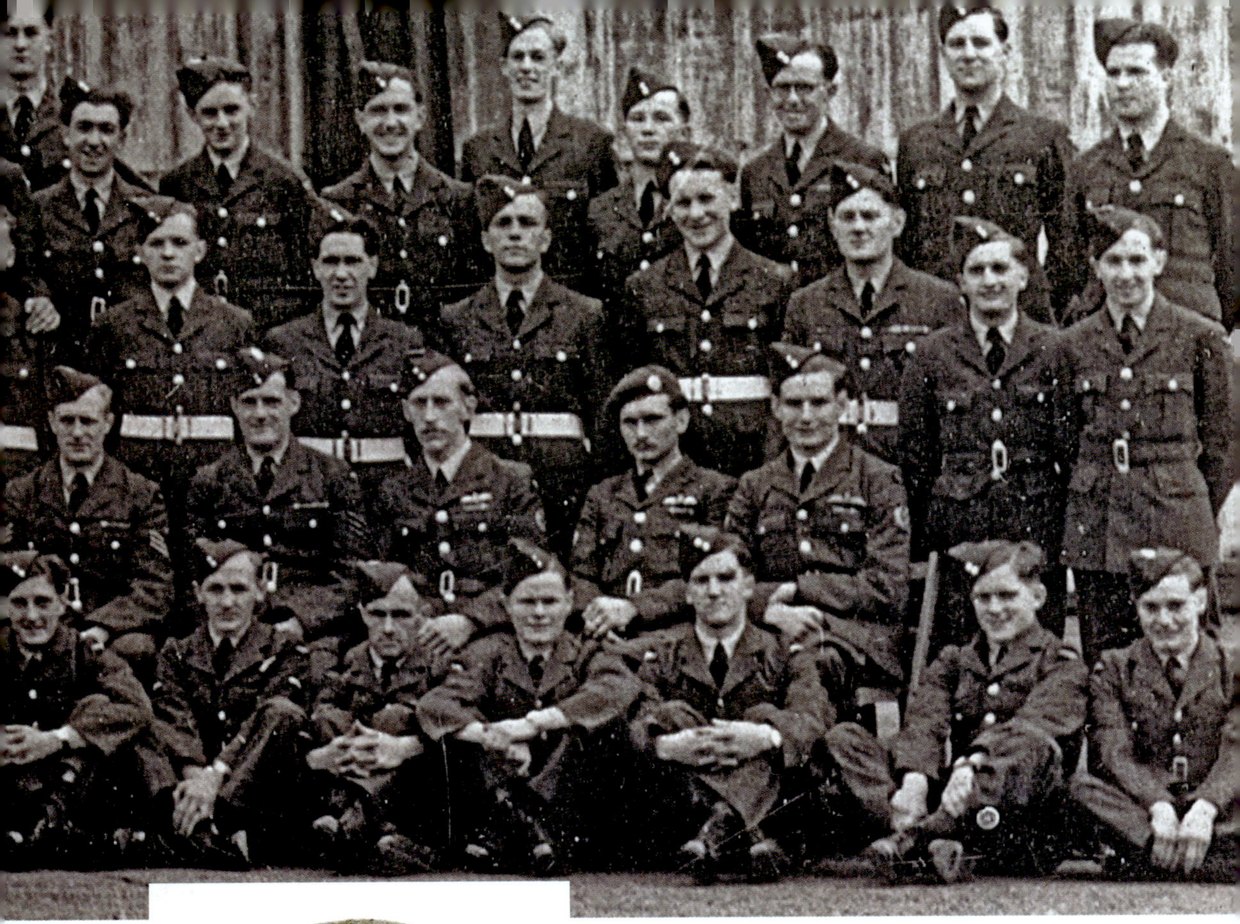

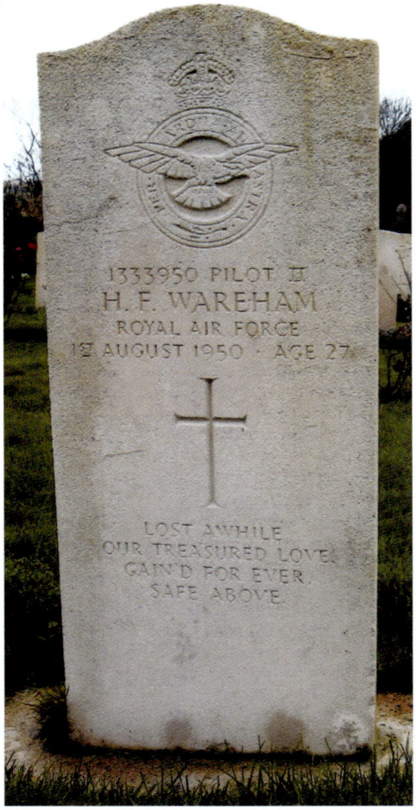

A group of 595 Sqn. personnel at Pembrey in1948. Frank Wareham is seated in the second row, second from the right, wearing a beret. To his right is Claude Fryer. LEFT: The last resting place of Frank Wareham at St Augustine's Churchyard, Heanton Punchardon, North Devon.

Evan later visited the scene of the crash and found a self-rescue crowbar lying in the grass; probably discarded by the pilot after extricating himself from the crumpled airframe. The crowbar formed part of Evan's tool box for many years.

An engine strip down identified the cause of its failure as a seized fuel regulator which starved the Merlin of petrol.

Just over 18 months later Frank Wareham lost his life in a similar accident after his squadron moved to RAF Chivenor in North Devon. On August 1, 1950 while taking part in an Army co-operation exercise near Welcombe, his Spitfire, TE452, crashed during a low-level turn while attempting to force land in a field. He is buried at St Augustine's churchyard, Heanton Punchardon, which overlooks the former airfield at Chivenor.

A metal detector sweep of the field where SM348 crashed showed no trace of any impact, but directly under the disfigured tree which the Spitfire hit, two pieces of copper sheathing, used to protect the leading edge of the aircraft's wooden propeller blades, were found.

JUNE 17 1949

AIRCRAFT: **Spitfire TB998**

Unexplained accident during aerobatic flight

February 11, 1949 saw 595 Squadron renumber to 5 Squadron. The change was in title only as the unit continued its work in Army co-operation.

An unexplained accident involving the squadron occurred at around midday on June 17 when a trainee pilot, F.O. A.H. Hill, was carrying out aerobatics near Pembrey with other pilots.

Fellow squadron pilot Claude Fryer remembers that the weather conditions that morning were hazy up to 10,000ft. Above this altitude the visibility would have been excellent due to the clear air.

F.O. Hill's Spitfire was last seen entering the haze in an inverted position before spiral-diving into the ground on the northern banks of the Gwendraeth Estuary. He failed to bail out and was killed on impact. It is possible that he lost control of the Spitfire after becoming disorientated while in the hazy conditions.

F.O. Hill had been posted to 5 Squadron to gain flying experience on Spitfires prior to joining an Operational Training Unit.

Corporal George Walsh was on duty in the control tower at Pembrey when one of the other pilots participating in the aerobatics reported the accident over the radio. George arrived with the rescue team from the base to find that there was no fire as the Spitfire had buried itself in a sand dune only yards from the Ferryside to Kidwelly railway line.

Today the location of the crash site is adjacent to the boating slipway near the Carmarthen Bay Holiday Village entertainment complex.

JAN
10
1950

AIRCRAFT: **Anson VP531**

Power workers watched aerial disaster unfold

In 1950 the Avro Anson was still in use by the RAF as a training aircraft. Anson VP531 was a Mk.19 model and on the strength of 58 Squadron, a photo-reconnaissance unit based at RAF Benson in Oxfordshire.

At 10:30 hrs on January 10, 1950 P.O. J.B. Skey, Master Navigator S. Powell and Gunner K. Brand took off from Benson for a navigation exercise. The first half of the flight went well, but early in the afternoon, while flying over Carmarthen Bay, the weather quickly deteriorated with cloud bases dropping to 400ft above the sea. Concerned that the weather would get even worse P.O. Skey decided to set course for RAF St Athan and wait there for the weather to clear.

On the way the Anson entered a dense bank of fog and the crew became lost. More worrying to them was the Anson's fuel supply which was running low and as the minutes ticked by a ditching seemed inevitable.

At 14:15 hrs the Anson was glimpsed briefly by construction workers at the site of the Carmarthen Bay Power Station. Flying at an altitude of less than 60ft it narrowly avoided disaster when it flew between two tall pile-driving machines with only inches to spare at each wingtip. It then disappeared into the fog with both engines spluttering and was heard to crash into the estuary a short distance from the coast.

With great skill P.O. Skey had been able to keep the aircraft in level flight and ditched the Anson about half a mile from the shore. Having landed on the water intact the crew wasted no time in vacating the sinking aircraft and inflating the survival dinghy. As the three drifted away in their dinghy they watched as the Anson disappeared below the fast moving water. They had survived one catastrophe, but were now at the mercy of the sea. While being buffeted along by the ebbing tide the crew noticed a line of steel anti-invasion posts left over from the war, this gave them a sense of direction to paddle towards and soon they reached the shore. Despite being soaked to the skin and freezing cold the trio managed to walk across the Ashburnham Golf Links to the main road where they hitched a ride on a lorry to Burry Port Police Station.

As they recovered from their ordeal at the police station another drama was unfolding in the estuary. On hearing the Anson crash a DUKW, used at the Power Station building site, and a small boat from Burry Port had set out from the shore independently to go to the assistance of the downed aircrew, but due to the fog both had become lost and were now in need of assistance themselves.

An ingenious idea by two local electricians of erecting a portable lighting unit at the Power Station site to act as a reference point proved a success, by nightfall the DUKW, with the small boat in tow, had homed in on the beacon like a moth around a light bulb.

Anson VP531 had ditched approximately half a mile off shore at a point midway between Burry Port harbour and the old derelict harbour at Pembrey. Up until the late 1970s part of the aircraft's fuselage would become exposed at low water on extreme spring tides, but a word of warning to any would-be visitor to the site, the waters here run fast and can be very dangerous.

MAY 7 1951

AIRCRAFT: Vampire VV196

Steep dive claimed life of air-to-ground attack pilot

In October 1949, 5 Squadron, formerly 595 Squadron, departed from Pembrey and moved to RAF Chivenor on the North Devon coast. From here it moved back across the Bristol Channel to Llandow in March 1951 before being disbanded later in the year. It might have been assumed that Pembrey would once again have settled down to a period of peace and quiet, but the air-to-ground firing range to the north of the base was still very much active.

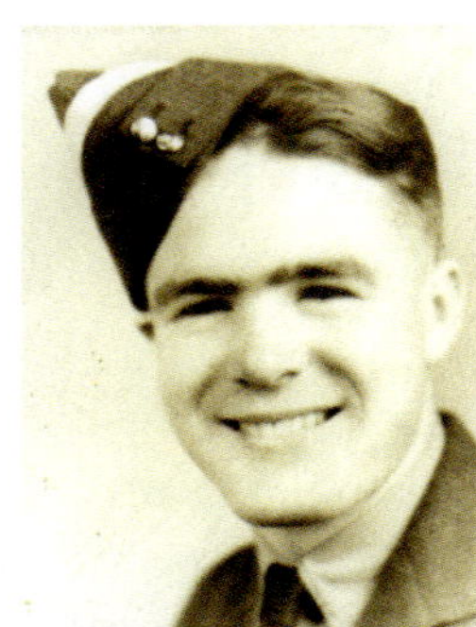

In the late afternoon of Monday May 7, 1951 Sgt. Eddie Campbell of 614 Squadron (Royal Auxillary Air Force), Llandow, was carrying out air-to-ground firing practice at the Pembrey range in Vampire VV196. During the course of his firing practice that afternoon he had been warned on two separate occasions that recoveries from his attack dives

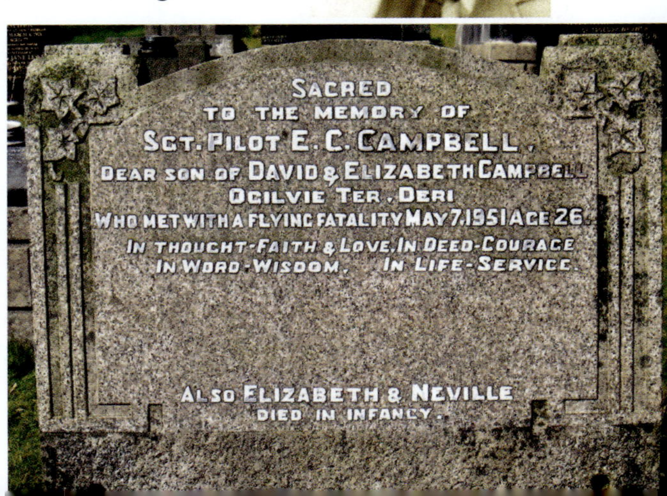

Sgt. Eddie Campbell pictured during his initial pilot training in Arizona, USA, towards the end of Second World War. RIGHT: The headstone on his grave at Brithdir cemetery, Bargoed.

on the targets were being left too late. On one occasion his Vampire had cleared the ground at an altitude of only 150ft. His subsequent recoveries were carried out at a much safer height, but at 18:10 hrs, on his 10th and final attack of the day, he once again pulled up too low. Climbing back up in a steep, nose-up attitude his Vampire was seen to roll three times before losing speed and falling into the sea out of control.

A rescue operation was initiated, but neither the pilot nor aircraft could be found until the tide receded. Retired RAF fireman Tom Gallagher of Kidwelly attended the incident and recalled searching Cefn Sidan beach until the wreckage was uncovered by the ebbing tide at around 01:00 hrs the following morning. VV196 had crashed on the beach at approximately three-quarters of a mile south of the range control tower. The cause of the accident was attributed to the aircraft having entered a high speed stall on pulling up from the dive onto the target, from which the pilot had been unable to recover.

Sgt. Campbell was an experienced pilot and had served in the regular Air Force during the Second World War, transferring to the Royal Auxillary Air Force at the end of hostilities. He came from Deri, near Bargoed and is buried under a private headstone at Brithdir cemetery, near the town.

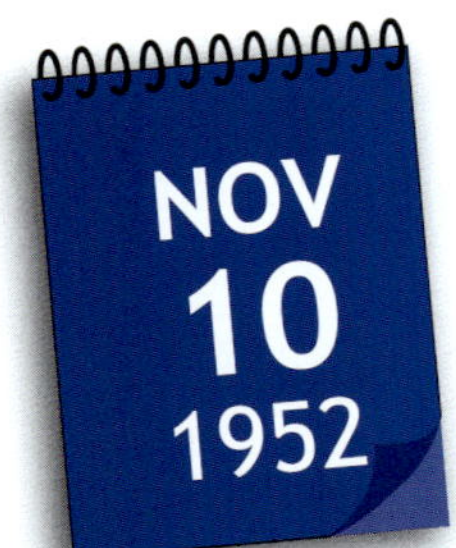

AIRCRAFT: Vampire WG798

Second crash brought reprimand for pilot

By November 1952 Pembrey had re-opened as a military airfield and was in the process of acquiring training staff and ground crew to support the forthcoming Operational Conversion Unit. At 09:50 hrs on November 10, Flt. Lt. R.K. Moores took off from RAF St David's in Vampire WG798 on a ferry flight to 202 Advanced Flying School at Valley, via Pembrey to refuel.

On joining the circuit above Pembrey at around 10:00 hrs Flt. Lt. Moores noticed that one of the 'short' runways was in use. Unable to make radio contact with the control tower because of an unserviceable radio set, he orbited the airfield to ascertain if it was possible to use the considerably longer main runway. During the Vampire's third circuit of the airfield it ran out of fuel and Flt. Lt. Moores was forced to glide down. Misjudging his approach he overshot the airfield and ended up in the adjacent forestry plantation. Though uninjured himself, the Vampire was a write-off and he was later reprimanded for his actions as this was the second occasion he had been involved in such an accident.

MAR 9 1953

AIRCRAFT: **Vampire WA243**

Faulty fuel dump caused string of Pembrey mishaps

October 1952 had seen the inception at Pembrey of 233 Operational Conversion Unit. During the Korean War the government had realised the need to increase the number of jet fighter pilots in the RAF and as a direct result 233 OCU was formed.

In December 1952, No. 1 Vampire training course commenced with 11 student pilots and within a month had completed over 300 training sorties between them.

In January 1953 a serious problem started to affect the unit's fleet of Vampires. A number of unexplained engine failures had led mechanics to believe that the station fuel supplies were somehow to blame. An inspection of the underground fuel dump confirmed their theory. When sampled, the fuel from the dump was found to be contaminated with sand, paint and rust particles. The tanks were refurbished, only for the problem to re-emerge a few months later, before finally being eradicated.

On the morning of March 9, the unit suffered its first flying accident. P.O. William Brown was taking part in a formation flying exercise at 15,000ft. Just before 10:00 hrs he was seen doing a barrel roll before his Vampire entered a high speed dive and crashed to the ground under full power. P.O. Brown made no attempt to either correct the dive, or to bail out. The accident report gives mention to the pilot's low tolerance of G-forces and that he may have blacked out during the dive.

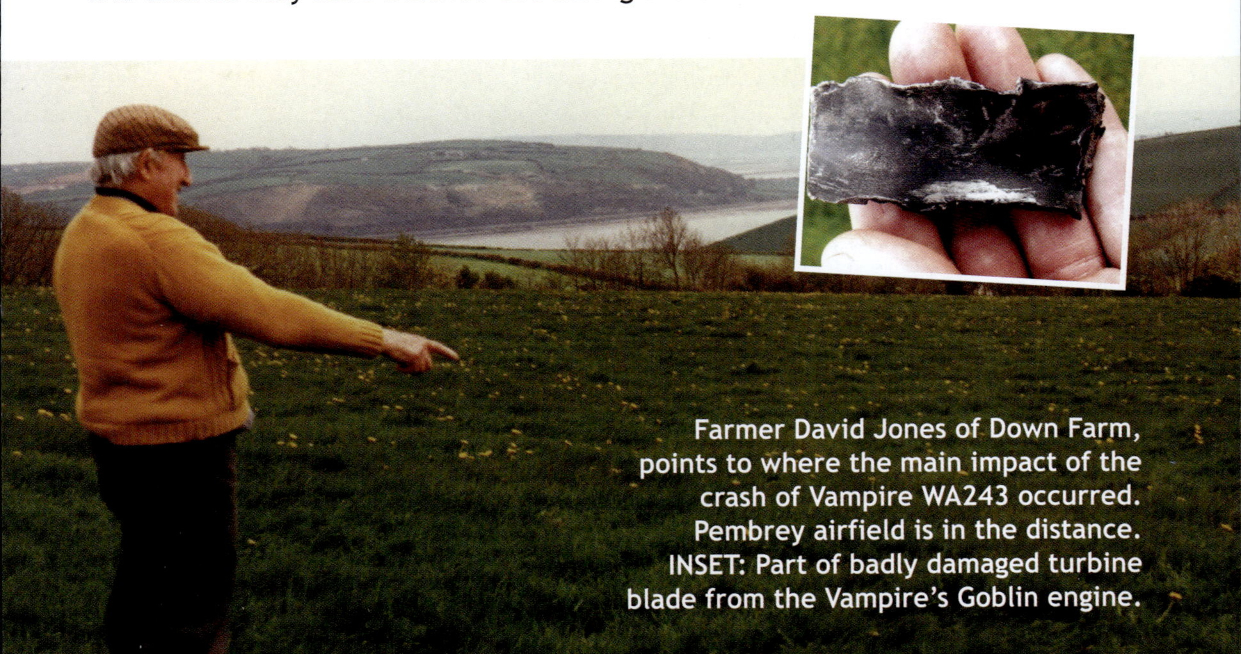

Farmer David Jones of Down Farm, points to where the main impact of the crash of Vampire WA243 occurred. Pembrey airfield is in the distance. INSET: Part of badly damaged turbine blade from the Vampire's Goblin engine.

Vampire WA243 struck the ground in a field at Down Farm near Llanstephan, making a 10ft deep crater and spreading wreckage over three fields.

The aircraft had completely disintegrated and farmer David Jones remembers the deep hole and thousands of small pieces of aluminium which littered the field after the crash. A few days after the accident one of Mr. Jones's dairy cows suddenly became unwell and died. A post-mortem revealed that the heifer had eaten some of the Vampire's electrical wiring.

When I visited the site many years ago the field had recently been ploughed and a few small fragments of plexi-glass, turbine blades and aluminium were found on the surface. Somewhere deeper below the ground still lie the aircraft's 20mm cannon which the recovery crew failed to find.

SEP 22 1953

AIRCRAFT: **Vampire WZ478**

Fire warning light followed take off

Part of the training syllabus at 233 OCU required student pilots to be regularly assessed by their instructors on instrument rating proficiency checks. These assessments were carried out in Vampire T.11 aircraft, a two-seater variant which allowed student and instructor to sit side by side.

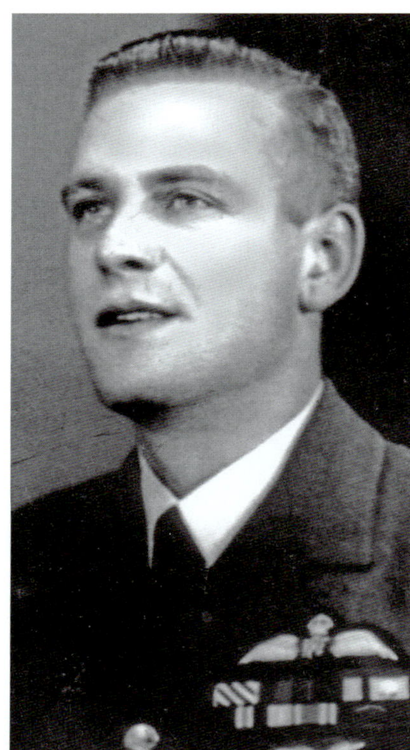

Sqn. Ldr. Lionel Wakeford.

At 11:22 hrs on Tuesday, September 22, Sqn. Ldr. Lionel Wakeford, Officer Commanding of the technical wing, took off in Vampire WZ478 with student P.O. W.H. Williams on just such an assessment flight.

Immediately after take off Sqn. Ldr. Wakeford's attention was drawn to a 'fire' warning light on the instrument panel. The warning light indicated that there was a fire in the Vampire's engine bay and he wasted no time in contacting the control tower for permission to make an emergency landing. Flying at 2,000ft over the Gwendraeth Estuary the Vampire was seen to make a series of 'S' turns in order to reduce his height and speed prior to landing. At 11:27 hrs the aircraft straightened out and with its undercarriage down proceeded to land. At this point flames could be seen coming from the engine bay by witnesses on the ground. With only 50 yards to go to reach the safety of the runway, control of the aircraft was lost and the Vampire crashed in flames. After some delay the fire tenders arrived and extinguished the fire, but it was too late to save the crew.

Sqn. Ldr. Lionel Wakeford had joined the Air Force as a junior apprentice at RAF Halton in 1930, aged just 15. At the outbreak of the Second World War he was serving as a Sergeant-pilot at RAF Heliopolis in Egypt, flying Bombay aircraft with 216 Squadron in the eastern Mediterranean.

Returning to the UK he initially flew Wellingtons before becoming an early member of Bomber Command's Pathfinder Force, flying Mosquitos with 139 Squadron. At the end of hostilities he had accumulated over 2,400 hours of flying and held the rank of Squadron Leader with a DFC, being Mentioned in Despatches on two occasions.

After the war he served with 29 Squadron which flew Mosquito night fighters before transferring to 233 OCU on its inception in 1952. Following the accident he was buried at St Illtyd's Churchyard, Pembrey, while P.O. Williams was laid to rest at his home town of Erith in Kent.

OCT 9 1953

AIRCRAFT: **Vampire VZ106**

Missing jet puzzled searchers for a week

Just over a fortnight later 233 OCU lost another student pilot, P.O. John Baldock. At around 17:10 hrs in the late afternoon of Friday October 9, John Baldock and fellow student, P.O. C.G. Keil, were returning to Pembrey on completion of a cine gun attack exercise. P.O. Baldock, who was leading the pair above a solid undercast, let-down through the cloud to establish their position. P.O. Keil followed him down, but had to pull up sharply to avoid hitting high ground. On regaining altitude P.O. Keil scanned the horizon for his leader only to find himself alone.

After eventually finding his way back to Pembrey, he landed and expressed his concerns for P.O. Baldock. Staff in the control tower waited anxiously for VZ106 to arrive in the circuit, but as the minutes turned to hours both aircraft and pilot were posted as missing.

At sunrise the following day a full-scale search for the missing Vampire was initiated, both on the ground and in the air. The search was centred around an area 30 miles north-east of Pembrey in the Brecon Beacons, the last plotted position of VZ106. Over the weekend the airborne operation was

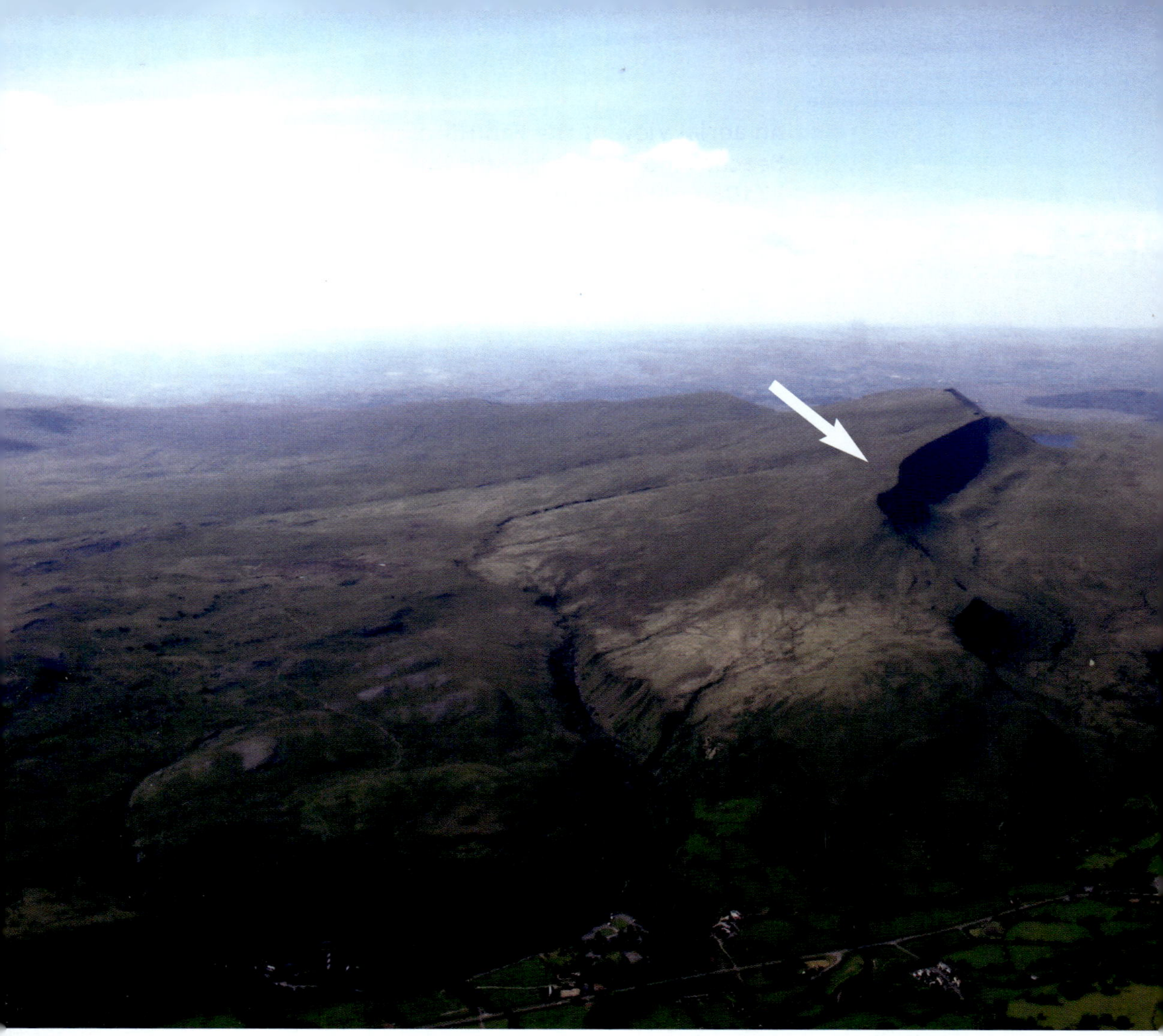

augmented by scores of young air cadets eager to volunteer as observers in the search aircraft.

Poor weather on the Monday temporarily halted the search, but the following day it resumed and despite conflicting reports from members of the public claiming to have seen the aircraft in the Elan Valley district of Mid Wales, the search area remained centred in the Beacons.

On Thursday October 15, nearly a week after the aircraft disappeared, Islwyn Jones and his father, David, of Tir Capel Farm, Trecastle, went onto the Fan Hir escarpment to round up a flock of sheep and bring them down to their winter pasture. Leading their ponies up the steep track above Llyn y Fan Fawr they noticed a number of low flying military aircraft in the area, but at the time were unaware of the news relating to the missing jet.

On reaching the plateau between Fan Hir and Fan Brycheiniog the pair saw an unusual man-made shape below them near the source of the River Haffes. VZ106 and P.O. Baldock were no longer missing.

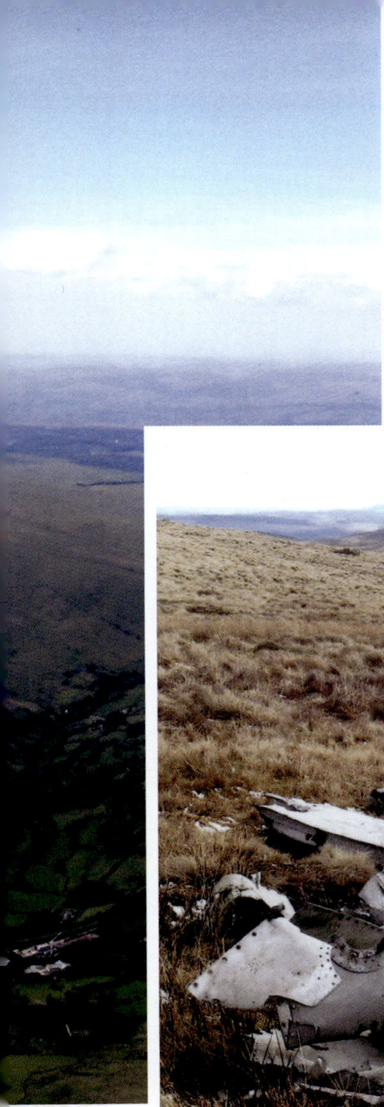

An aerial view of the Fan Hir escarpment in the Brecon Beacons looking north with the crash site of Vampire VZ106 indicated by the arrow. BELOW: wreckage of the aircraft and bottom, Ian Hodgkiss holds up one of the aircraft's 20mm cannons. Now deactivated, it is on display at Kidwelly Industrial Museum.

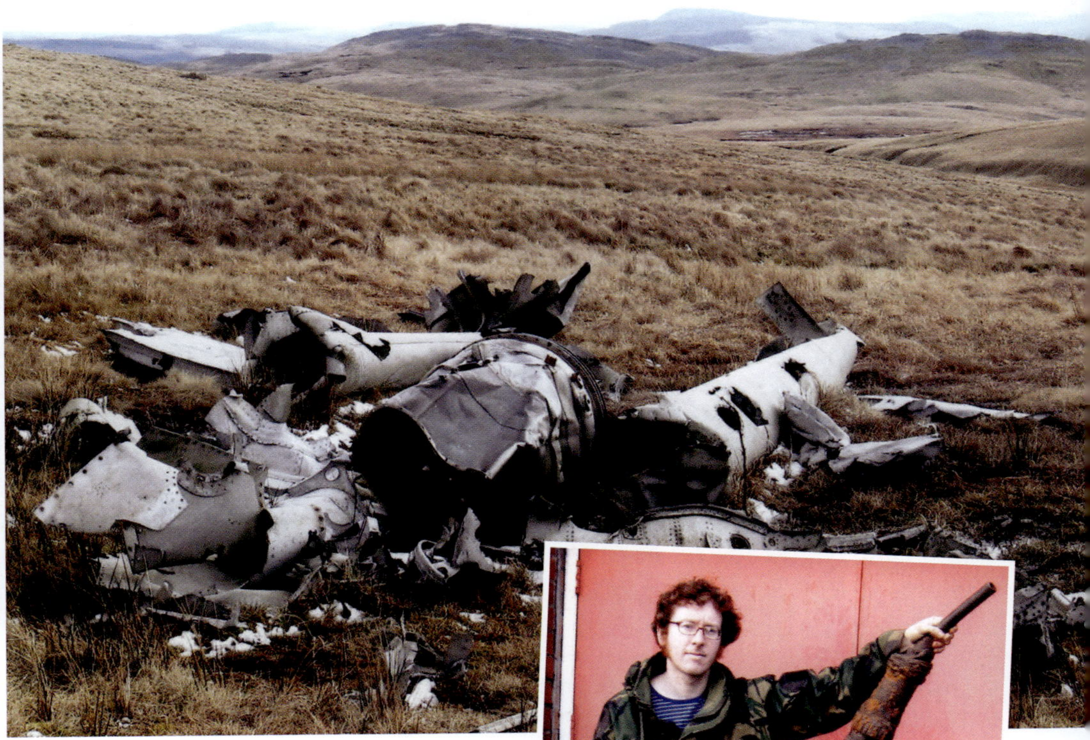

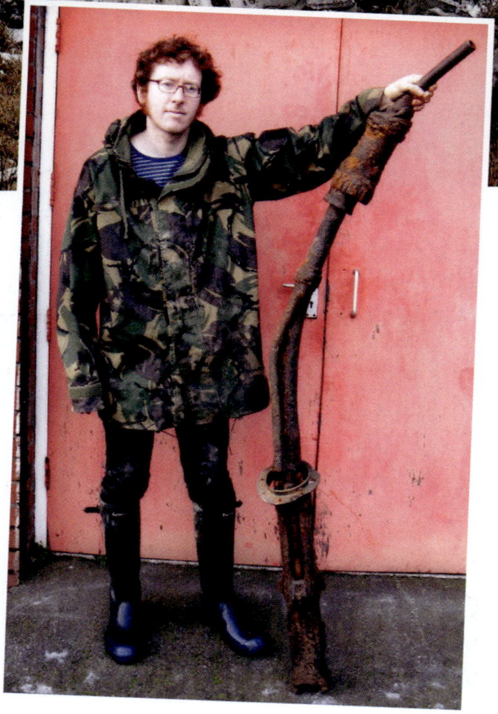

The pilot's body was brought down the mountain on horseback by Islwyn, who rode to the forestry houses at Glasfynydd to raise the alarm. Later RAF personnel arrived and persuaded Islwyn to take them back up Fan Hir to the spot where he had found the wreckage.

Due to the logistics involved in recovering the crashed Vampire from such a remote area it was left there and still remains there to this day. For those who know where to look its

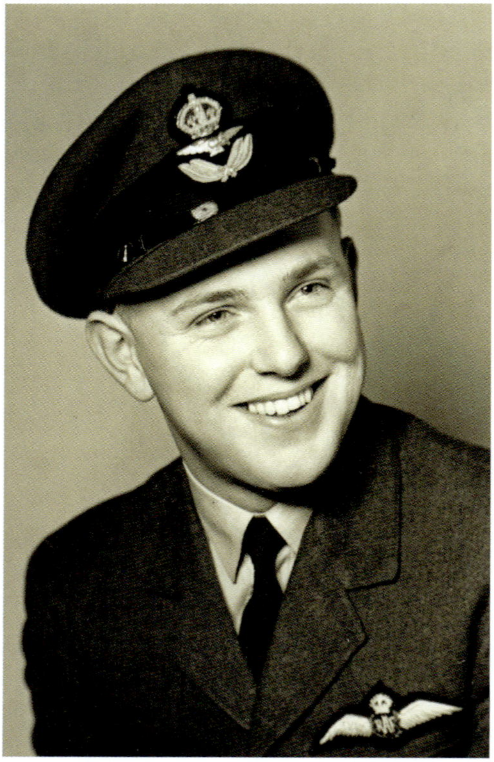

Pilot Officer John Baldock.

outline can be viewed on the internet website Google Earth. Those wishing to make the arduous trek up the mountainside can find the crash site at grid reference SN 82656-20042.

VZ106 had been built by English Electric at its Preston factory and served in the Middle East before being handed over to 233 OCU a few months before its loss.

John Baldock came from the Portsmouth area and had a keen interest in aviation from an early age, his father also having served in the RAF during the Second World War. He attended Chichester High School for Boys and was a member of the local Air Training Corps.

In 1949, under the influence of his mother, the family emigrated to Vancouver, Canada, to avoid John's conscription into military service. However, John, who disapproved of his mother's motive, applied to enlist in the RCAF though he was unsuccessful. The family then returned to the UK and John gained a commission for officer training at RAF Cranwell. He is buried at St Illtyd's Churchyard, Pembrey and his grave has a private headstone.

Islwyn Jones continued to live in the Brecon area and recalled vividly the events of October 1953. On a lighter note he remembered that his pony was so exhausted after ascending and descending the Fan Hir escarpment, that it took a full week for it to recover from its exertions.

OCT 13 1953

AIRCRAFT: **Tiger Moth N6914**

Brecon Beacons search claimed second victim

The search for Vampire VZ106 had, ironically, claimed the loss of another 233 OCU aircraft, though luckily its pilot and passenger escaped unhurt. On October 13, Flt. Lt. Bruce Wingate and Major Hugh Mercer, an Army officer attached to RAF Pembrey, were airborne in Tiger Moth N6914 assisting in the search for the lost Vampire.

They were in the vicinity of the western Brecon Beacons, not far from where VZ106 was eventually found, when the pair spotted a patch of scorched earth in a shallow valley at Cwm Pedol near Brynamman. Flt. Lt. Wingate took the Tiger Moth down for a closer look, but the area in question turned out to be the remnants of where a farmer had previously burned-off some overgrown vegetation. On attempting to regain altitude the Moth failed to climb over the long ridge overlooking Cwm Pedol due to down-drafts flowing over the lee side of the mountain. Unable to get out of the valley Flt. Lt. Wingate skilfully landed the aircraft on a flat piece of ground in Cwm Pedol before both crew left the Tiger Moth and headed off in the direction of Pantyfynnon Farm, further down the valley, in the hope of contacting Pembrey by telephone.

It was not long before news reached the nearby village of Brynamman that an aeroplane had landed on the mountainside. Within a short space of time many curious inhabitants from the village are reputed to have walked up to Cwm Pedol and claimed a souvenir from the aircraft. So intense was the pilfering that not much remained of it by the time the recovery crew turned up the following day.

When the recovery crew arrived in the area they stayed at Pantyfynnon Farm for over two weeks, a seemingly long time considering that there was very little salvage work for them to carry out. RAF records state that the Tiger

Only a small amount of wreckage of ill-fated Tiger Moth N6914 – including the 'silent' picket left behind by the recovery crew – remains on the mountainside at Cwm Pedol above Brynamman.

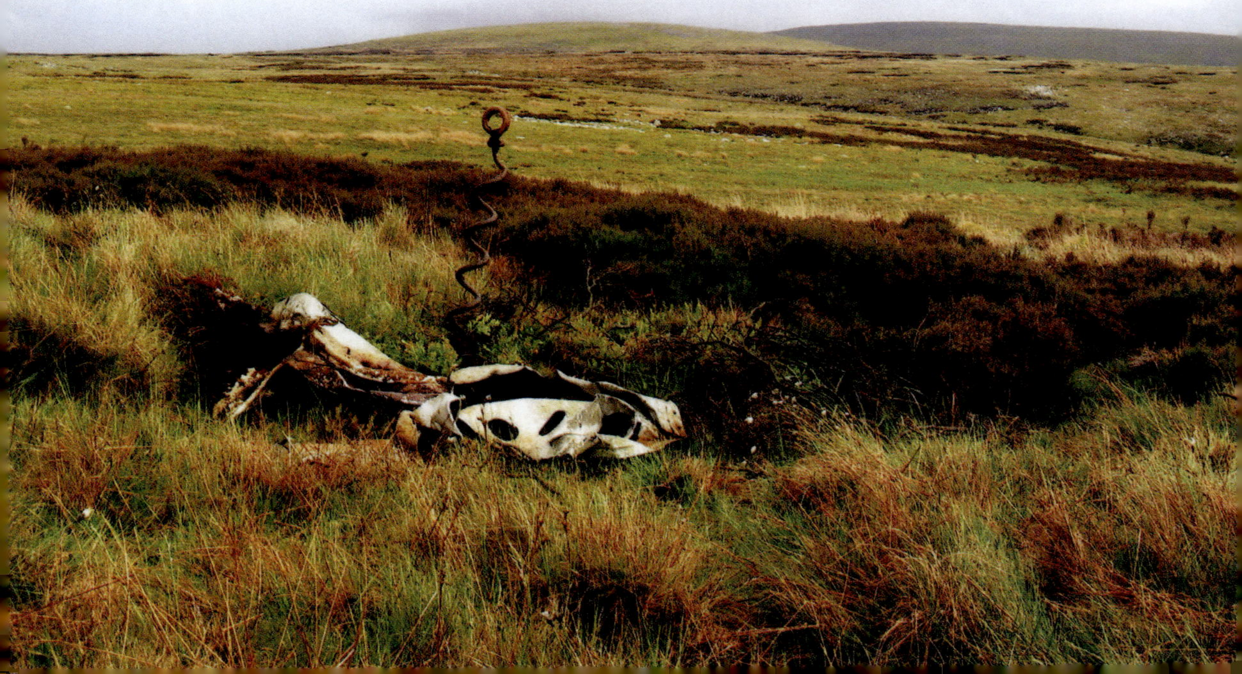

Moth was 'destroyed at site.' Their lengthy stay at Pantyfynnon was perhaps due to the culinary skills of farmer's wife Anna Thomas proving to be better than that of the Airman's Mess at Pembrey.

Despite being given a rough idea of where the crash site lay by Mrs. Thomas's son, Meirion, who currently farms Pantyfynnon, it took me no fewer than five visits to finally locate the site. Thanks to a sketch drawn by local resident Tony Lockley and his wife, Mary, I was able to find the few remaining remnants of the aircraft on the featureless moorland. Interestingly, the site was marked by a silent picket, left behind by the recovery crew back in 1953. Up until a few years ago the Tiger Moth's Gypsy engine could also be seen amongst the heather, but has since disappeared. No doubt a large collection of artefacts are probably stashed away in the attics of grown-up Brynamman schoolboys!

JAN 7 1954

AIRCRAFT: **Vampire WA277**

Engine failure survivor tells of his lucky escape

Over six years since the loss of Vampire VF302 at Pembrey, Goblin engines were still suffering failures due to impeller fractures. One pilot who lived to tell the tale after such an accident on January 7, 1954 was student Pilot Officer Mike Allaby.

"After lunch I took off again for another session on the firing range," recalled Mike. "There was ice on the runway, so my partner and I took off separately rather than in the usual formation, in case one of us skidded during the run. I went first.

"There were often rumbling and clicking noises as the undercarriage retracted, but this time, at a height of no more than about 50ft there was an immensely loud bang and something white flashed passed the cockpit. People on the ground told me later that there was a bang, a cloud of white smoke and then a sound like tin cans falling onto a corrugated iron roof.

"The engine rpm gauge showed zero, moving the throttle had no effect whatsoever, and my squeaky voice cried 'Six-eight, my engine's failed'. You have to admire Air Traffic Controllers, they remain calm under all circumstances. I had an immediate reply; 'Roger, six-eight. Land straight ahead.' They were giving me permission!

"There was a slight problem, in that a small wood lay straight ahead, but there was a field to my right and my options were few. In the course of about 10 seconds I turned towards it, closed the fuel cocks, turned the ground-flight switch to the ground position, opened the canopy and lowered

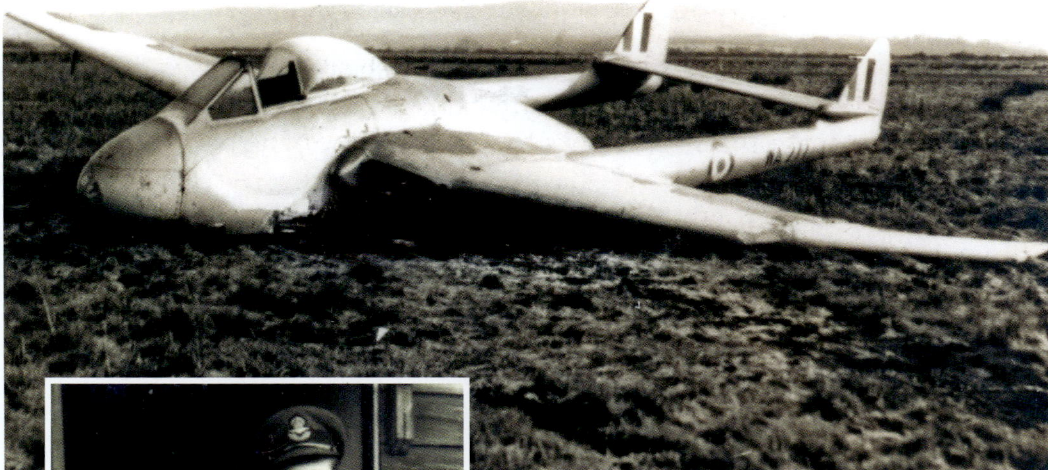

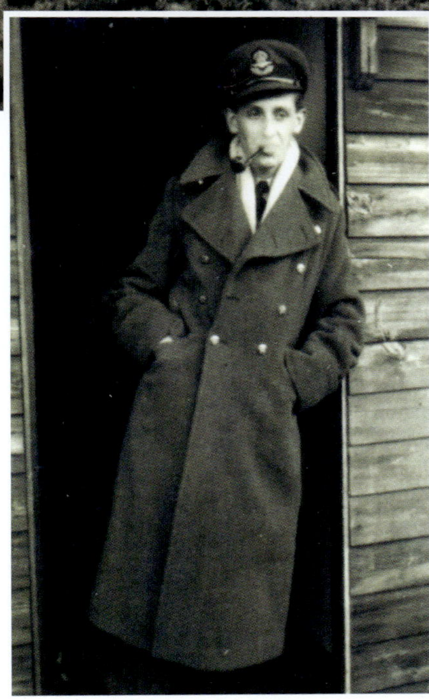

Vampire WA277 after its belly landing near Commissioner's Bridge, Kidwelly.
INSET: The ill-fated aircraft's pilot, P.O. Mike Allaby.

the flaps. Then I saw the power lines just in time to heave the dying aircraft over them at about 90 knots and very close to stalling.

"I must have stalled and knocked myself out for a moment when I hit the ground, because the next thing I remember was sliding along the ground with lumps of turf and mud flying past me. The aircraft finally slewed to the left and stopped, and I climbed out and ran, for fear it would explode. Both main fuel tanks were full and the guns were fully loaded and cocked. A few whisps of smoke rose from the air intakes, but there was no fire, so I returned for a closer look.

"That was when I discovered that beneath the aluminium paint the nacelle housing the cockpit, engines and guns, was made partly of plywood. It had broken and there were splinters.

"It was when I tried to leave the field that I discovered it was surrounded on all sides by small rivers. My Wing Commander, who had appeared from nowhere and who was standing excitedly across one of the rivers, shouted at me to 'jump lad!' So I did and we made our way to the road, where a local farmer commented dryly 'floods at 'igh tide'. It did too, and then it froze.

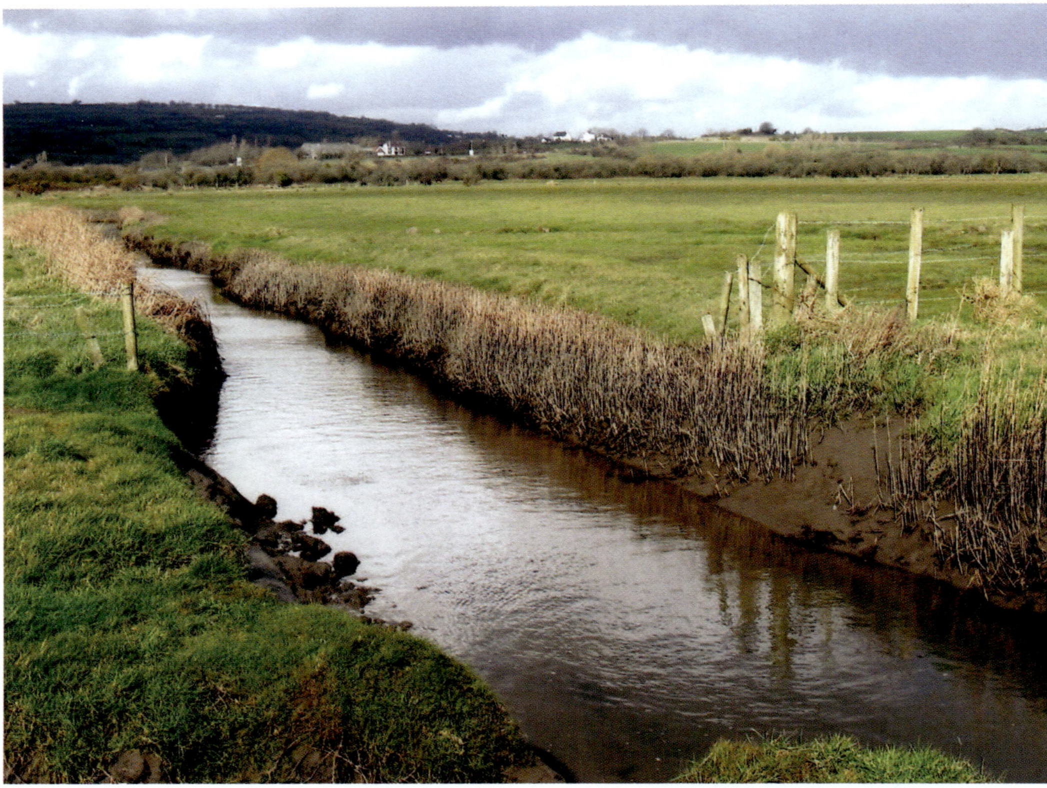

One of the 'small rivers' which Mike Allaby encountered on exiting the marsh with his Wing Commander. Vampire WA277 came down on the right. The main Pembrey to Kidwelly road is approximately 100 yards away, to the left.

"I must have been one of the very few people to have made a wheels-up landing in a Vampire and lived to tell the tale. I was told that the people at de Haviland were delighted with me.

"The engine had been destroyed by the failure of its impeller – the large fan at the front of the engine which compressed the air entering the combustion chambers. One blade had snapped causing the whole structure to shatter. Apparently there had been a number of such failures, but this was the first one from which they had been able to find out what was causing them."

Mike Allaby had been at Pembrey when P.O. John Baldock's Vampire went missing the previous October. Taking part in the ground search, Mike remembered a more light-hearted moment in the operation.

To feed the RAF personnel cooks had set up a field kitchen beside a road with a huge cauldron boiling eggs, which they handed out with hunks of bread. The problem was, as the eggs were removed they kept putting more in to replace them, and soon had no idea which were cooked, and which were not. One Squadron Leader had a pocketfull of broken raw eggs which displeased him immensely.

OCT
12
1954

AIRCRAFT: **Vampire VZ309**

Three pilots hit the silk during aerial exercises

The majority of Vampire jets were not fitted with ejector seats and should the pilot have cause to leave the aircraft in an emergency while airborne, he had to do so manually. During the months of July and October three 233 OCU pilots were forced to 'hit the silk' and although all of them abandoned their aircraft successfully only one pilot came down in the Carmarthenshire countryside.

At 11:00 hrs on October 12, F.O. John Knapp took off from Pembrey as the No. 2 of a pair on a cine gun attack exercise. On completion of the exercise at around midday he lost his leader in cloud, so climbed to 16,000ft to try and contact Pembrey on his radio for a homing bearing. Failing to contact his base, he was however able to communicate with the Royal Naval Air Station at Brawdy who guided him into their circuit.

Overhead at Brawdy F.O. Knapp found the weather too bad to attempt a landing and was vectored onto a heading which would take him back to Pembrey. While following this bearing east, at 12:18 hrs, after being airborne for an hour and 18 minutes, the Vampire's Goblin engine cut out from a lack of fuel and F.O. Knapp was forced to bail out. Drifting down through the cloud from 9,000ft he eventually landed unhurt on the hillside above Sittim Chapel, overlooking the small hamlet of Felin Gwm Isaf, north of Nantgaredig.

Vampire VZ309 made landfall three miles to the north-west at Cwm Egwad, near Rhydargaeau. On striking the ground the aircraft exploded making a six foot crater at the bottom of a steeply-sided valley. Retired farmer, Myrddin Jones, formerly of Blaen Cwm Egwad Farm, recalled that the Vampire fell only a matter of yards outside the boundary of his land.

Fifty years later Myrddin could still pinpoint the exact location of the crash from the high ground above the valley floor. Following his directions I descended the steep and heavily overgrown ravine which makes up Cwm Egwad. On reaching the bottom I was surprised to find many identifiable Vampire components laying around on the surface – a nose wheel, complete with tyre, exhaust jet pipes and many other pieces of twisted aluminium.

Myrddin also recalled that only the lighter parts of the aircraft were hauled up the side of the ravine by the recovery crew; the heavier items, including the remains of the Goblin engine, were buried in the crater formed by the crash. John Knapp went on to complete his Vampire course at Pembrey,

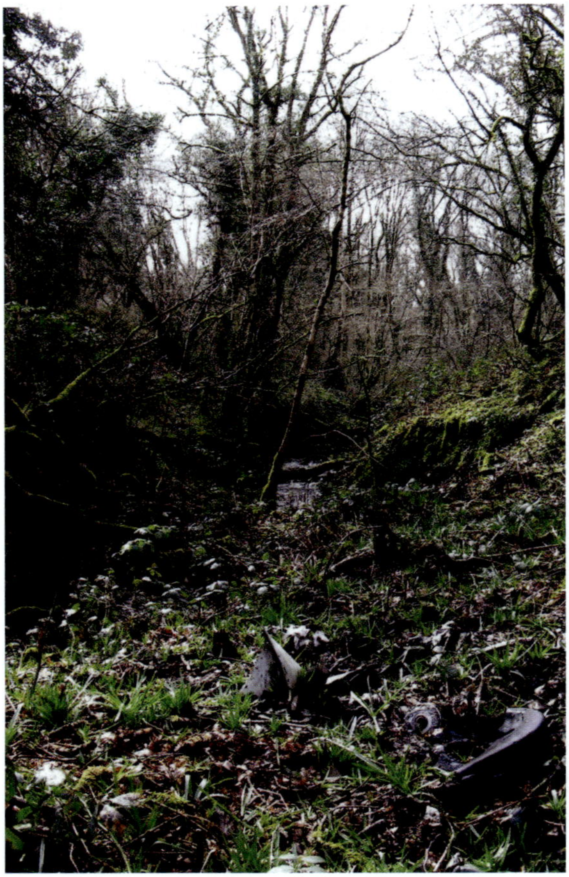

A tyre and various pieces of twisted aluminium visible on the floor of Cwm Egwad. Access to the bottom of the ravine is made difficult by the dense vegetation and steep incline.

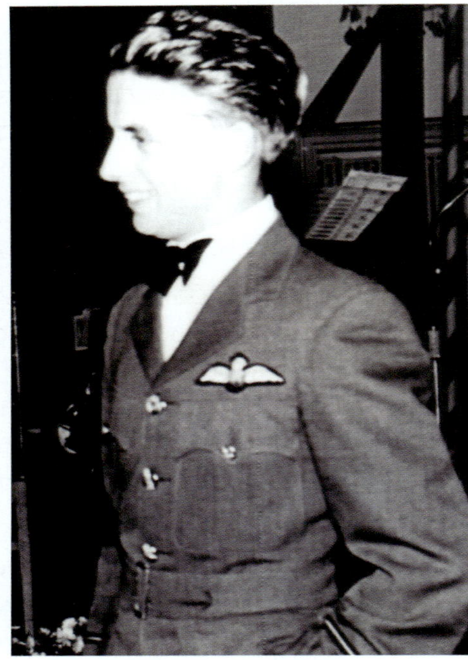

Flying Officer John Knapp.

which was only the beginning of a remarkable career in the RAF. After leaving Pembrey he was posted to 145 Squadron at Celle in Germany, where he flew Venoms in anticipation of a Russian invasion during the Cold War years.

During the early 1960s he converted to fly Vulcan bombers with various units in Lincolnshire, Rutland and South Yorkshire; again a counter measure for any anticipated breakthrough by the Russians in the east.

From the late 1960s until his retirement in 1992, he was stationed at RAF Brize Norton, still flying large aircraft, first piston-engined Belfasts and then VC10 passenger jets. As a VC10 pilot he was one of only a few Category A pilots qualified to fly dignitaries, including the Queen and Prime Minister, around the world. At the automatic retirement age of 55 he was retained for a further seven years, finally retiring in 1992 at the rank of Squadron Leader and having completed nearly 40 years of service.

His son Stephen recalled that despite his father's length of service, of which only six months were spent on ground duties, he didn't experience many events as serious as his bail out over Wales in 1954, even though he was a Falklands veteran and came under shell-fire while at an Iraqi airfield on one of his last missions. John Knapp died in 2005 on his 75th birthday.

NOV
17
1954

AIRCRAFT: **Vampires VV229, VV552, WA362**

Training staff fail to return after collision

On November 17, 233 OCU lost two of its training staff in a collision over the sea off Mumbles Head, near Swansea. One of them, Wing Commander Holland, was the unit's Officer in Command of flying.

At 11:15 hrs that day, Wing Commander R.H. Holland, was making a mock attack on a formation of four other aircraft, in Vampire VV229. Pressing home his attack at too short a distance, the Wing Commander's aircraft collided with the No. 3 of the target formation, Vampire VV552 flown by Flt. Sgt. P.W.D. Green. Both Vampires were seen to fall out of the sky and crash into the sea south of Mumbles. The No.4 of the formation, F.O. G.T. Orde in Vampire WA362, was unable to take evasive action before he flew into the debris caused by the colliding aircraft, but managed to land his damaged aircraft back at Pembrey.

Despite an extensive sea search which lasted for many days, no trace of either pilot was ever found; both being listed as missing, presumed killed.

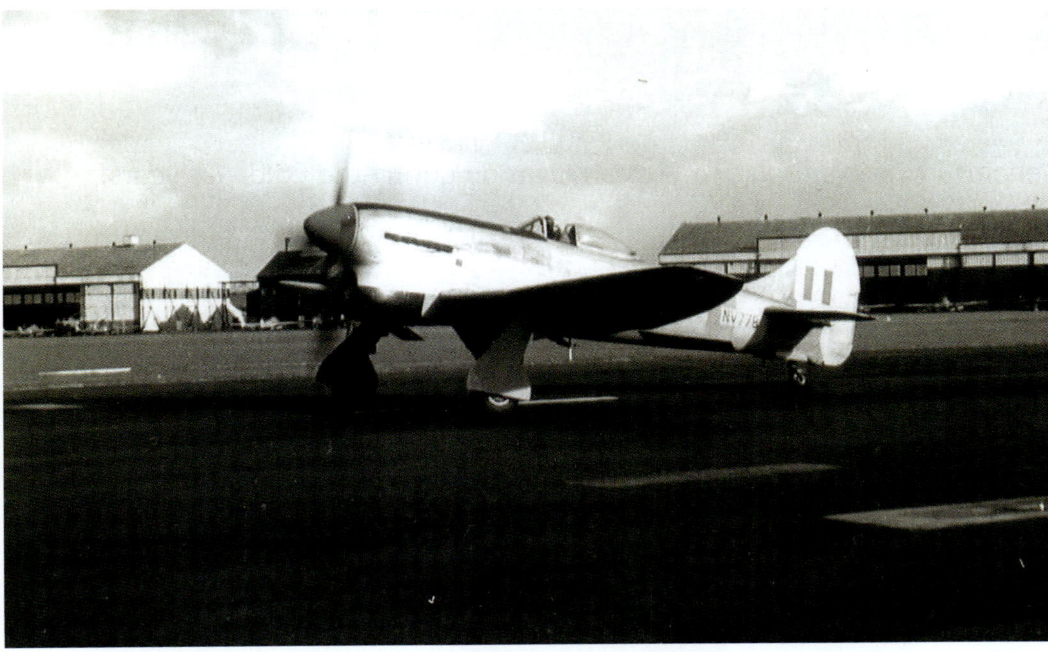

Tempest NV778 of 233 OCU's target-towing flight, seen here at Pembrey in 1954. This aircraft was flown on many occasions by Sgt. Johnnie Walker of Carmarthen. It now hangs from the ceiling in the Milestones of Flight hall at the RAF Museum in Hendon. Its colour scheme depicts its time with 233 OCU.

DEC 19 1955

AIRCRAFT: **Vampires VV566, VZ871**

High altitude alarm that led to mid-air collision

The following year another collision occurred over the Sennybridge ranges near Brecon, but due to the altitude at which the pilots were flying, both succeeded in bailing out.

At 09:15 hrs on the morning of December 19, 1955, student pilot P.O. R.D. Knight and instructor, Flt. Sgt. Emrys George, took off from Pembrey on a battle formation exercise; flying in Vampires VV566 and VZ871 respectively.

Thirty minutes into the exercise and flying at an altitude of 30,000ft, P.O. Knight's attention was drawn to a high jet-pipe temperature reading on his instrument panel. Taking his concentration away from flying straight and level in close formation, his port wing dropped and struck the starboard wing of Flt. Sgt. George's Vampire, VZ871.

As a result both aircraft sustained severe wing damage and each entered an uncontrollable spin. Unable to regain normal flight, both pilots bailed out, landing within a mile of each other in the midst of the remote Crychan Forest, north east of Llandovery.

The two pilots were soon picked up by forestry workers who had followed their descents and, shortly after, taken to the West Wales General Hospital at Glangwili, Carmarthen for a medical check. Later that day they returned to Pembrey with only slight injuries from their ordeal.

The two spinning Vampires came down on the southern boundary of the Crychan plantation at a place known locally as Graig yr Wyddon, just north of the A40 between Llandovery and Trecastle.

One had crashed onto spruce trees and started a serious fire, the other came down within four hundred yards, in open farmland at the edge of the forestry. By sheer coincidence the Vampire which set fire to the spruce trees had fallen near a gang of forestry workers who quickly surrounded the blaze and stopped it from spreading.

In March 1998 I was shown the area in which the two aircraft came down by retired forestry worker Donald Jones. Despite the fact that over 40 years had passed since the accident it was still possible to make out the charred stumps of fire-damaged trees among the more recently planted conifers. Closer inspection of the burned area revealed aluminium aircraft parts.

Four hundred yards away Donald pointed out where the other Vampire had crashed. At the time of the accident it was an open field on the edge of the

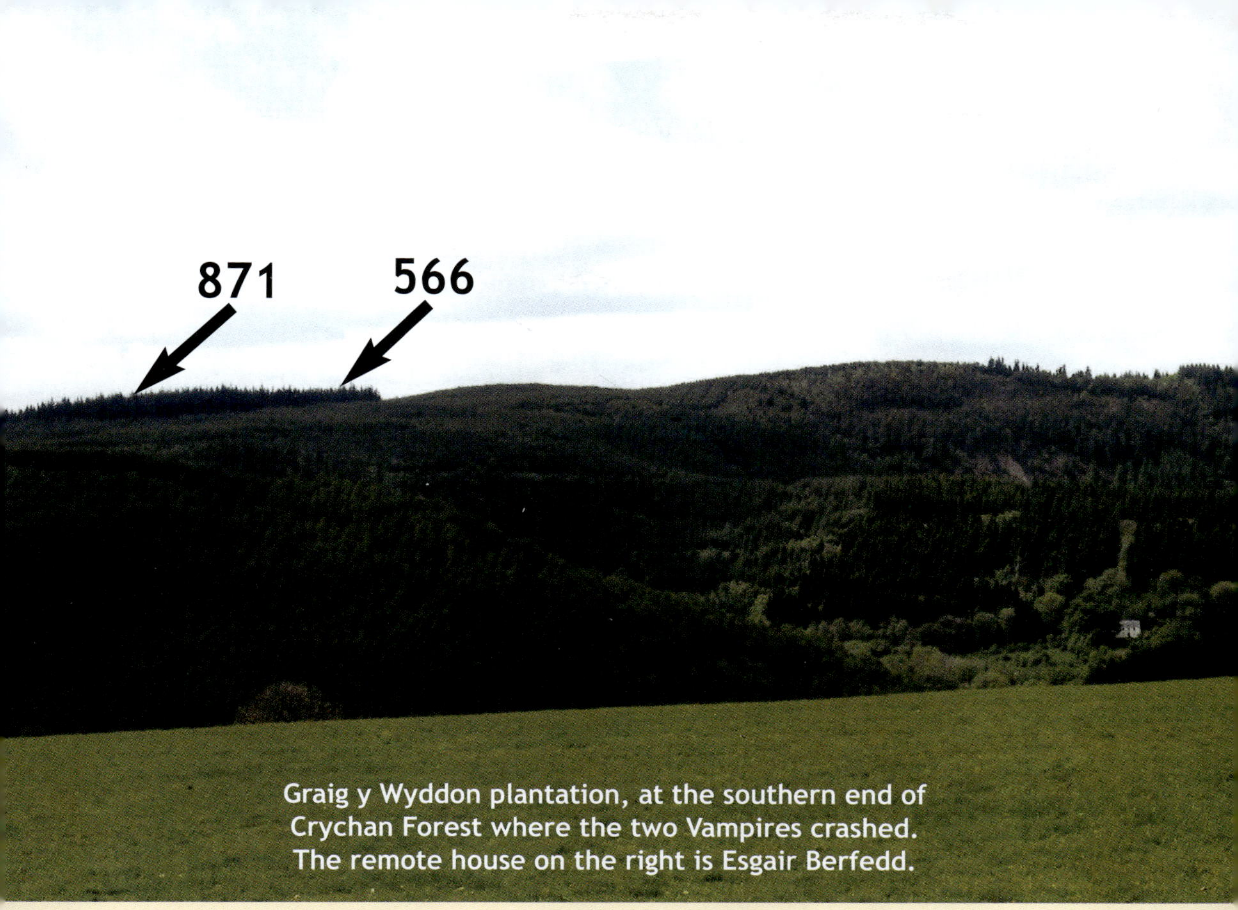

Graig y Wyddon plantation, at the southern end of Crychan Forest where the two Vampires crashed. The remote house on the right is Esgair Berfedd.

plantation, but had since been planted with trees. Donald recalls that despite falling from a great height this aircraft remained fairly intact and didn't catch fire. Due to the thick undergrowth and the probability that the ground would have been deeply ploughed prior to the planting of the trees, I gave up any hope of finding evidence of this aircraft.

Trying to establish which of the aircraft came down in either location was solved when I found a small piece of aluminium in the burned area of forestry. Clearly stamped on its surface were the letters 'EEP', an abbreviation for English Electric Preston. As VZ871 had been a de Haviland-built aircraft, then this was more likely to be P.O. Knight's Vampire, VV566, which records show was built at the English Electric factory at Preston. As with F.O. John Knapp (Vampire VZ309), Flt. Sgt. Emrys George also had an exceptional time in the RAF. In an astonishing career spanning 44 years, Emrys first enlisted as an engine mechanic in early 1939. Re-mustering in the war years to become a pilot, he gained his 'wings' in 1942 in Rhodesia under the Empire Air Training Scheme. From here he joined 261 Squadron and for the rest of the war flew Thunderbolts in the Far East.

His post-war service included flying Spitfires and later Hornets in the Malayan Emergency where he earned a Mention In Despatches and the Distinguished Flying Medal. From 1952 until 1957 he was posted to 233 OCU as a staff pilot, initially for target-towing duties, but later as an instructor. The accident in December 1955 above the Crychan forest was not the first time Emrys had walked away from a life-threatening situation. On November 4, 1948 he was at 8,000ft in a Hornet when both engines failed. With great skill he managed to force land the aircraft in a field near Derby with no injuries to himself.

With the disbanding of 233 OCU in 1957 he returned to Malaya where he undertook psychological warfare missions with 267 Squadron in Dakota aircraft. These duties included flying low over the dense jungle in aircraft fitted with a very large public address system. The idea being that the insurgents would give up and surrender to the local police force. On a more lighthearted note, Christmas carols were broadcast from the aircraft around their base during the festive period. While in Malaya he also flew Hornets & Tempests with 33 Squadron.

Returning to the UK in 1961 Emrys was forced to take a compulsory desk job with Air Traffic Control for a brief period before returning to flying in 1962. During the 1960s he flew passenger aircraft including VIP flights in and out of London. On returning from an overseas posting to Malta in 1968 he was commissioned to the rank of Flying Officer.

Another desk job with Air Traffic Control followed, before a posting to Wildenrath, Germany in the mid 1970s. From then until his demob in 1984, Emrys once again undertook ATC duties by which time he had attained the rank of Flight Lieutenant.

On leaving the Air Force he had been Mentioned In Despatches twice and awarded both the DFM and a Queen's Commendation.

FEB 13 1956

AIRCRAFT: **Vampire VV544**

Pilot escapes after engine flame-out at 2,000ft

As far as mishaps were concerned, 1956 was a relatively quiet year for 233 OCU though at 11:07 hrs on February 13, Sqn. Ldr. H. Ambrose was forced to make an emergency wheels-up landing on Cefn Sidan beach. This was made necessary because of an engine flame-out at 2,000ft over the sea soon after take off. Sqn. Ldr. Ambrose emerged unhurt, but VV544 sustained damage to its fuselage and port wing.

Throughout the spring of 1956 Hawker Hunters were progressively phased in as training aircraft to replace the obsolete Vampires.

JUN
22
1956

AIRCRAFT: Anson VV914

Mouse found in crash plane's engine cowling

At 10:48 on the morning of Friday June 22, Anson VV914 of 3/4 Civilian Anti-Aircraft Co-operation Unit based at Exeter was taking off from Pembrey on a flight to Plymouth when the starboard engine lost power at an altitude of 150ft.

The aircraft's engine was feathered, but, unable to turn around and land at Pembrey on one engine, the pilot opted to make a forced landing on the edge of the Gwendraeth marshes.

The pilot, Flt. Sgt. G.M. File, and the sole passenger on board, Colonel Nicholls of the Army School of Artillery at Manorbier, both escaped unscathed. A field mouse found inside one of the Anson's engine cowlings fared less favourably. The crash site is now a water treatment works at the side of the track which leads to Kidwelly Quay.

JUN
20
1957

AIRCRAFT: Hunter WT563

Stricken plane nearly smashed into train

The year 1957 was only a fortnight old when two staff pilots from 233 OCU collided over Broadway Farm, Llangennith on the Gower Peninsula. At 16:12 on January 14, Flt. Lt. R.W. Hayes and another staff pilot were practising close formation flying in Meteors WE887 and WH457 when they struck each other while carrying out steep climbing and descending turns.

Flt. Lt. Hayes successfully ejected from WE887, but somehow the drogue chute on his ejector seat became entangled and his main parachute failed to deploy. He was killed when he hit the ground, still strapped into his seat. Meteor WH457, though seriously damaged, was able to land back at Pembrey.

During March 1957 orders were received at Pembrey that 233 OCU was to be disbanded in July after completion of No.8 Hunter course. Ironically, this course suffered the only Hunter loss by the OCU. At 09:30 hrs on June 20, student pilot P.O. F.W.R. Jacques and his instructor were taking off from Pembrey in separate aircraft for a battle formation exercise.

The pair took off simultaneously, but at 400ft P.O. Jacques's Hunter, WT563, banked towards and under his instructor's aircraft before crashing onto the main Carmarthen to Llanelli railway line, approximately 200 yards east of Kidwelly Station. Miraculously it avoided hitting a passenger train from Carmarthen about to leave the station when the accident happened.

P.O. Jacques ejected from the Hunter, but did so at height of only 50ft above the ground. Although surviving for a short while, he died from his injuries at the scene. Two days later his funeral took place at St Illtyd's, Pembrey.

Examination of the wrecked Hunter suggested the cause of the crash to be false anchorage of the port aileron, which restricted its movement.

A view of the railway line from the east-bound platform at Kidwelly Station. P.O. Jacques's aircraft crashed just beyond the signal box, where the track curves around to the right. INSET: The headstone of P.O. Jacques at St Illtyd's Churchyard, Pembrey.

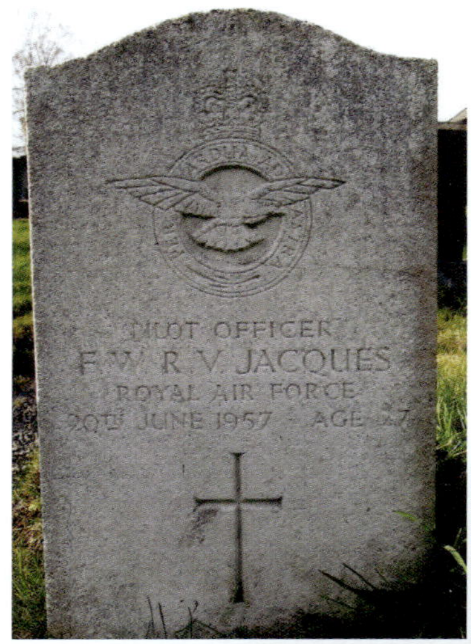

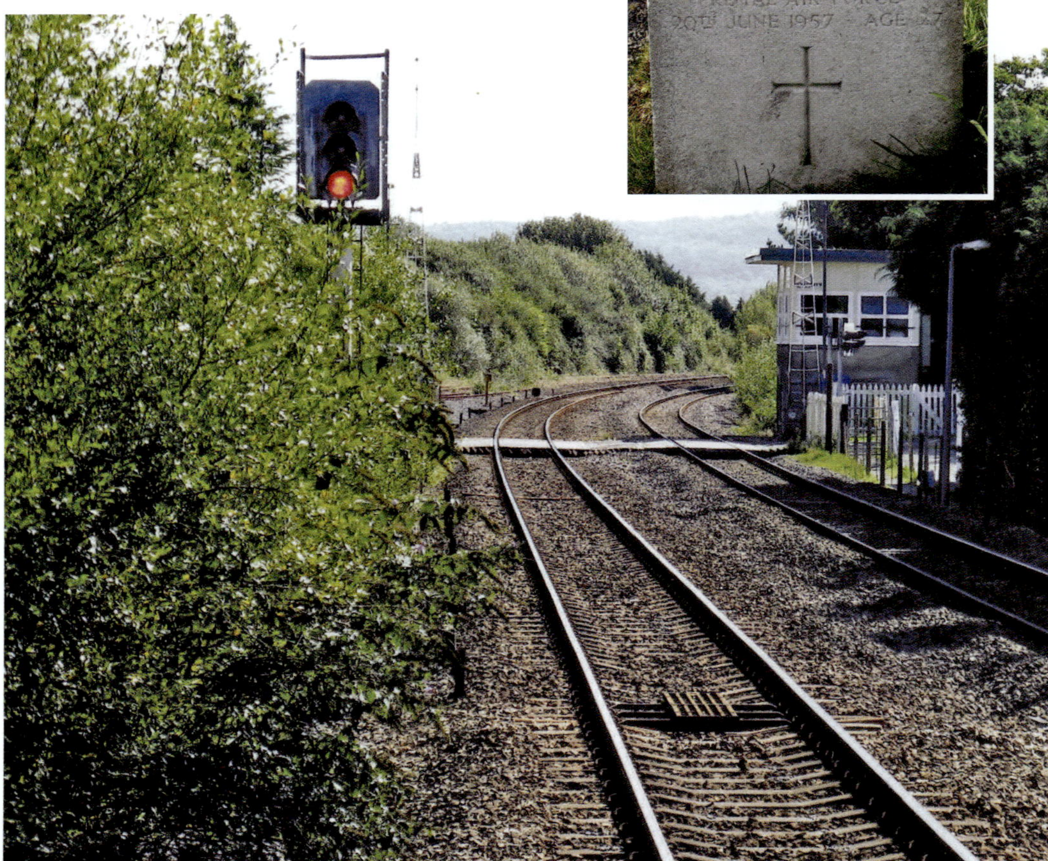

When this condition was simulated on a test rig it revealed a similar flight pattern to P.O. Jacques's aircraft just after take off.

Interestingly, on July 10, a Vickers Viking airliner, derived from the famous Wellington bomber of Second World War, took off from Pembrey with Princess Margaret on board, returning to London after a royal visit to Carmarthenshire. The aircraft, VL247, had the distinction of being the last military plane to leave Pembrey's runway before 233 OCU disbanded, the station itself closed three days later. On 1 January 1969, 233 OCU was resurrected as a Harrier training squadron at RAF Wittering, Cambridgeshire.

It was to be another 40 years before Pembrey airfield was to become operational for flying. Not though, through the RAF, but by the financial investment of local businessman Winston Thomas. On August 22, 1997 the eastern-end of the former airfield was officially opened as Pembrey Airport by the then First Minister for Wales, Ron Davies.

The western section of the former airfield has been developed into a popular Motor Sports Centre. Buildings dating back to the early years of the base can still be seen near RAF Pembrey Sands, the current Royal Air Force establishment which services the needs of the air-to-ground firing range. Most prominent among these is the distinctive air gunnery training dome. This has long since been relegated to the role of a cattle shelter. Elsewhere in the area, refurbished hangers and a solitary wooden accommodation hut are also clearly visible.

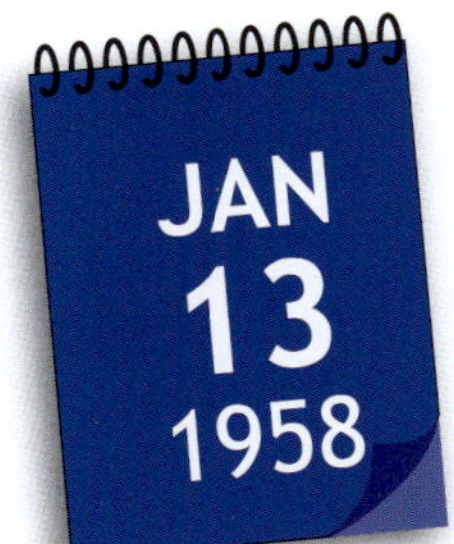

AIRCRAFT: **Canberra WE117**

Hero pilot saves village from certain disaster

By strange coincidence the next flying accident to occur in Carmarthenshire also happened within a few hundred yards of a railway station. On January 13, 1958 Flt. Lt. James Wallace, a test pilot with 38 MU at St Athan in the Vale of Glamorgan, was airborne in Canberra WE117 on a routine air test.

At 14:45 hrs, 15 minutes into the flight, the Canberra was seen flying in a westerly direction at only 500ft over Garngoch Common, Swansea. The witness also heard the engine cut out. The Canberra entered a dive to starboard and minutes later crashed onto marshland near Llangennech railway station on the Carmarthenshire side of the Loughor Estuary. On hitting the ground the jet exploded, rocking the foundations of many buildings in Llangennech village and forming a crater over 30ft deep in the soft mud. Debris was scattered for hundreds of yards in all directions.

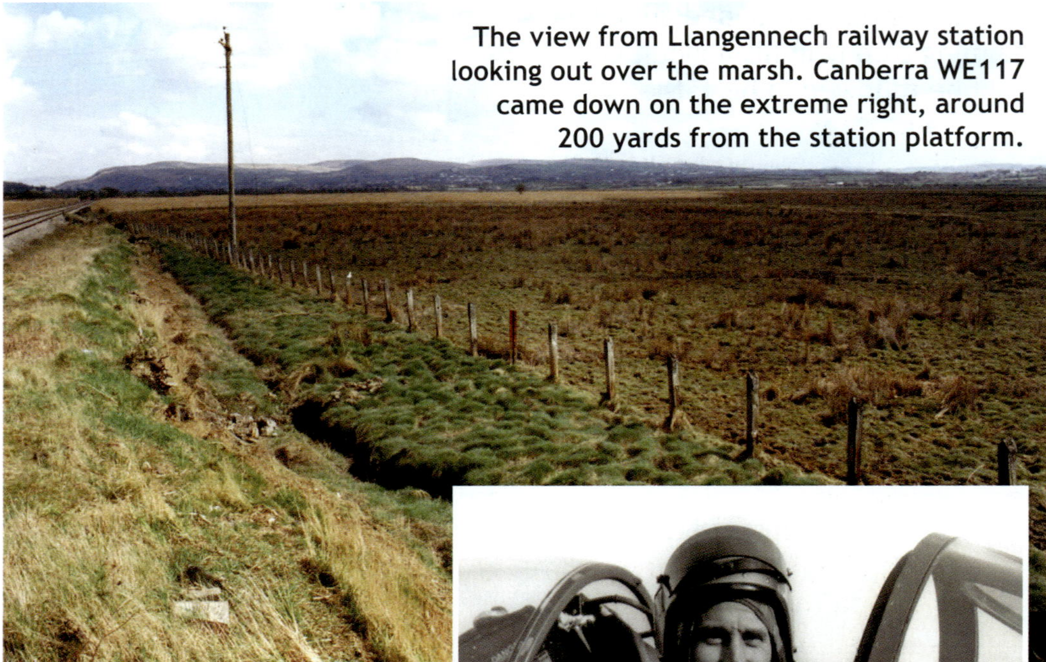

The view from Llangennech railway station looking out over the marsh. Canberra WE117 came down on the extreme right, around 200 yards from the station platform.

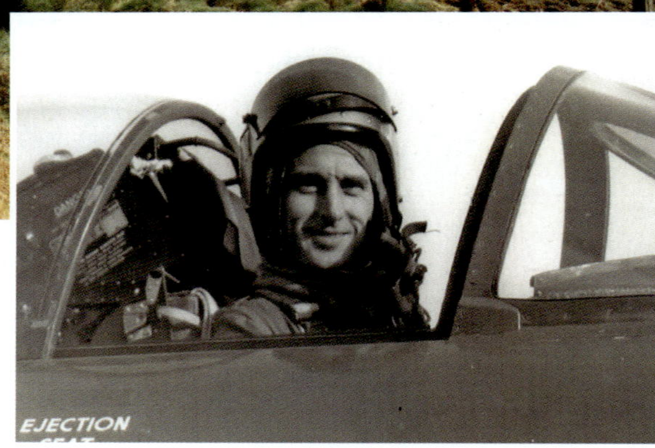

James Wallace in his role as a post Second World War test pilot.

Onlookers described how, during the last few seconds of its flight, the Canberra veered off its collision-course with Llangennech before crashing, a brave act by the 35 year old pilot, which no doubt saved many lives. Would-be rescuers, including my father, rushed to the scene to render assistance, but on arrival at the edge of the crater the main wreckage was already disappearing under the surface. My father recalls that the only recognisable parts which lay above ground was a pair of undercarriage wheels.

In the cold and fading mid-winter dusk a wider search of the marsh was made for the pilot, but it was the following day before his body was found.

Today any sign of the main impact point has long since disappeared due to the changing nature of tidal mudflats and the creation of drainage channels in the area. All around the crash site however can be found small pieces of corroded aluminium. On a visit to the site some years ago I uncovered a large fragment of a compressed air cylinder which had exploded like a bomb in the crash, testament to the force of the impact.

James Wallace was born in South Shields, Tyne and Wear. Along with his academic achievements, while at High School he became a champion swimmer winning many medals for the school. On his death the Wallace family initiated and funded an annual school swimming trophy in his honour. On leaving school he followed in his father's footsteps and became a draughtsman at the Swan Hunter shipbuilding yard, but in July 1941 enlisted as a pilot in the RAF. On completion of his training in Southern Rhodesia he served with 103 Squadron, Bomber Command. At the end of hostilities he married and returned to his pre-war occupation as a draughtsman. It wasn't long before his passion for flying prompted him to re-enlist into the RAF, this time as a test pilot. Serving first at Linton-on-Ouse, he and his young family then moved to St Athan in 1952 where they stayed until the time of his accident. His daughter, Jane, recalls many trips aloft with her father carrying out 'circuits and bumps' over the airfield in the station Auster. He also participated in the Open Days at St Athan, thrilling the crowds at the well-attended event.

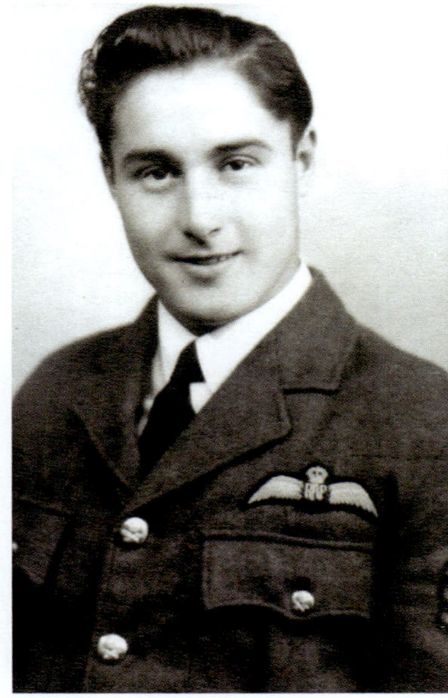

James Wallace as a Sgt. pilot during the Second World War.

In November 1957, just two months prior to the crash at Llangennech, his services to the RAF were recognised when he was awarded the Air Force Cross at Buckingham Palace. James's flight on the fateful day of the

A proud moment. James Wallace and family at Buckingham Palace, November 1957. INSET: Jane Wallace with the author at Llangennech, during October 2010.

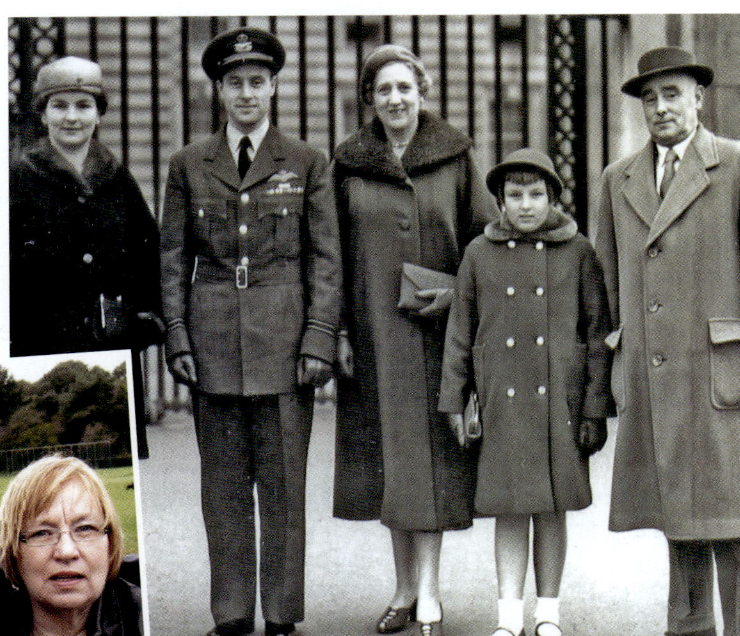

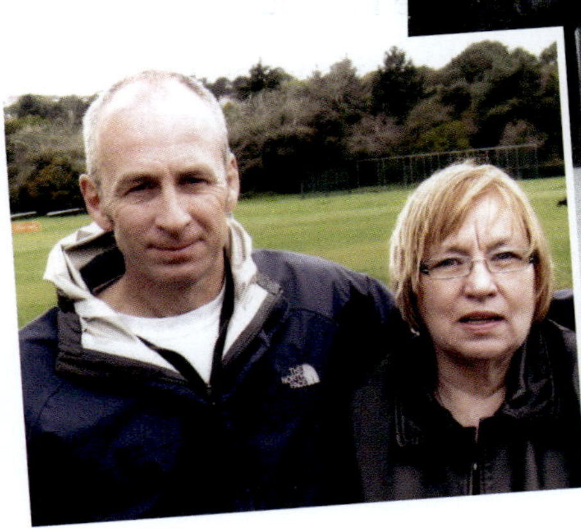

accident was to be one of his last as a test-pilot, for he was shortly due to transfer to the RAF's prestigious Queen's Flight. He is buried at Llantwit Cemetery, Boverton, just a short distance away froms the RAF base of St Athan from where he took off for his ill-fated flight.

SEP 4 1967

AIRCRAFT: **Hunter XG198**

Wildfowlers get an unexpected shock

Ten years after 233 OCU disbanded, its sister unit at RAF Chivenor, 229 OCU, was still very much in existence. At 09:20 hrs on September 4, 1967 Flt. Lt. T.M. Sharp took off from the base in Hunter XG198 as No.2 in a pair, for a rocket attack exercise at the Pembrey air firing range.

Crossing the Bristol Channel in a matter of minutes the pair entered the range on the Gwendraeth Estuary and made a successful low-level pass on the target area. On pulling away the pair became separated as Flt. Lt. Sharp's aircraft encountered broken cloud while gaining height.

XG198 was next seen from the ground by Fred Lyne and Erwyn Williams who were travelling by car along the Pembrey to Kidwelly road on their way to do a spot of wildfowling on the northern shore of the estuary. At a point just past the turning for the airfield the Hunter came into view on their left

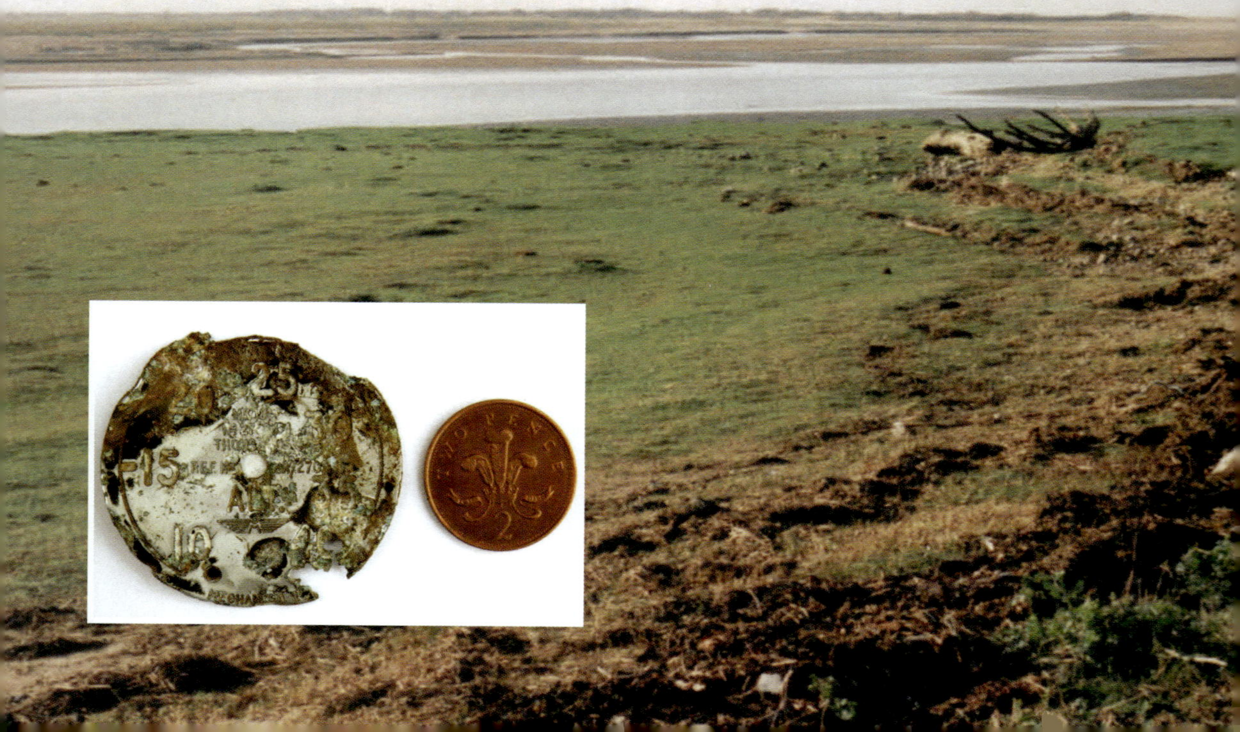

flying extremely low and parallel to them. Following the course of the railway line the aircraft then disappeared from view over the marshes. So concerned as to the Hunter's low altitude, Fred and Erwyn stopped the car at the railway underpass near the Pinged junction and crossed under the railway line onto the Banc y Lord embankment on the other side of the line.

From here they could see a pall of black smoke rising from the high water mark at a point between Penallt Farm and the Carmarthen Bay Holiday Village; the Hunter had crashed.

Arriving in the vicinity of the crash Fred and Erwyn were shocked to find that the Hunter had come down only yards from the hide that they had intended to use that morning and had they not have been late, they would have both been inside the hide when the aircraft crashed.

Flt. Lt. Sharp had made no attempt to eject and was killed. So severe was the impact that debris from XG198 was scattered far and wide, some parts being found among the boats moored in front of the holiday village.

In 1994 Fred and I carried out a metal detector search of the area. Among the many corroded pieces of metal found was the face of an altimeter gauge, the height scale still legible.

The foreshore below Penallt Farm where Hunter XG198 crashed. Carmarthen Bay Holiday Village is in the distance to the right, while the RAF air-to-ground firing range is on the left. The hide where Fred Lyne intended to shoot from was located just behind the camera. INSET LEFT: An altimeter instrument face found after a metal detector sweep of the crash site. INSET RIGHT: Two stainless steel turbine blades from the Hunter's engine, corroded by the salt water.

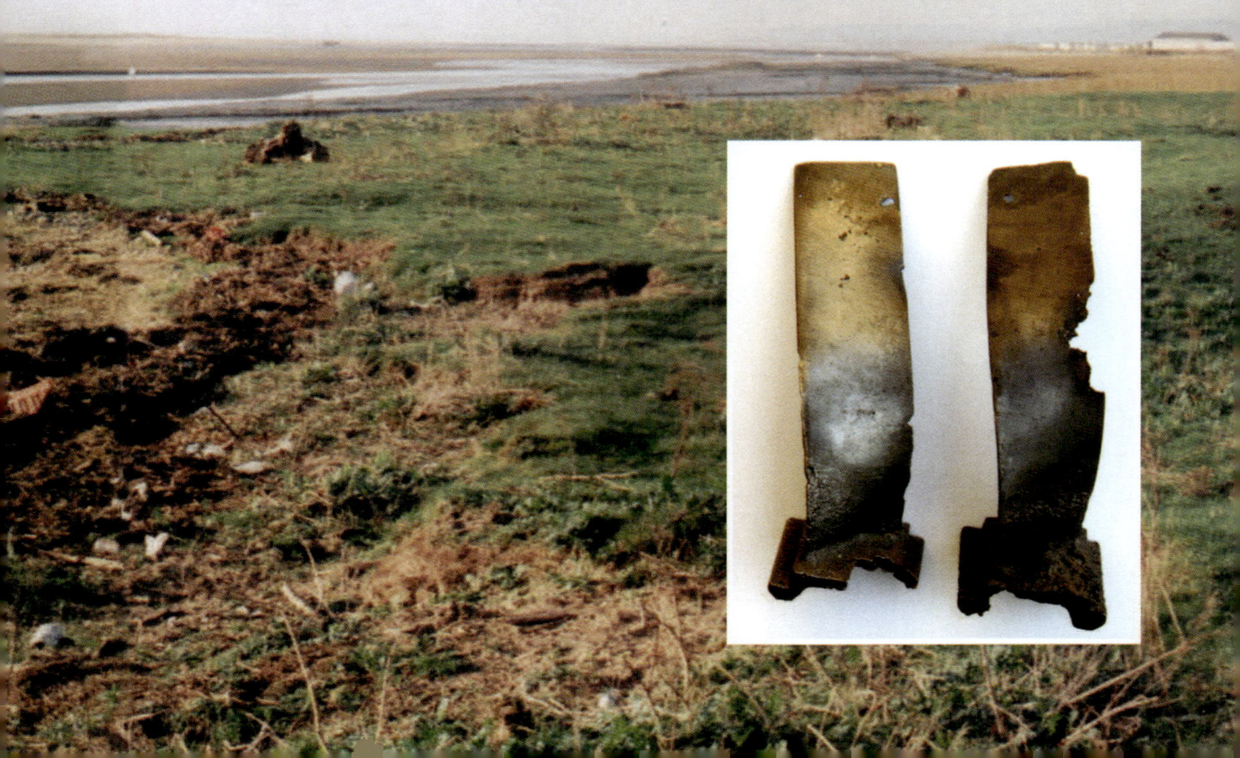

An inquiry into the accident failed to reveal a conclusive outcome, though it was suggested that the pilot might either have lost control due to an unestablished cause, or become disorientated.

Flt. Lt. Sharp had accumulated nearly 300 hours of airtime, of which 52 hours were on Hunters. He was 23 years of age. Hunter XG198 had previously been used by the Blue Diamond display team, the predecessors of the RAF's prestigous aerobatic display team, the Red Arrows.

MAY
1
1971

AIRCRAFT: **Piper Arrow 28 D-EHBR**

Flying friends distracted football spectators

Saturday May 1, was a fine and sunny spring day over South Wales. Many avid football spectators in the Ammanford area were concentrating on their game when the sound of an aircraft engine racing high above them drew their gaze skyward.

The engine belonged to a Piper Arrow coded D-EHBR which had taken off earlier that day from Egelsbach airfield, Frankfurt, in what was then the Federal Republic of Germany. On board were four friends who had chartered the aircraft for the weekend and were travelling to the Shannon area of Ireland for a fishing trip.

At 11:00 hrs the Arrow's pilot, Wilhelm Klohoker, landed at Lydd Airport in Kent to refuel. On approach a technical problem with the aircraft's radio necessitated a long wait at the airfield before permission was eventually gained to continue on to Shannon without radio communication.

At 12:40 hrs Klohoker took off from Lydd on the final leg of their journey to Ireland. By around 14:15 hrs the Arrow was cruising straight and level at 6,000ft above Ammanford when it was seen to enter a shallow dive. It recovered with a gentle climb, but then entered a much steeper and more severe dive. The recovery from this second manoeuvre was so abrupt that it resulted in the port wing shearing off at the fuselage. The Arrow then spun out of control to the ground killing all four on board.

From the ground many people had been watching the aircraft, their attention being initially drawn to it by the sound of its 'racing' engine. One of them was Winston Richards of Pen Waun Hafog, on the outskirts of Ammanford. In his back garden at the time he witnessed the final seconds of the Arrow as it came down in a field near Cwmbach Farm, not far from the Saron to Llandybie road. The wing that broke away, along with part of the tail, was later found four hundred yards away to the north of the main road.

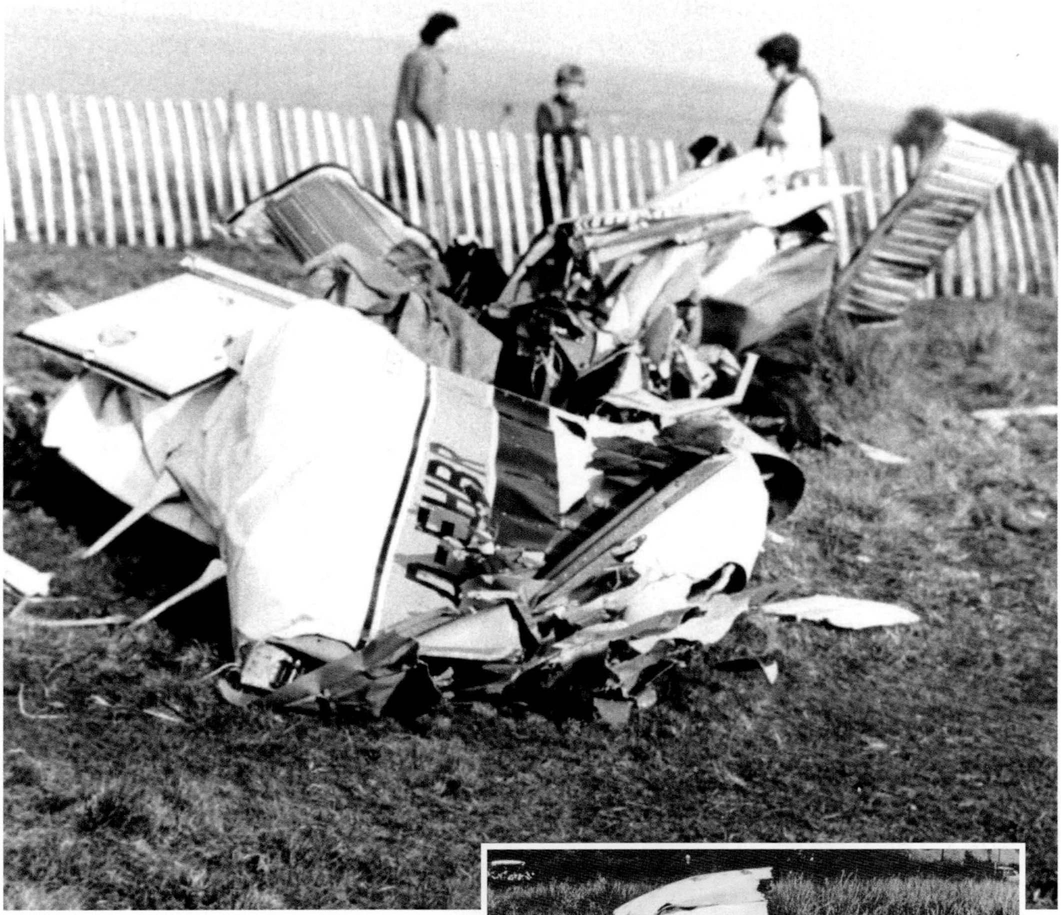

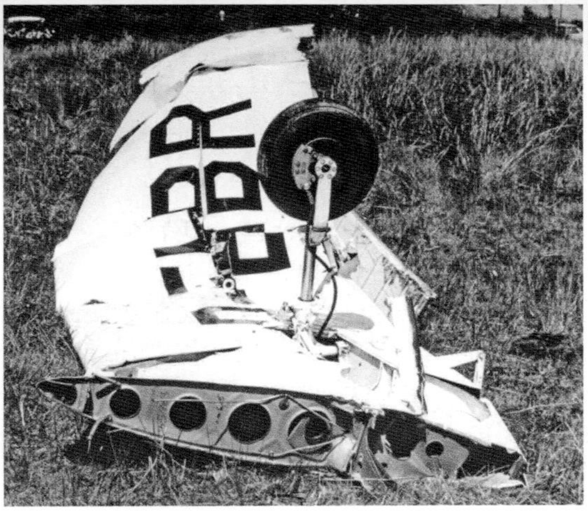

The crumpled wreckage of the Piper Arrow's fuselage, its registration code D-EHBR clearly visible in the foreground. INSET: The aircraft's port wing, sheared off as a result of the recovery from the steep dive and landed in a field approximately 400 yards north of the main impact point near Cwmbach Farm.

Examination of the wreckage failed to reveal any defect in the aircraft's construction. Puzzled by this finding investigators turned to the autopsy reports of the Arrow's occupants. It was found that the front seat passenger, Anton Block, had a history of coronary heart disease and had recently, possibly inside the aircraft, suffered a heart attack. Given that Arrow D-EHBR was fitted with dual controls, it became a reasonable possibility that he did indeed suffer a heart attack while in the aircraft and in the process fell forward onto the control column in front of the passenger seat. This would account for the two dives which the aircraft entered prior to the loss of the port wing.

Gethin Thomas of Llandybie showed me the location of the crash site. At the edge of a large hay field, half way between Cwmbach Farm and Pen Waun Hafog, a shallow depression marks the spot where the Arrow fell to earth.

MAR
12
1980

AIRCRAFT: **Harrier XW765**

Buzzard strike brought down Maple flag flyer

On March 13, 1980, the South Wales Evening Post newspaper contained an article informing its readers of a military low flying exercise which was taking place over parts of Mid Wales. The exercise involved predominantly Harrier aircraft and was planned as a prequel to the NATO 'Maple Flag' manoeuvres held annually in northern Canada. For Ernie Randell and his family at Blaen Cwm Farm just outside Lampeter the warning had come a little too late.

The previous morning, March 12, Flt. Lt. Peter Barton took off in Harrier XW765 from his 3 Squadron base at Gutersloh, Germany, to participate in the forementioned exercise. After refuelling at RAF Wittering he continued west to the mountains of Mid Wales. At around 16:00 hrs while flying at low level to the east of Lampeter the Harrier suffered a bird strike to its canopy. The bird, later identified as a buzzard, glanced off the Harrier's canopy and was immediately ingested into the aircraft's Pegasus jet engine. Though not causing any significant damage to the engine it had interrupted the airflow through the intakes, causing the engine to surge.

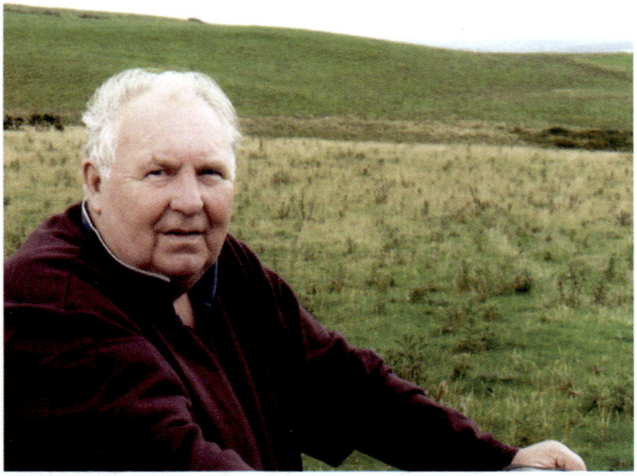

Ernie Randell of Blaen Cwm Farm. Less than an hour prior to the crash his wife Mary had been helping to deliver lambs in this field. The Harrier crashed into the hillock behind.

Flt. Lt. Barton instinctively put the Harrier into a climb and jettisoned the external fuel pods. Having gained over

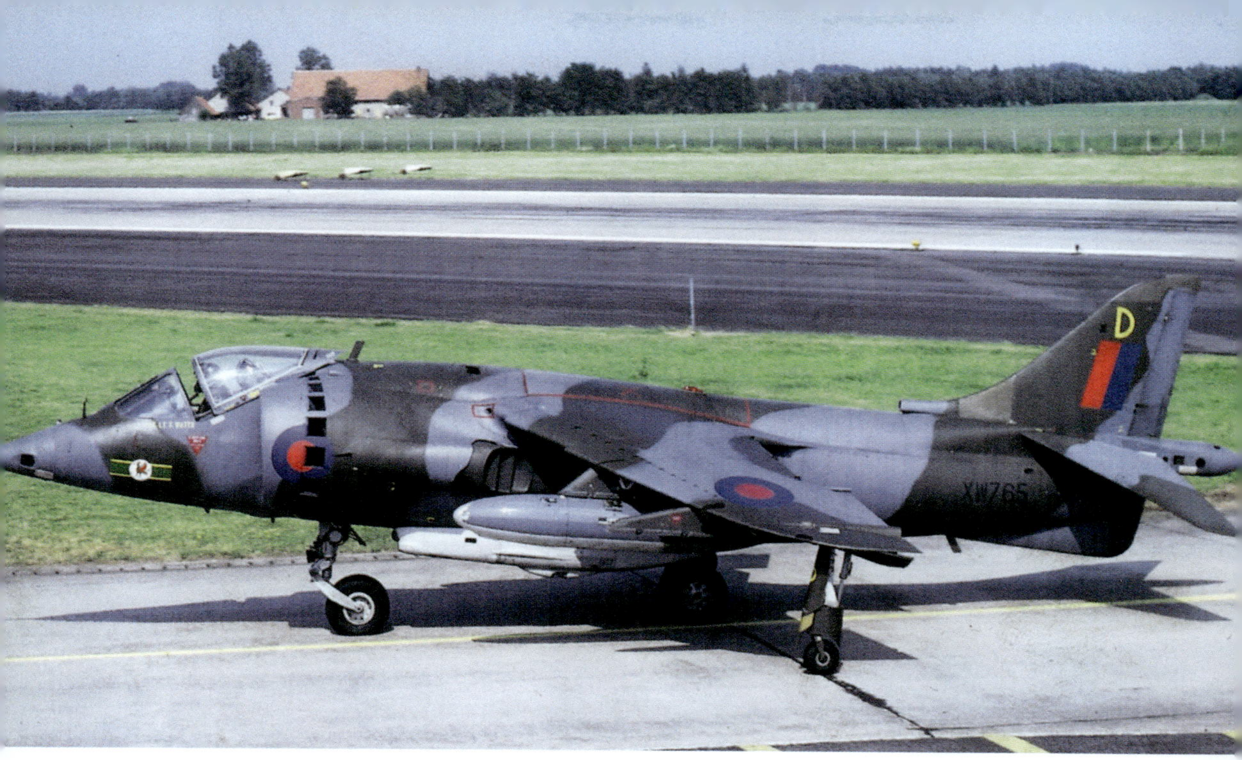

Harrier XW765 at Hopsten airfield, Germany. June 1977, just three years before a buzzard brought it down to earth with a bump.

1,000ft of valuable altitude his next priority was to shut down the surging engine and attempt to manually restart it. This he achieved, but the Harrier had lost too much altitude before sufficient thrust could be produced. To give some idea of the time scale involved, from the moment the buzzard was ingested to the time that the Harrier hit the ground was only a matter of 45 seconds.

At Blaen Cwm Farm Ernie Randell was standing in his yard when he heard a sound not unlike a plumber's blow-torch backfiring. He looked up and saw XW765 in its final moments of flight. Ernie watched as the Harrier passed low overhead on a northerly track, before crashing into a field about a mile away. Seconds before the impact he noticed an object break away from the aircraft. He had just witnessed Flt. Lt. Barton's successful ejection.

Taking only a few minutes to reach the crash site Ernie first came upon the pilot, who apart from a few minor cuts and bruises, appeared fine. Some 200 yards away lay the wrecked Harrier which had impacted on the side of a low hill and spread itself for some distance. The only recognisable piece of the aircraft being the tail section which had come to rest near a stone cairn at the brow of the hill. A short while later other aircraft circled the spot, most noticeable was a Nimrod which stayed in the vicinity for over an hour.

Peter Barton was not the only person to have had a lucky escape that afternoon. Less than an hour before the crash Ernie's wife Mary had been delivering lambs close to where the Harrier came down and had only left a nearby field to go and collect their children from school. Mary had also seen XW765 pass overhead while travelling along the lane which links the farm to the main road. The external fuel pods jettisoned before the crash fell harmlessly in fields at Garth Llwyd Farm a few miles to the south.

During the Falklands Campaign in 1982 Harriers were used extensively and low level training such as that carried out over Mid-Wales proved invaluable for British pilots.

In 2008 Ernie Randell showed me the spot where XW765 had crashed. Around a small crater in a grazing field small pieces of twisted aluminium can still be found.

AUG 5 1982

AIRCRAFT: Hunter XL593

Routine training flight landed in farmers field

By 1982 the Hunter had been in RAF service for almost 30 years. The last major user of the aircraft was No. 1 Tactical Weapons Unit, a training establishment based at RAF Brawdy on the Pembrokeshire coast.

At around 09:00 hrs on the morning of August 5, 1982 Hunter XL593, a Mk T7 side-by-side trainer, had taken off on a routine training flight. On board were Group Captain P.D. Oulten, who was completing a short refresher course, and his instructor, Flt. Lt. M.B. Stoner.

Fifteen minutes into the sortie, XL593 was just north of Carmarthen when the crew's attention was drawn to a high jet pipe temperature indication. Coupled with a low oil pressure gauge reading Flt. Lt. Stoner took control of the aircraft and transmitted an emergency call

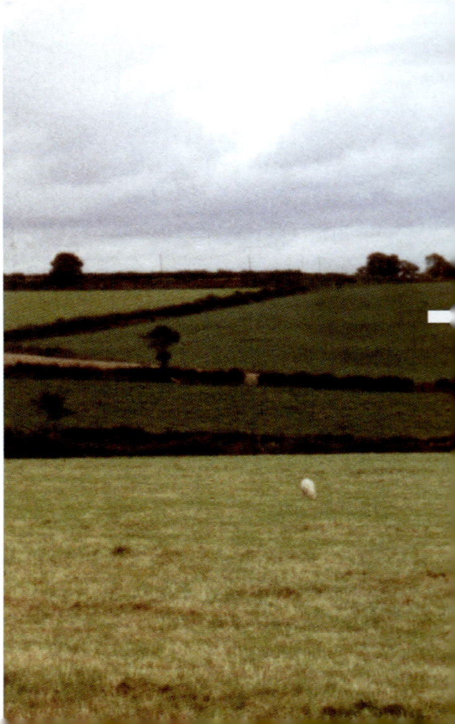

Hunter XL593 travelled for a considerable distance before coming to rest, almost intact, at the point arrowed. At the time of the accident there was also a hedgerow dividing the large field in the centre of the photograph. Esgerfa Farm is out of view to the right. The farm visible in the photograph, above the crash site, is Plas Newydd.

back to Brawdy. His intention was to land as soon as possible at the nearest available airfield.

At an altitude of 4,000ft Flt. Lt. Stoner assumed that the Hunter had suffered an engine surge. He followed procedure and after shutting down the aircraft's Avon engine, restarted it. Still the jet pipe temperature gauge rose with no noticeable increase in thrust.

Losing height, the crew abandoned their plans to put down at an airfield and instead sent a May-Day call stating their intention to eject. The Hunter was put on a heading for the coast and one last attempt was made to shut down and relight the engine.

Again this failed to solve the problem and at 1,500ft Flt. Lt. Stoner ordered his student to eject. On seeing the Group Captain's seat fire, he himself left the aircraft. Both crew landed safely in the Blaen y Coed area, approximately five miles north west of Carmarthen. After being abandoned XL593 flew on straight and level for just over a mile before making a perfect belly landing in a field at Esgerfa Farm. Passing low over the Talog to Carmarthen road the unmanned Hunter ploughed through two hedgerows before coming to rest almost intact. Though still in one piece the heavy landing had ruptured

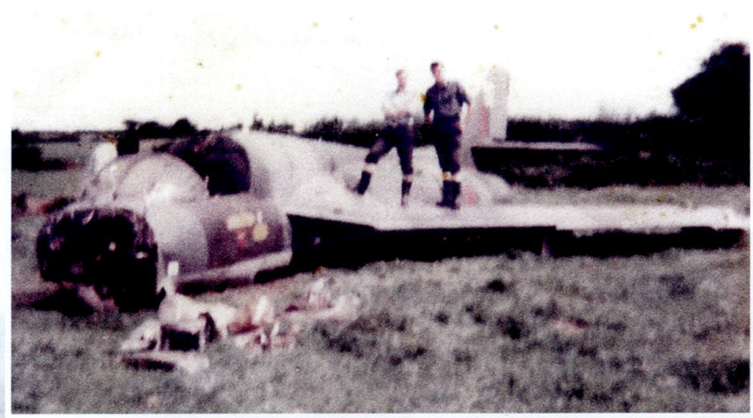

Two airmen pose for a photograph on the port wing of Hunter XL593. The nose section seems to have taken the brunt of its passage through the two hedgerows.

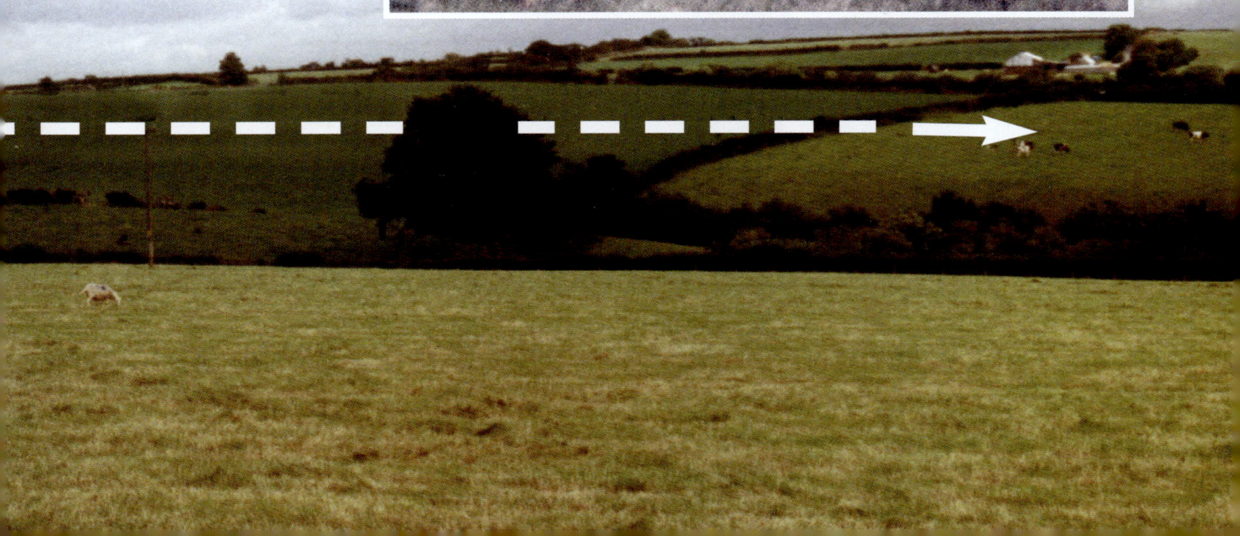

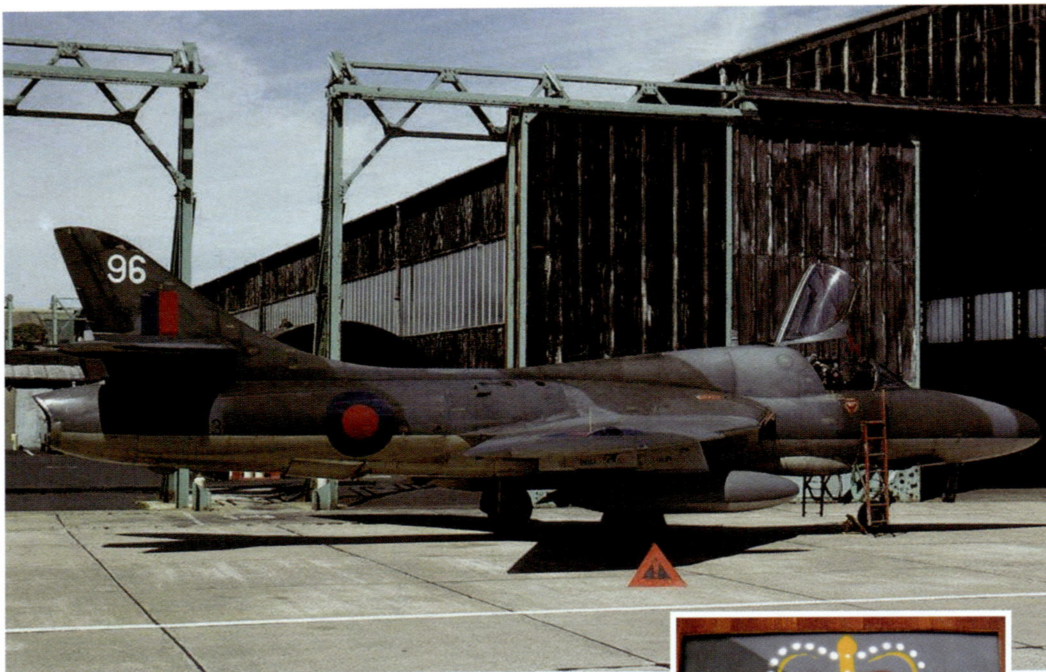

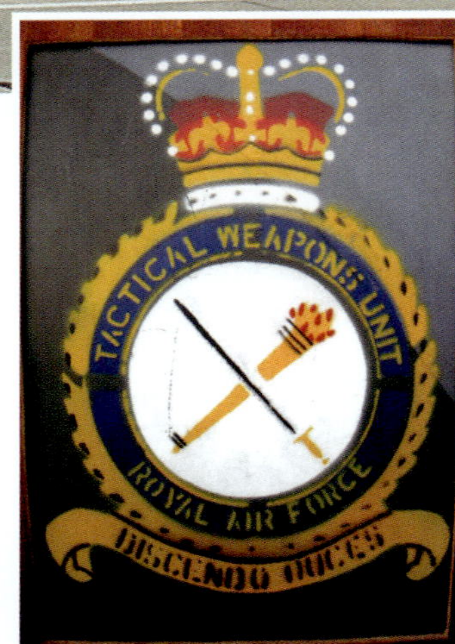

Hunter XL593 at RAF Chivenor in July 1974. INSET: The unit crest of 1 Tactical Weapons Unit cut from the fuselage of the aircraft and presented to the Convery family of Esgerfa Farm as a momento. Its motto, Discendo Duces translates as 'Through learning you will lead.'

its fuel tanks and led to the soil in the immediate area around the aircraft becoming heavily contaminated. An investigation into the accident established the cause of the high jet pipe temperature reading and subsequent loss of power to be attributed to a fractured rotor blade on the compressor turbine of the aircraft's Avon engine. The fractured blade was ingested into the engine which brought about its eventual failure.

Though incorrect on their assumption of an engine surge, both Flt. Lt. Stoner and Group Captain Oulten were commended for their cool-headedness in dealing with the situation.

At Esgerfa Farm today no visible trace can be seen of where Hunter XL593 came to rest. The contaminated soil around the aircraft was dug up and replaced, while the damaged hedgerows were removed more recently to enlarge the fields. However, Emily Convery, the owner of the farm, was able to show me the TWU crest neatly cut from XL593's fuselage and presented to her as a momento by the recovery crew.

JUL 8 1983

AIRCRAFT: **Hawk XX195**

Forty thousand homes suffered in jet incident

Nearly a year after the loss of Hunter XL593 a near-miss involving another TWU aircraft occurred within two miles of Esgerfa Farm. Just after midday on Friday July 8, 1983, Lloyd Davies of Llethr Moel Farm was busy making hay on what turned out to be the hottest day since the memorable heat wave of 1976. Looking across the field in the bright sunshine he caught a glimpse of a Hawk jet on an easterly heading pulling sharply up out of the narrow Nant Ring valley a few hundred yards away. In Lloyd's own words: 'it looked like a trout rising to a fly'.

As he squinted against the strong sunlight he saw a flash come from the aircraft, but thought nothing of it until he drove his tractor into the adjoining field. Here, close to the gateway, he came across three high-tension cables lying on the ground in front of him. They had been severed by the low flying Hawk.

Arriving back at the farmhouse Lloyd was met first of all by a policeman before his yard became the focal point of operations with power workers and press reporters milling around for most of the day.

The damaged cables were replaced within a matter of hours, but the disruption caused had been phenomenal. Newspaper headlines quoted the figure of 40,000 homes affected in an area west of a line drawn between Carmarthen and Aberystwyth.

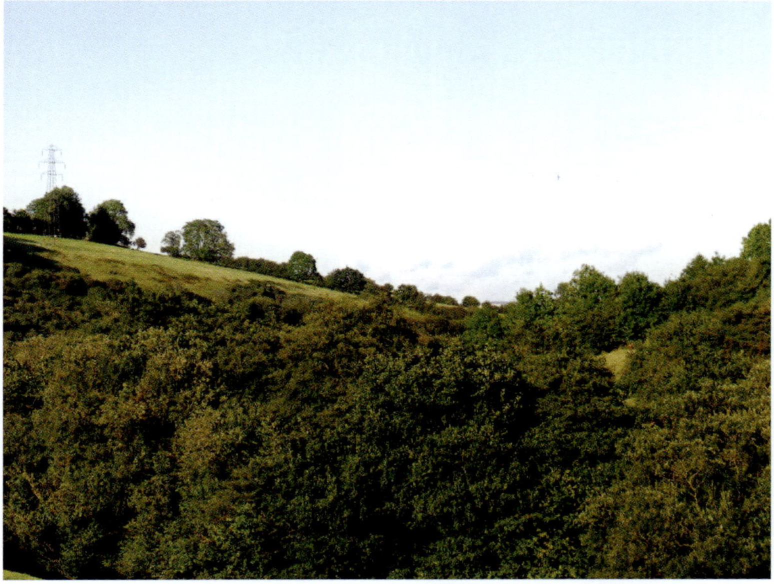

The high-tension cables running above the Nant Ring valley, near Cynwyl Elfed, are almost invisible against the sky in this photograph. The pylon, top left, stands in the field where Lloyd Davies found the severed cables.

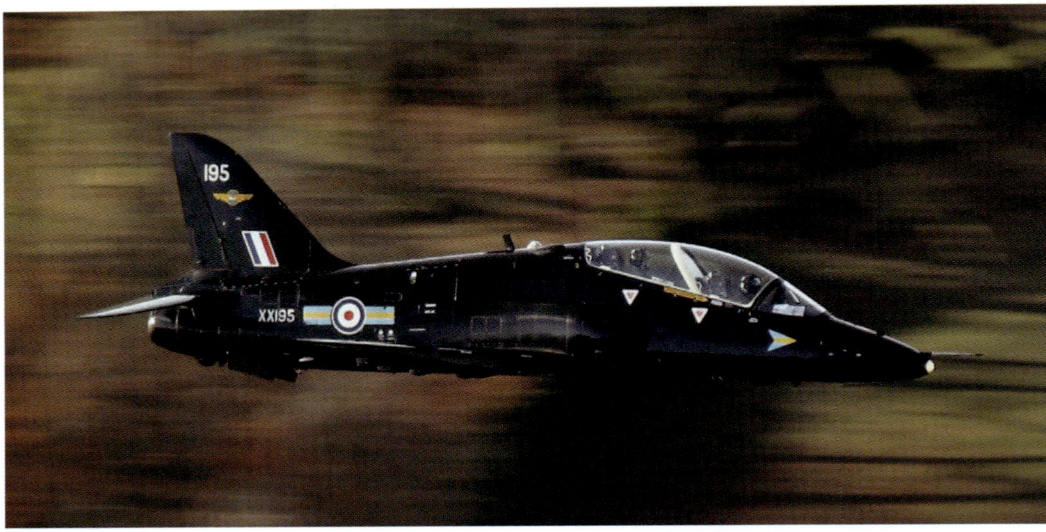

Hawk XX195 looking none the worse for its encounter with high-tension cables which disrupted power to thousands of homes in 1983.

The aircraft involved was Hawk XX195 of 2 TWU, which had been on a low-level training flight from its base at RAF Chivenor. After striking the cables the crew made an emergency landing at its sister unit at Brawdy where an inspection of the airframe revealed only superficial damage.

The RAF inquiry laid the blame squarely on the shoulders of the two crew who were unaware of the clearly marked hazard on their low flying chart and hadn't seen the cables in time to avoid them. Perhaps the glare from the strong sun that day also contributed to the accident.

XX195 first flew with the RAF at Brawdy in 1978. After over 30 years of service it is currently based at RAF Valley on Anglesey with 4 FTS.

JUN
5
1989

AIRCRAFT: Sea King XV699

Helicopter crash lands on village playing field

In the early morning of Monday June 5, 1989, two Royal Navy Sea King helicopters of 826 Squadron were returning to their base at Culdrose, Cornwall, on completion of an exercise in Scotland. After having refuelled at RAF Valley the two aircraft continued their journey south across Wales. At 09:00 hrs, while south-east of Carmarthen and at an altitude of 1,500ft, the captain of Sea King XV699, Commander Mike Mason, detected a vibration through his seat. Initially neither of the aircraft's two pilots noticed the series of jolts, but as they became more pronounced the helicopter was slowed while the second Sea

King drew alongside to make a visual inspection; nothing unusual was noticed. Concerned about the helicopter's safety, Commander Mason ordered his 1st pilot, Lt. Alan Novelli, to lose height immediately and look for a suitable landing field.

Though bordered on three sides by a housing estate, school and aged person's complex, the level surface of the football pitch at Pont Henri was chosen and as a precautionary measure a 'Pan' urgency message was transmitted over the helicopter's radio to the nearest airfield. At this point the aircraft was behaving normally and responding to the pilot's control inputs. However, minutes later at 09:09 hrs, when XV699 was only 20 feet above the ground and in its final moments before touch-down, lateral control of the helicopter was lost. It yawed sharply to the right, spun through 180 degrees and struck the ground before heeling over onto its port

Sea King XV699, covered in fire-fighting foam, lies on its side on the football pitch at Pont Henri, just yards from some of the homes on a housing estate where one of the helicopter's rotor blades ended up wedged into a road drain cover. The school is just out of view to the right.

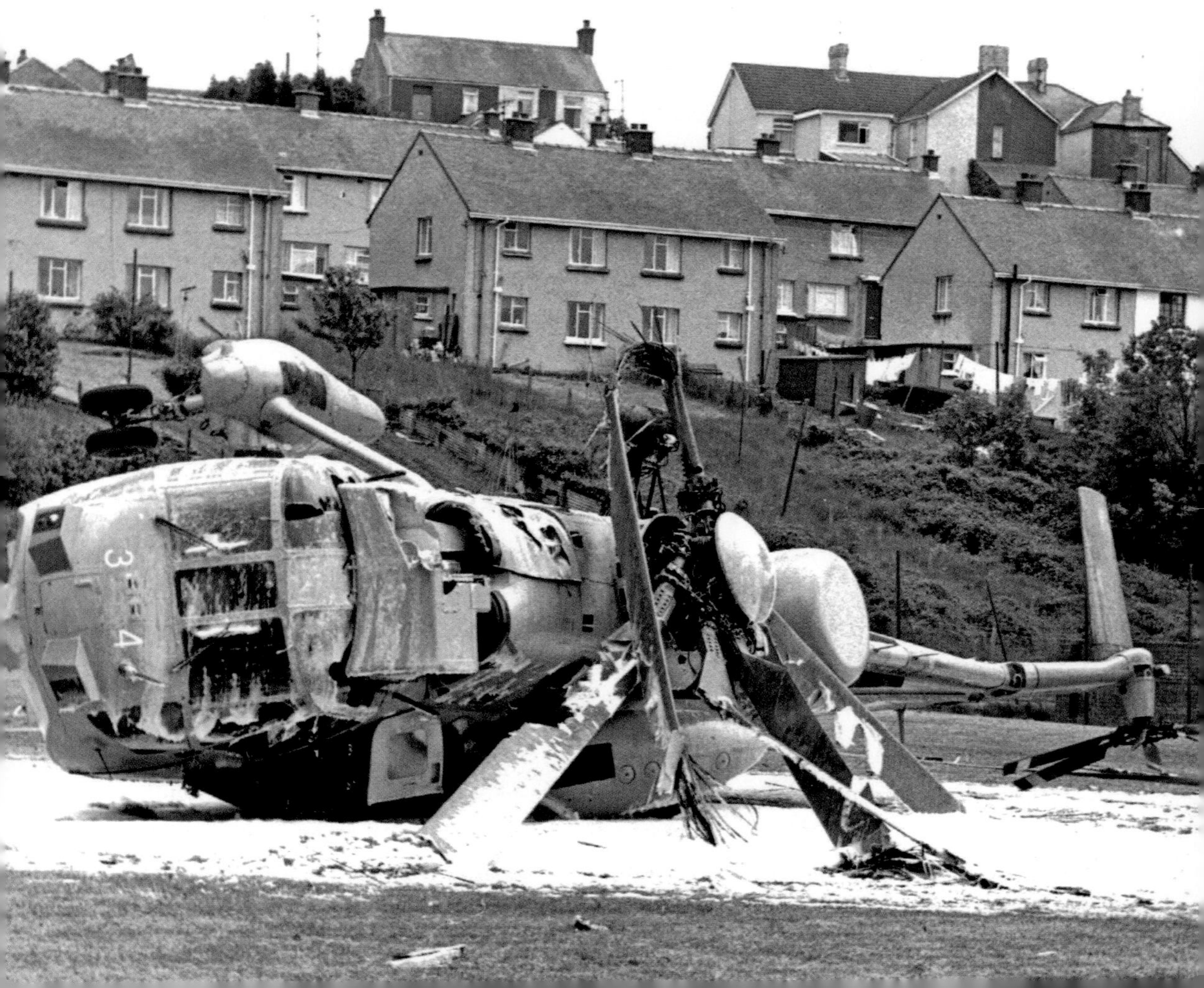

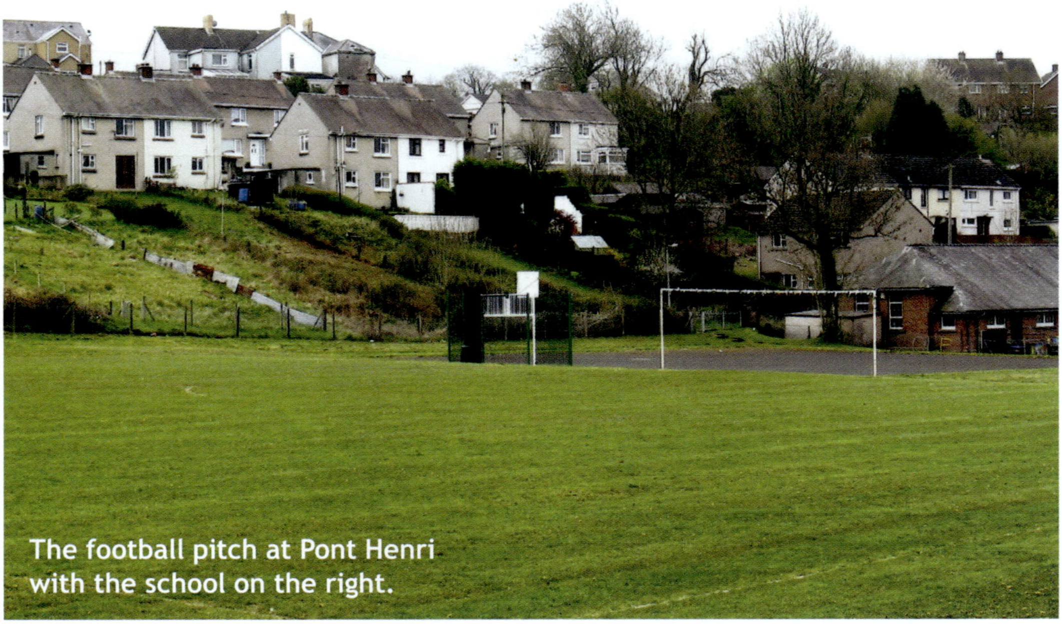
The football pitch at Pont Henri with the school on the right.

side. Miraculously there was no fire, enabling the four crew and eight passengers on board to exit the aircraft unharmed. The second helicopter landed alongside to render help, but took off a short while later to re-establish radio communications.

Despite the main rotor blades fracturing on impact and being thrown some distance into the neighbouring housing estate, there were no civilian casualties. As it was Monday most of the younger children of the village were attending lessons at the local primary school, located less than 100 yards away from where the helicopter crashed.

On hearing the unusual noise from the stricken helicopter as it approached Pont Henri, headmistress Pat Rowlands, sensed immediately that all was not well. With the assistance of her teaching staff all 67 pupils were evacuated from the main building and took cover behind an outside wall at the far end of the school while events unfolded on the nearby football field.

Damage to property in the village was minimal, mostly confined to the Coed Mawr area overlooking the playing field. Here steel bolts and washers had smashed windows and embedded themselves into internal walls. Perhaps the most striking realisation of how lucky the inhabitants of Pont Henri had been that day was the sight of a 15ft length of main rotor blade protruding skyward from a metal street drainage grating.

Over the following days Sea King XV699 was defuelled, hoisted onto a low-loader and transported by road to Lee-on-Solent where an investigation into the crash took place. The investigating team were able to establish that the cause of the accident was attributed to a lack of lubrication to the splines attached to the tail rotor driveshaft.

Hardened and compacted grease in the driveshaft assembly had prevented the egress of fresh lubrication which allowed the driveshaft splines to wear excessively. This wear eventually prevented the splines in the driveshaft from meshing together to propel the tail rotor.

Sea King XV699 was subsequently deemed repairable and is still in service with the Royal Navy. In October 1989 Lt. Alan Novelli and his crew made a return visit to Pont Henri in another Sea King, to thank the villagers for their help during the incident.

Since this incident there have been more than 20 serious flying accidents in Wales, mostly involving low flying military jets, though none of these have occurred in Carmarthenshire.

. . . and finally, two aviation mysteries

All of the flying accidents recorded in this book have taken place either in Carmarthenshire or just off its coastline. Of these, the reasons for the vast majority have been relatively easy to explain. They have been attributed to either pilot error, mechanical failure or in some instances inclement weather. There are two further aviation tales linked to the county however, that have attracted attention more for the mystery elements in them than anything else.

JUN 23 1942

AIRCRAFT: **Focke-Wulf 190 Werke No. 5313**

An unintentional gift for Pembrey airfield

Perhaps one of the most extraordinary events to happen in Carmarthenshire during the Second World War was the unscheduled arrival at Pembrey of the Luftwaffe's most recent and highly prized fighter aircraft, the Focke-Wulf 190.

In 1942 Reich Marshall Hermann Goering had been so concerned about the possibility of the Allies gaining secret technical information about the potent fighter that he issued strict orders that on no account were FW 190 pilots to cross the English Channel into mainland Britain for fear of one falling into enemy hands. At a time when the FW 190 was outperforming even the most recent mark of the Spitfire, the unexpected appearance of a fully functional example on the tarmac of an airfield in South Wales must have quickened the heartbeats of Air Ministry officials throughout Whitehall.

The Focke-Wulf's flight to South Wales began in the early evening of June 23, 1942 at Morlaix airfield in northern France. Oberleutnant Armin Faber and a section of his squadron, Jager Geshwader 2, had been scrambled to intercept a formation of Boston bombers which were about to attack their base on the Brest Peninsula.

The ensuing aerial dog-fighting with the escorting RAF fighters stretched all the way back across the English Channel to Salcombe on the coast of South Devon, where Faber shot down his first Spitfire of the day. Another encounter to the west of Exeter lead to a second Spitfire falling to his guns. The Czech pilot of this second aircraft, Flt. Sgt. Franta Trejtnar, managed to bail out before his Spitfire hit the ground, but broke a leg on landing. Franta Trejtnar can perhaps be credited with forcing Lt. Faber further north and west than he had anticipated. Reich Marshall Goering's orders had been well and truly breached. With an unserviceable radio set, short of fuel and in Faber's own words: 'the air full of Spitfires,' the reality of not being able to return to his base on the Continent started to sink in. Furthermore, not wanting to aggravate a previous spinal injury in the process of baling out he resigned himself to landing at the nearest airfield and walking into captivity.

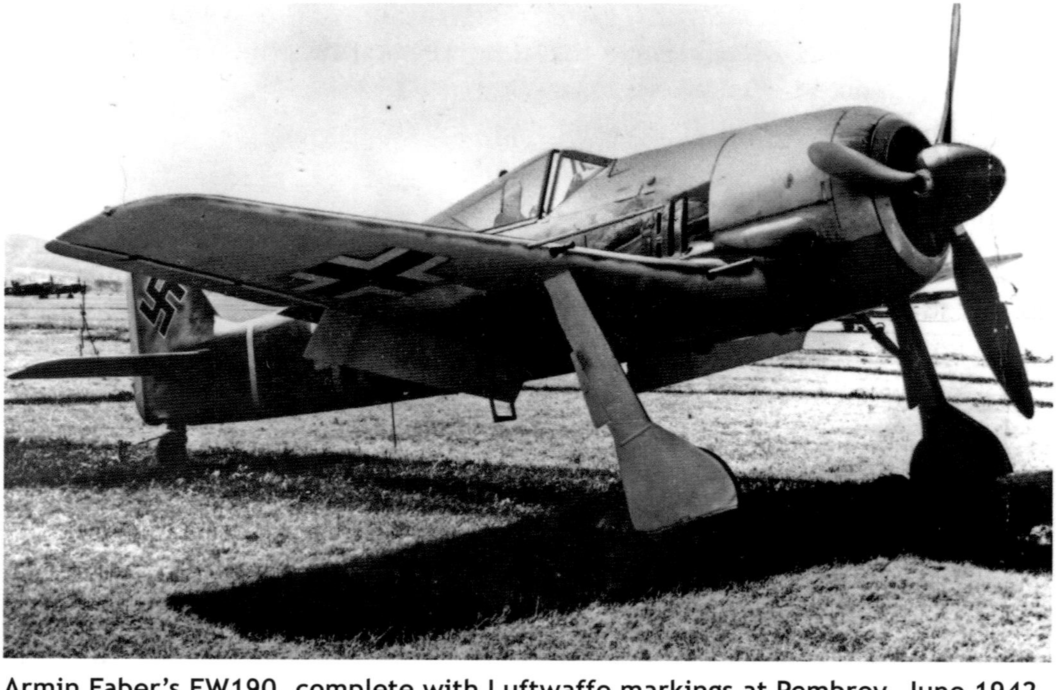

Armin Faber's FW190, complete with Luftwaffe markings at Pembrey. June 1942.

Faber's FW190 in RAF markings at the Royal Aircraft Establishment Farnborough with its chief test pilot at the controls.

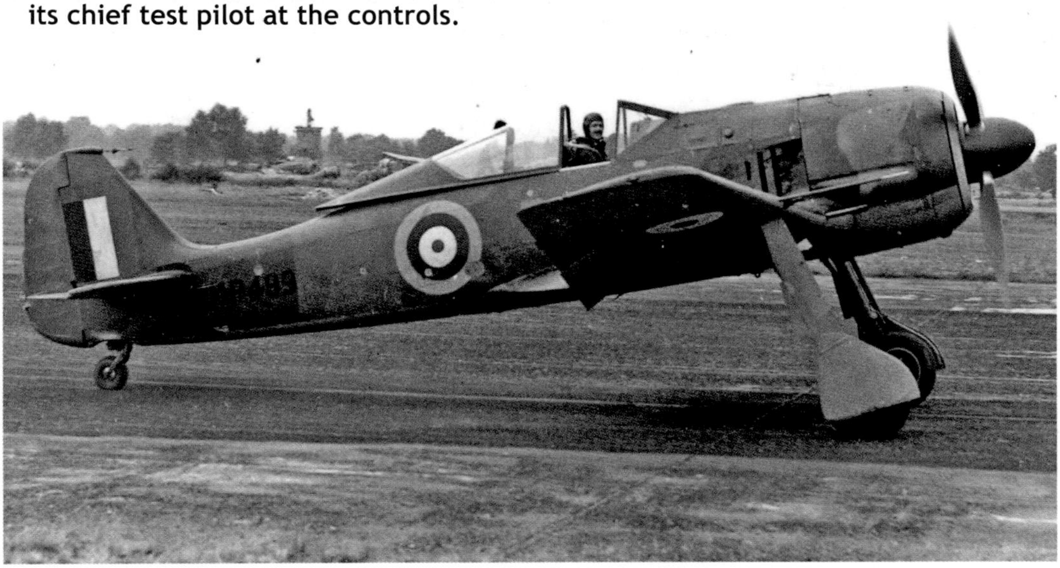

Having an English grandmother may have made his thoughts of internment in Britain much easier to cope with.

At this point in time there is a misconception by many people that Armin Faber, on sighting the Bristol Channel in front of him, mistook it to be the English Channel.

A file held at the National Archives documenting an interview with Faber soon after he landed at Pembrey, confirms that he knew full well that he was about to put down on British soil.

Also held at the National Archives is the Operational Record Book for RAF Fairwood Common. An entry relating to Faber's arrival at the Officers' Mess at Fairwood later that evening records the following:

'The pilot's story is that after shooting down two Spitfires he was forced north and running short of petrol landed at the first available aerodrome, which happened to be Pembrey. He was escorted to Fairwood Common and was a guest of the Officers' Mess for about two days until he was sent to London for interrogation.'

One of the first sightings of Faber's FW190 in South Wales was made by a young schoolboy in the Pontarddulais area. Islwyn Thomas, then just eight years of age, was playing in the back garden of his home at Ar Fron on the eastern side of the village when he saw what he thought was a spitfire flying low from the direction of Graig Fawr to the north. As the aircraft flew overhead, it banked slightly allowing Islwyn to glimpse the distinct Luftwaffe cross painted on the side of its fuselage. It then flew over Goppa Hill and dissapeared toward the Loughor Estuary. Minutes later, at 20:25 hrs it was again spotted and identified as an FW190, by an Observer Corps post near Laugharne which relayed the news to its Command Headquarters at Carmarthen. RAF Pembrey were duly informed of the intruder with the words: 'it's coming your way' and just as the message was being received, the aircraft was spotted flying near Pembrey Mountain before making a low pass over the airfield.

Due to the large number of parked training aircraft and the outline of the station's buildings, the anti-aircraft gunner's defending Pembrey airfield were unable to take aim at the Focke-Wulf as it flew past. When a clear view did present itself the gunners withheld firing as Faber started to lower his undercarriage, supposedly while inverted. Minutes later the aircraft was on the ground and the engine shut down. It may have been the case that Faber had tried to destroy the Focke-Wulf by means of a self destruction device during the few minutes it took for an armed squad to rush out and apprehend him. If so this failed and he had presented the RAF with an unintentional gift.

Word of Armin Faber's arrival at Pembrey spread like wildfire in RAF circles and over the following days senior officers, eager to get a closer look at the formidable aircraft, flooded into Pembrey.

The Focke-Wulf was dismantled and taken away by road to the Royal Aircraft Establishment at Farnborough where it was re-assembled and given the RAF serial number MP499. Its airframe was repainted in air force livery and sported roundels. Taking to the air in British hands on July 3, it was later evaluated against Allied fighters at the Air Fighting Development Unit at Duxford.

The only remnant of this historic aircraft to survive into modern times is part of the cockpit, which is currently exhibited at Shoreham airfield in Sussex.

By strange coincidence, on the very day that Armin Faber arrived at Pembrey, the Air Ministry received detailed plans for a daring commando-style raid on an airfield in France to capture an airworthy Focke-Wulf 190. Operation 'Air Thief' was the brainchild of Commando officer, Captain Philip Pinkney, who relied on his friend, Spitfire test pilot Jeffrey Quill, to fly the aircraft back to Britain. Due to the intervening circumstances the plan was turned down.

Armin Faber survived the war. After a period of internment as a POW in Canada he feigned epilepsy and was repatriated back to Germany before the end of hostilities. Not much is known about his life post-war.

DEC 9 1944

AIRCRAFT: **Lancaster ND707**

Sgt Trevor Jones - the aviator who vanished

In the afternoon of Saturday, December 9, Pilot Officer R.H. Chittim and his crew of six took off in Lancaster ND707 from their 166 Squadron base at RAF Kirmington, Lincolnshire. The recently formed crew were taking part in a routine, daytime cross country training flight which would take them across South Wales. After being posted to 166 Squadron from an operational training unit only days previously, on December 6, this was to be the crew's first flight on the strength of a front line bomber squadron.

At around 16:00 hrs they were at 24,000ft and over the Brecon Beacons when the pilot experienced extreme turbulence, probably the result of entering cumulonimbus thunder clouds. In the confusion as the aircraft tumbled out of the sky, four of the crew took to their parachutes and bailed out; landing in the Llanddeusant area on the northern side of the Black Mountain.

Back on board the Lancaster P.O. Chittim skilfully regained control of his aircraft at 8,000ft and landed at RAF Fairwood Common with the remaining crew.

Informed of the news that four crew had bailed out, a search party was organised and set off from Fairwood to retrieve them. Three were found fairly quickly, but as the night drew on, no sign of the fourth crew member, 19-year-old, Flight

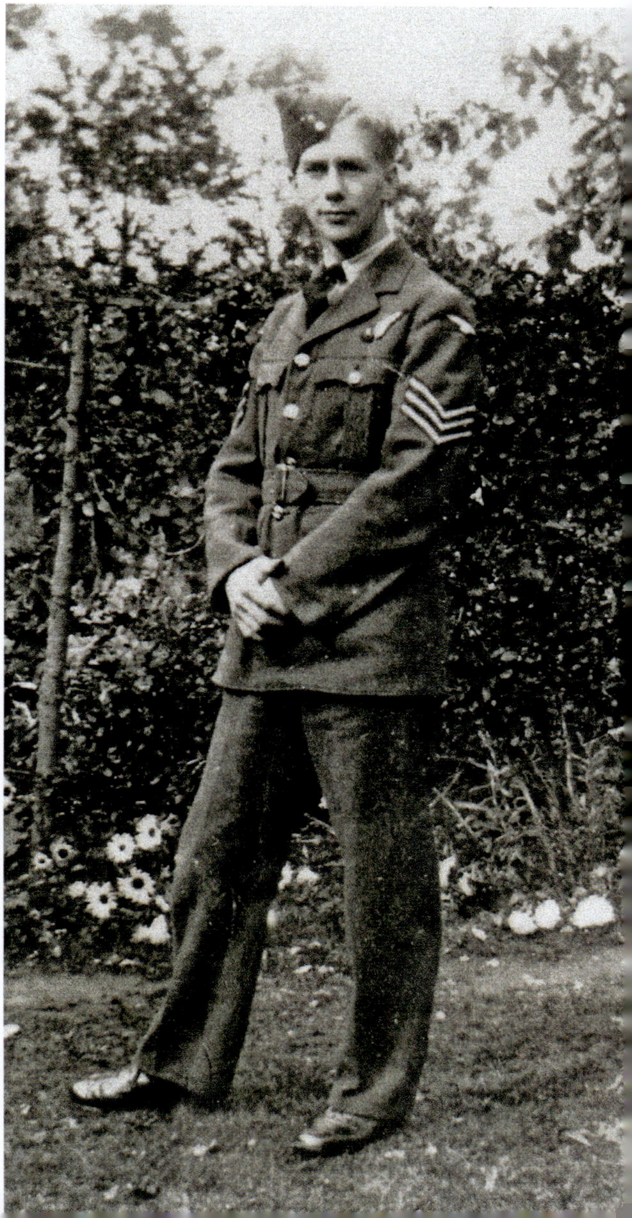

Sgt. Trevor Jones — the aviator who vanished.

Engineer, Sgt. Trevor Jones, could be found. Hopes of finding Sgt. Jones were later raised when his parachute, harness and flying helmet were found near Llyn y Fan Fawr lake by George Smith, the teenage son of a reservoir keeper, who from his home at Crai reservoir, had seen a parachute descending along the northern end of the Fan Hir escarpment in the fading light. By nightfall of the following day, December 10, there was still no sign of the missing airman. This prompted the Air Ministry to broadcast an appeal for help in finding Sgt. Jones via the BBC news on Monday, December 11.

The text of the BBC news broadcast stated: 'On Saturday afternoon four members of the crew of an RAF aircraft bailed out near Swansea. Three have been found safe, but the fourth, a Sergeant, is missing, possibly injured and suffering from loss of memory. The Air Ministry is anxious to get any news of the airman. Will anyone able to give information please communicate with the nearest Police or RAF station.'

The BBC broadcast failed to raise any new leads as to the whereabouts of Sgt. Jones. Though now scaled down, search parties were still out actively

The ravine-scarred landscape in the area where Sgt. Jones' body was found. Pentre Gronw Farm is up on the high ground to the left. Army manoeuvres were carried out on the floor of the valley, where the sheep are grazing.

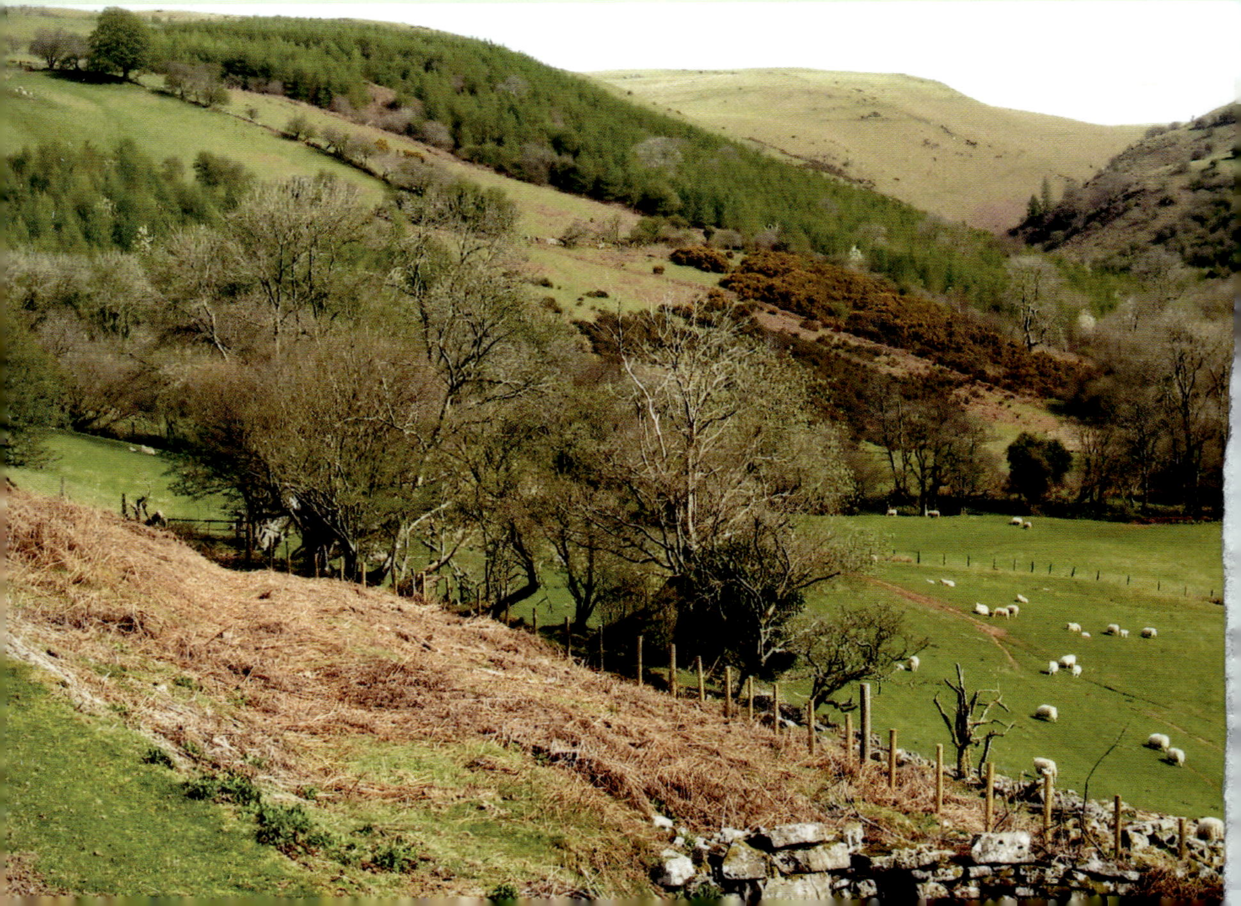

looking for Sgt. Jones as late as December 21. In the midwinter twilight of December 25, Christmas Day, farmer Gwyn James was attending to his sheep near the derelict hillside farmstead of Pentre Gronw, high above Myddfai, when he discovered the body of an airman lying just off the track leading to the old farm buildings. The long search for Trevor Jones was over.

The police from Llandovery were called and his body carried down the mountainside on a fencing hurdle, before being laid out in Myddfai Church overnight. On Boxing Day his body was transferred to Fairwood Common and a few days later laid to rest near his home at Hucclecote, near Gloucester.

The reason Trevor Jones remained undiscovered amongst the harsh winter landscape of the Black Mountain for over two weeks will never be known. The further such mysteries are researched, the more questions than answers seem to be brought to light.

Some clues to a resolution of this particular mystery include the fact that when Sgt. Jones was found by Gwyn James he had a severe open fracture of his leg. Was this the result of his initial parachute landing, or a later fall? His RAF flying suit was also worn through at the elbows and torso area; the result of crawling on this stomach for some considerable time perhaps?

The distance from where George Smith located the abandoned parachute and harness is over four miles from Pentre Gronw Farm. The terrain between these two locations is boggy, uneven and extremely remote, but after all, whose parachute had George

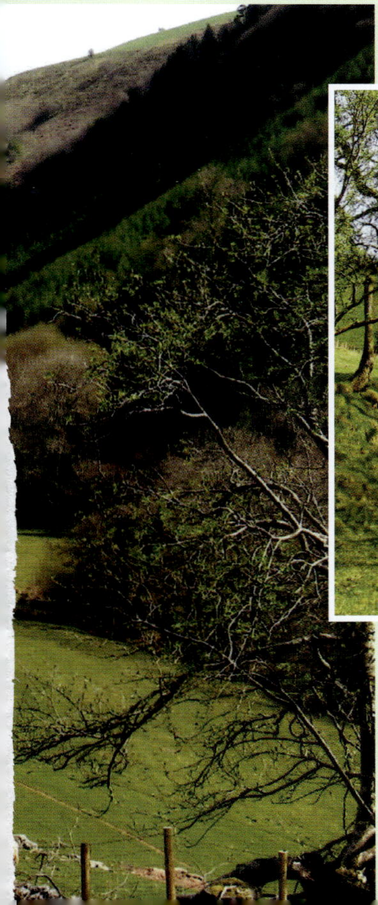

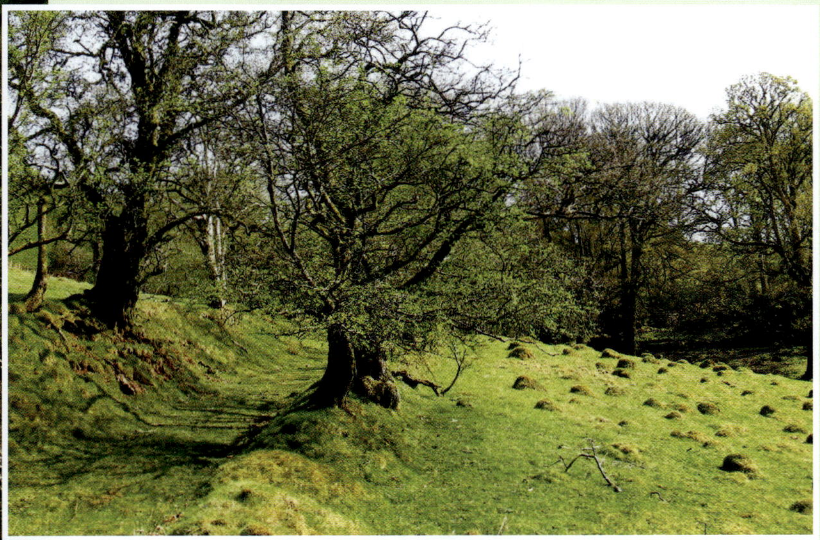

The body of Trevor Jones was found by farmer Gwyn James just to the left of this track leading to Pentre Gronw Farm. Its ruins, among the trees on the right, may have given shelter to Sgt. Jones and are where Peter Foot found the used ration packs.

Smith really found. Was it Trevor Jones's, or maybe one of the other crew members. There is also the question of whether Sgt. Jones had landed closer to Pentre Gronw Farm and perhaps sheltered in the derelict farmhouse awaiting help. Myddfai resident and wartime evacuee, Peter Foot, a nephew of farmer Gwyn James, recalled that in the days following the incident he visited the spot where Trevor Jones's body was discovered and found discarded ration packs in the immediate area and in the derelict farm buildings at Pentre Gronw. It is a well-established fact that the human body can survive for a long period of time without proper sustenance, providing that water is available. In the damp environment around Myddfai water was in plentiful supply.

The area in which Sgt. Jones spent his last days was sometimes used as a live firing range for Army manoeuvres, even the wreckage of a shell-pocked tank lay close by. Had he heard the sound of gunfire or mortar shelling and somehow thought that he had landed in occupied territory and had perhaps been trying to evade capture. If he had indeed landed in the Llyn y Fan Fawr area, he may have also come across the wreckage of a Lancaster (W4929) which crashed in 1943, perhaps even assuming that this was his own aircraft.

By 1944 it was common practice for aircrew to carry a whistle, usually attached to the collar of their uniform. Assuming that Sgt. Jones had such a whistle, why did he not use it to attract attention of his whereabouts?

Another sad aspect of this story is that just over a week after the discovery of Trevor Jones's body at Pentre Gronw, P.O. Chittim and most of his original crew were killed while on a raid to Nuremburg in Lancaster ND635. Only Sgt. Lillis, the rear gunner, survived the mission. He was captured and became a prisoner of war. Sgt. Abrams didn't take part in the raid.

**CREW LIST: P.O. Chittim RH (Canadian) Pilot, KIA Jan 2, 1945;
Sgt. Jones TC, Flight Engineer; Flt. Sgt. Pearson GH, Air Bomber, KIA Jan 2, 1945;
Sgt. Tarlton JD, Navigator, KIA Jan 2, 1945; Sgt. Abrams GA W.Op/Ag;
Sgt. Morgan WJ (Canadian), MU Ag, KIA Jan 2, 1945;
Sgt. Lillis JC (Canadian) Rear Ag, POW Jan 2, 1945.**

'To live on in the hearts of others is not to die'